# REPORT TO THE ACADEMY

## (RE: THE NEW CONFLICT OF THE FACULTIES)

GREGG LAMBERT

CRITICAL STUDIES IN THE HUMANITIES

Series Editor — Victor E. Taylor

Address all requests to:
  The Davies Group, Publishers
  PO Box 440140
  Aurora, CO  80044-0140
  USA

*Library of Congress Cataloging-in-Publication Data*

  Lambert, Gregg, 1961-
    Report to the academy : re—the new conflict of the faculties / Gregg Lambert.
      p. cm. — (Critical studies in the humanities)
    Includes bibliographical references.
    ISBN 1-888570-61-X (alk. paper)
    1. Education, Higher—Philosophy. 2. Universities and colleges—United
  States—Faculty—Attitudes. 3. Postmodernism and higher education—United
  States. 4. Subjectivity—Social aspects—United States.   I. Title. II. Series.

  LB2322.2 .L36 2001
  378.73—dc21

                                                                    2001037263

Printed in the United States of America
Published 2001. The Davies Group Publishers, Aurora  CO  80044-0140

1 2 3 4 5 6 7 8 9 0

Outline of the report:

Critical Studies in the Humanities
Victor E. Taylor, Series Editor

This open-ended series provides a unique publishing venue by combining single volumes issuing from landmark scholarship with pedagogy-related interdisciplinary collections of readings. This principle of cross-publishing, placing scholarship and pedagogy side by side within a single series, creates a wider horizon for specialized research and more general intellectual discovery. In the broad field of the humanities, the Critical Studies in the Humanities Series is committed to preserving key monographs, encouraging new perspectives, and developing important connections to pedagogical issues. *Proposals for submission should go to the Series Editor, Victor E. Taylor, Department of English and Humanities, York College of Pennsylvania, York, PA 17405-7199.*

# MEMORANDUM


Re: *Who speaks* for the university today?

**To Whom It May Concern:**


The objectives of the following *Report to the Academy* are twofold:

1. To examine some examples of what I will call the discourse of the contemporary university in the United States;
2. To interrogate the legitimacy and the authority of a new *subject* who, today, has emerged within the public sphere to speak *for* the university.

Although this new subject, this "university faculty," can most immediately be identified with a class of administrators, and even faculty who assume this role in their respective colleges and departments, it need not be limited to the individuals who occupy these positions in the university. Throughout this report, I maintain the conceptual ambiguity that belongs to the Kantian concept of "faculty," which designates both the possible relationships that exist between objects and subjects (i.e., the 'faculty' of knowledge designates the different relationships possible for a representation), as well as the source of specific kinds of representations, or object-relations (i.e., a particular faculty legislates over objects that are subject to it). Within the framework of the university, the concept of faculty undergoes a further definition in that the totality of relationships that belong to the representation of knowledge are formalized and historically arranged. Needless to say, this "historical arrangement" itself becomes the source of ambiguity, since the representation of knowledge is dynamic rather than static; there are always new relationships (and thus new subjects of knowledge) that are not yet *subject to* the current arrangement of faculties.

The subject I wish to address, therefore, is what Foucault had earlier defined as a "subject of discourse" referring in this case to any subject who assumes the task of *positioning* the modern university within the vast and conflicting field of ends that are imposed upon it by society, politics, technology, culture and economy. In addition to the university administrator who officially assumes this task, there is also the contemporary philosopher (or "theorist"), cultural critic, and a variety of public intellectuals who can often be heard speaking *of* or *for* the university today. The faculty who assumes responsibility for this task recalls the earlier argument by Kant in *The Conflict of Faculties* (*Der Streit der Facultäten*, 1798) in which the faculty of philosophy bears the full authority for the following tasks:

1.  To "position" — although not necessarily the executive power to "institute" — the idea of the university. I will discuss below how this distinction between the two forms of power (the juridical and the executive, or administrative) in the conception of "philosophical right" is often overlooked.
2.  To "critique" any architectonic or institutional arrangement of the principles of "university reason" according to those forms of reason that Kant defines as "private" (historico-political, economic, religious).

I underline the fact that such an ideal subject can no longer be recognized from within the disciplinary discourse of the faculties themselves. Unlike the Kantian prescription, the discourse of the university is no longer the free creation of its faculties, who no longer speak a public language. Likewise, the subject of the university no longer crystallizes in the language of the classical philosopher who determines its *ends* within a speculative accord with the ends of society. This, I argue, has introduced a fundamental problem in the architecture of the contemporary university: a failure in the discourse of sufficient grounds (or principles) caused by the absence of a faculty whose juridical task is to protect the ends of the university from being reduced to purely finite, economic, politico-ideological, and culturally determined "ends," (i.e., private forms of interest). The problem of sufficient reason, as earlier philosophers might have phrased this, may help to address the weakness or the inability of the current faculties (specifically, the faculty of philosophy, which would include most of the modern disciplines of the Humanities and Social Sciences) to protect the university from becoming an instrument of *techné*, a functional apparatus, a tool, or a piece of equipment charged with providing information, or generally with "doing something with a view toward something else."

As we can see in many contemporary universities, there is a danger when this determination of what could be called "university reason" becomes all-encompassing and is even charged with instituting and reorganizing the historical faculties within a common architecture, which in turn creates a situation where the faculties are often evaluated and funded along a criteria that French philosopher Jean-François Lyotard first defined as "performativity." Lyotard's early analysis in *The Postmodern Condition: A Report on Knowledge* addresses the failure of the "university" itself as a master narrative of the Enlightenment which can no longer prop up its architecture and now is in the process of being submitted to what Kant had earlier called "private purposes." However, in some respects Lyotard himself does not seem to take into account the survival of these narratives that continue to inform the institutional practices and ideological divisions of cultural knowledge. In the forward to the English translation, critic Fredric Jameson remarks their staying power and identifies them as the institutional symptoms of what he will call here and elsewhere "the political unconscious."

More important than this somewhat simple pronouncement of the absence (even perhaps "death"?) of the earlier philosophical subject from among the faculties who can be identified with the discourse of the university itself is that, in the wake of this subject's disappearance, we still find the persistence of a language which can be associated with an earlier authority, even though this language is often reduced to the various clichés and metaphors of an eighteenth century understanding of the idea of the university. The decline or incredulity concerning certain "master narratives" (including the universal nature of reason, or the perpetual progress of history, etc.) is a condition over which most postmodern critics seem to agree. In fact, this incredulity is informed by the different polemics that mark our era of criticism, which has become distinctively "post- (even "anti-) Enlightenment." At the same time, these very critics do not also question, as a result of the claims concerning the bankruptcy or even concupiscence of "old European concepts" (Habermas), whether this might undermine the very place from which they are speaking: the contemporary university. That is, as a result of the avowed rejection of Enlightenment principles, few have questioned whether or not the very principles of social critique upon which the modern university is founded (or funded) can any longer be "rendered to reason" in the earlier sense of this term. We might begin to understand the recent developments that are impacting universities and colleges both nationally and abroad — particularly in Europe, Australia, and elsewhere in the world — as tangible evidence that contemporary societies themselves are disinvesting the social institution of the university from some of its earlier ideological and critical functions, whether these earlier functions are understood in relation to what Jürgen Habermas has called the "bourgeois public sphere," or in terms of a more direct alliance with the modern nation-state as Bill Readings, following Lyotard, has argued in *The University in Ruins*. A third possibility is the determination of the contemporary university in terms of what some critics have perceived as a site for staging the national competition over knowledge and labor in an emerging global marketplace. Whichever explanation one finds most credible, Lyotard's earlier thesis is being dramatically performed by the manner in which current universities are gradually being re-configured (or re-tooled) by a new set of social objectives. This has caused a certain conflict to break out between an earlier understanding of the university and this new rationale, more economic in nature, which is responsible for adapting and conforming the social institution to a new set of priorities.

Throughout this report I will address the current situation in terms of the decline of an earlier philosophical authority or "principle of reason" (Derrida) and the replacement of the classical philosopher by the modern day administrator who has assumed many of the speculative duties of the former in addition to having executive power over the institution and the faculties themselves. As my subtitle indicates, this has resulted in what I call a "new conflict of faculties" concerning the historical mission of the university and its relationship to the dominant interests of the surrounding society, a conflict that returns us to the original terms of Kant's earlier *Conflict of the Faculties* in a somewhat uncanny but nevertheless highly relevant manner. Ultimately, the current conflict is a bit unusual in the sense that my primary question will concern precisely what form this conflict has taken or must take in order precisely *to fit the situation at hand.* This question opens an investigation into the very concept of "the critical" itself in the final part, as well as an assessment of the idioms of the critical by which conflict over the form of the social bond is both understood and waged today. In a certain sense, my entire argument can be seen as a kind of mock trial in which I provide various expert witnesses (most of them philosophers) to speak to the issues at hand. Therefore, the guiding question at the conclusion of this report will be *What is the nature of the conflict today and what is the idiom of the critical that might best correspond to it?*

### Note to the reader

*The* Abstract *and* Summary & Transition *sections, which frame each of the three parts of this report, can be read independently of their corresponding sections. This is also true of the final summary and outline of the five principle arguments of the report, which can be read first.*

## Part I *The University in the Ears of its Publics*

*Left to itself, a spontaneous (technical) practice produces only the 'theory' it needs as a means to produce the ends assigned to it; this theory is never more than a reflection of this end, uncriticized, unknown, in its means of realization, that is, it is a by-product of the reflection of the technical practice's end on its means. A 'theory' which does not question the end whose by-product it is remains a prisoner of this end and of the 'realities' which have imposed it as an end.*
— Louis Althusser, *Pour Marx*[1]

*"The quality of the University is under great threat. We must take charge of change."*
— Former University of California President Jack Peltason.[2]

### *Abstract*

*Rather than seeing the decline in authority suffered by certain faculties today (mostly located in the disciplines of the Humanities) as a relatively recent development as many have argued, I show that it can already be pre-figured in Kant's original appeal to the sovereignty of a higher authority to rectify the imbalance of power between the higher and lower faculties. I discuss how Kant saw the very nature of conflict as essential to both the creation of new knowledge in the university, as well as to continued assessment of archival knowledge that is maintained and reproduced by the historical disciplines. Kant's entire argument can be understood simply as proposing a manner of governing or legislating this conflict between the faculties in order to prevent what he defined as the "illegal forms of conflict" from being employed in a manner that would threaten the autonomy of the faculties. I suggest that the rise of an administrative subject today who is charged with defining the university's relationship to the larger society — with managing the conflict of faculties — may signal a change in the epistemological conditions of knowledge. In this part, my discussion will be limited to how recent restructuring efforts by university administrators have begun to shape one public institution, the University of California. I believe that this local example may have some relevance concerning what is already taking place nationally, particularly in "land-grant" and larger research universities in the United States. This example will also be important in light of the fact that these new models of organization, often referred to by the terms "corporatization" and/or "privatization," are now being exported globally and are being instituted from Australia to South Africa. My discussion of the principles behind this restructuring is based on a report that was issued from a long-range planning and goals- setting conference that took place in the summer of 1993, which was charged with speculating on the future of the university with a view to future changes in its mission and traditions.[3] In my discussion and analysis of this report, I will frame some of the implications of this contemporary example in comparison with two historical and philosophical perspectives. The first historical perspective is Kant's original argument of* The Conflict of the Faculties, *which I take up in order to make certain general inferences with regard to the contemporary subject of the university. The second perspective I take up is Jacques Derrida's more recent reflections on this subject, delivered at Cornell in 1983, the text of which was published that year in the journal* diacritics *under the title "The Principle of Reason: The University in the Eyes of its Pupils."[4]*

## I(a) *The conflict of cultures*

In late summer of 1993, a group of sixty members of the leadership of the University of California (mostly regents, administrators, and other university officials) gathered to discuss the current crisis in the University caused by the "severe setbacks" in state funding during the late 1980s. According to the mission statement of the conference, "those circumstances [i.e., the decrease in state funding], plus the accelerating changes in the state, nation, and world, call for a fundamental assessment of the university's future course."[5] The objective, therefore, was to frame "substantive ideas and proposals relating to the task of *preserving, adapting, and sometimes changing fundamentally* the university's position and role in an uncertain and probably difficult future."[6]

The following passages are excerpted from "Report: U.C. Long Term Planning Retreat, University of California, September 1993."[7] I will cite a passage from this report at length to foreground and provide an example of what could be seen as current university discourse, and to call attention to the presence of a certain discursive subject who seems to have emerged in the position vacated by the classical philosopher, even while taking up his language as well as the Platonic role of a pilot who navigates the ship of state by fixing its compass, according to a well-known and often cited phrase by Kant, on "the starry skies above us and the moral laws within."

I. *Context for Change: Positioning the University*

Most attention was dedicated to framing substantive ideas and proposals relating to preserving, adapting, and sometimes changing fundamentally the university's position and role in an uncertain and probably difficult future. At the same time, it was recognized that one ingredient of creative change is the university's capacity or incapacity to change. Obstacles to change can be found in the cultures of various groups in the university, in comfortable assumptions of continuity of external support, and in the sluggishness of existing structures and procedures. With respect to the latter, the following arenas were suggested as possibilities for investigation:

A. The adaptive capacity of campus units — academic departments, schools, colleges — in the process of change. Possible areas of concern are instructional improvement, curricular change, and faculty personnel practices.

B. It was recognized further that (a) many of the university's inherited structures and procedures have played a role in building and sustaining the university's excellence; (b) most structural arrangements in the university contain a mix of flexibility and inflexibility; (c) efforts to change long-standing university structures probably confront the strongest resistance to change. In light of such considerations, structural reforms should not be attempted on a headlong or wholesale basis. However, it would repay the university and its campuses to undertake selective task-force reviews for nodes of structural resistance and inflexibility, with an eye to improving institutional performance and streamlining adaptive capacity.

II. *Context for Change: Values of the University*:

As indicated, the most visible concerns of the retreat had to do with recasting university goals and policies. Participants also recognized that whatever changes occur will do so in the context of several still-viable values inherited by the university. In that context, participants reminded themselves of some of these values, and raised questions about how they themselves might require redefinition and reformation in the light of current and future changes. The following points emerged:

A. Despite the great need for economies in university programs and for directed applications of knowledge, the university and its publics should reaffirm the principle of the pursuit of knowledge irrespective of its immediate applications. Intrinsic to the idea of the university is that, in principle, no corner of knowledge should remain unexplored.

B. The principle of commitment to objectivity and dispassion in the search for knowledge is a cornerstone of the modern university. As the university seeks to expand and diversify both its sources of funding and the range of its applied research and service, it becomes especially important to reaffirm this principle. This may call for periodic examination and redefinition in areas such as the public nature of knowledge, conflicts of interest, the limits on conditions to be specified by external donors and supporters of university programs, and what counts and does not count as "service."

C. The principle of academic freedom also stands as a valued tradition of academic life, and calls for continuing defense commensurate with that status. That value, too, may be challenged anew as the boundaries of the university become more permeable in its relations with larger society.

D. At the same time, it is essential to recognize that academic freedom has never been coterminous with academic license or academic chaos. Academic freedom exists in the context of a number of understandings and limits. Chief among these is that freedom of choice in teaching and research is always defined in the context of departmental, campus, and university educational goals and policies. Furthermore, the realization of academic freedom is possible only in an organizational context that guarantees civility, mutual respect, and non-coerciveness from within and without. Those responsible for safeguarding academic freedom are equally responsible for safeguarding the institutional contexts in which that principle can flourish.[8]

Although nowhere identified, the participants of the long-term planning retreat assume the task of representing the perspective of the university in a time of crisis. This task is outlined from the first sentence and concerns "preserving, adapting, and sometimes fundamentally changing the university's position and role in an uncertain and probably difficult future." The subject, who is speaking both *of* and *for* the modern idea of the university, seems to have a clear view as to what the institution is becoming, even though this "view" (a total picture, perhaps even in the sense of a *Weltanschauung*, or "world-view") is only implicitly present as a form of unspoken consensus. This consensus remains bound to a private decision-making entity outside the public sphere of debate and, consequently, is nowhere presented, proposed, or outlined within the Report itself. *If such a total picture exists,* then it is only in the minds of those who are identified as "the participants" and who can be recognized as the *agents provocateurs* (even managers) of change. (As former president Jack Peltason announces, "*We* must take charge of change.")

Yet, without such a view, the Report could not speak of the obstacles to realizing such change, adaptation, and streamlining that this subject projects as both necessary and swift: "[M]ore generally, the relations between campuses and the system-wide administration should be the subject of continuous assessment, particularly in light of the anticipated pace of future changes." Even as the document seems to outline the need to re-structure and re-organize existing disciplinary units and fields of institutional knowledge in order better to serve specific interests on the part of its "publics," this subject also feels the need to erect certain barriers and articulate certain time-honored "values" in the name of a universal, rather classical, picture of university reason. In the very process of adapting and transforming the historico-institutional structure of the existing university system according to a new set of principles and presuppositions concerning the position of the modern university *vis-à-vis* its exterior "publics" and its indigenous "cultures," this subject feels compelled to remind itself of certain fundamental principles (credos, values) that would function as guard-rails to the rapidity and sweeping nature of this change, and would prevent the university from being de-structured in such a way that it would no longer resemble its historical form in its renovated, adapted, more stream-lined design. I will return to this below.

It is not hard to discern in the viewpoint this language embodies a certain leftover from a colonial administrative rhetoric that might help to clarify the technical meaning of the term "adaptation" with regard to the university's interior "cultures." The use of the term "culture" in reference to the intra-institutional collectives of faculty and students is, I think, technically precise from the perspective of what (or who) the Report identifies as "the University." As we know from anthropologist Jean-Loup Amselle, a large portion of the language and techniques of modern day administrations originated in colonial governments and has subsequently been adapted to the problem of "managing populations" in first-world institutions (along with the difference of perspective this implies between the administrator and the administered where there is no natural affiliation assumed). In fact, it is this perspective which promotes a more exaggerated separation between distinct groups and a tendency to pose this distinction in the form of conflict.[9] Consequently, there is a certain borrowing from the nineteenth-century anthropological definition of culture (with a small "c"), which is employed quite casually to explain the cause of those factors that are identified with the various expressions of "resistance to over-all change."

As we all know from the usage of the concept of resistance which seems to fit here, cultures are insular, rigid, hegemonic and inflexible structures which generate and maintain their own values through legitimation, prejudice, and by means of ritualistic systems of encoding and ceremonial language games. These values are often non-exchangeable with the values and language games of other cultures. From the larger perspective of "the University" itself, however, somehow distinguishable from its various interior cultures in the language of the Report, this non-exchangeability leads to what is defined as a "non-adaptive capacity" which introduces points of resistance and inflexibility into the structure, like "noise" in a cybernetic system. The effects produced by the different cultures are not consonant with its over-all objectives for changing and adapting the structure and are, therefore, determined as negative from this other perspective.

It is important to emphasize again that this discourse of the university no longer resembles the discourse of the philosophy faculty, who seem to be strangely absent from the place where the university can be heard speaking both to and about itself, concerning its future architecture, its long-term goals (*telos*), even about the historical and social function of the various knowledges and techniques that are produced by its various faculty "cultures" and, in a certain manner, reproduced by its student cultures as well. We can infer from the negative evaluation given to the various forms of dissonance and cross-speaking that emerge from and between these cultures that, from the perspective of this new university subject, the creation of new knowledge is no longer seen to be engendered by the instances of conflict between historical disciplinary partitions and fields.

*It is precisely the presence of a seemingly permanent conflict between faculties that seems to be responsible for many of the problems that university administrators confront in their attempts to communicate, in a coherent and unified manner, the position of* *the university before its various publics. Rather than being, as it is in the Kantian argument, the very event and even the "eventuation" of new knowledge and the reno- vation of historical and disciplinary knowledges through the creative strife (*polemos, conflict, war*), it is precisely the character of "conflict" among and between faculties that itself becomes the primary object of the new managerial task. According to this new subject, the conflict between intra-university "cultures" — not, here, its faculties — must be better organized, controlled, adapted, and regulated in order to avoid the possibility of increasing various misperceptions by the general public concerning the university's role and its service to the larger society.*

I have placed the above paragraph in italics to highlight the possibility that the entrance of this new faculty to *manage*, to *steer*, and to *mediate* the conflict of the other faculties may in fact signal a fundamental revision of the epistemological conditions of knowledge, particularly concerning the classical autonomy of the faculties themselves over matters internal to the discipline and their right to settle their own territorial disputes. The public discourse of the university, as opposed to the private languages engendered by its indigenous cultures, has become the responsibility of a specialized subject who bears the juridical and executive respon- sibility as well as the technical language with which "the University" speaks. This subject speaks indirectly to the various interior "cultures" that it might wish to inform (mostly, to stimulate change or to install a more "adaptive capacity" within their local and ritualized practices), or to the several "publics" that it might wish to address (clearly, as if with only one voice, and without what the Report determines as the traits of ambiguity that confound all culture-bound discourse).

Concerning what it transmits to its own cultures, the language of the Report is unequivocal. It is never a question of "discussion," "debate," or "consultation" with and among the various cultures of the university, but rather their "adaptation" and "capacity for adaptation," or conversely, their "resistance," "inflexibility," or "their permeability in relation to the larger society," as well as their "rigidities" and their "articulations" with similar or like cultures in the same institution or with other campuses. Therefore, in addition to the colonial genealogy that is implied here by the problem of managing cultural groups or indigenous populations, the second paradigm these terms belong to could be said to correspond to a cybernetic scheme, in which the viability of the various structures and cultures that inhabit and comprise the university are judged by their capacity for receiving new information. The argument of the Report outlines three obstacles to change in general: "Obstacles to change can be found in the cultures of various groups in the university, in comfortable assumptions of continuity of external support, and in the sluggishness of existing structures and procedures." Because the over-all objective will be to minimize and by-pass resistance as well as to "streamline adaptation," this would seem to imply that these obstacles must either be removed or adapted in order to institute "change" — "particularly," as the report states, "in light of the pace anticipated of future change." "In light of such considerations," the Report recommends, "structural reforms should not be attempted on a headlong or wholesale basis."

This last recommendation should cause some concern to those who are identified as the university's cultures. It implies that they should not expect a large part of "the structural reform" of the university to take place through its present governing systems (e.g. Department committees, Divisions, Academic Senates), through its long-term structures (e.g. tenure system, class and rank of already installed line-faculty), or through its current procedures (e.g. review and promotion, discussion and debate among and between its various departments and divisional disciplines over matters of curriculum). This is because, according to the language of the Report, existing structures and procedures are too rigid and sluggish to be effective vehicles of necessary change, and thus, more difficult to "adapt." If recent developments give any indication of a solution to this problem, the "new structure" will be installed in a piecemeal manner, and ciphered in terms of various "economies" that now exist in the institution (budgetary, curricular, research, alliance with industries or corporate donors, public or community service).

As distinguished from its internal cultures, the Report also speaks of the university and its "publics." Who are these publics? We know it is not the students, since the university never speaks to them, although it often speaks *of* them. This is an important question, because the public addressees of the university's discourse will determine the form of policy. "The public," the Report explains elsewhere, "is in reality multiple publics — members of the state and federal legislature, executives, concerned civic leaders, taxpayers, parents, the media, and various social movements — that hear what the university says with different ears and sometimes place contradictory demands on it."[10] If the problem that the university finds with its indigenous cultures is that there are too many voices, then here we might notice that the problem it finds with its publics is that they have too many ears. Therefore, the university seeks to "inform and communicate with its publics in areas of ambiguity and controversy," and "to augment its efforts to speak not only on behalf *of* itself, but *for* other educational segments," including, I imagine, those intra-institutional segments who must not be allowed to speak for themselves due to the presence of these contradictory demands which require a special expertise in addressing multiple constituencies — that is, the problems inherent in how civil and public space is structured within a postmodern media state.

In the sections that follow I will address the underlying principles of this highly specialized "discourse of the modern university" in order to gain a better view, perhaps, of the relationship between the new values that have emerged to define the function of "communicative action" (Habermas) within the public sphere and the eclipse of the classical *idea* of university reason.

I(b) *The return(s) of the philosopher*

In *The Conflict of the Faculties* Kant himself noted that the faculties themselves do not speak or address their debates before the public, which would be tantamount to placing "the people" in the seat of the tribunal to hear the appeal of opposing parties in a trial.[11] Kant's discourse is essentially paternalistic around this point: republican, not democratic. He writes that "the people" are not only incompetent to judge concerning the knowledge of the faculties, but are already inclined not to want to know anything about the subject matter of debates between academics. Such knowledge, he argues, is useless to them and would interfere with "the course of daily happenings," in which they have more of an interest.[12] Therefore, the discourse of the faculties is never addressed to the public, according to Kant, but only to the other faculties as well as to the membership of the various "workshops" (academies and scientific societies) that may comprise the historical and institutional representation of knowledge within the same faculty.[13]

It is for this reason perhaps that academic discourse bears a certain "heterogeneity" that marks its very appearance, including the logical and rhetorical forms that distinguish academic discourse from common speech. By its very nature, it is closed to the public. On the other hand, the subject of academic discourse concerns an essential form of "publicity" that is prior to its historical determination as a public form, a "publicity" (*Offentlichekeit*) that Kant, and Spinoza before him, identified with the spontaneous freedom of thinking alone. Of course, this is the subject of the philosophy faculty, but can also be found in the higher faculty of medicine since, as Kant says, "its texts cannot be sanctioned from higher authorities but can only be drawn from nature."[14]

For a moment, however, let us remain with the description of the Kantian architecture of the university as a point of comparison with our contemporary example above. In *The Conflict of Faculties*, those who are found in the position of addressing "the people" are identified, not with the faculty, but rather with what Kant calls the "*businessmen*, or technicians of learning."[15] This group is identified as forming a special class of the general *intelligentsia* (university graduates), comprised principally of graduates from the higher faculties — lawyers, jurists, government officials, and clergy — who are described by Kant as "instruments of the government, invested with an office for its own purpose (which is not exactly the progress of the sciences)."[16] Throughout his argument, Kant reveals the considerable amount of anxiety he feels toward this class, which underlines the rhetorical purpose of the entire argument of the first part of *The Conflict of the Faculties*, "The Philosophy Faculty versus the Theology Faculty." This anxiety can best be illustrated in the following passage:

> *As tools of the government* (clergymen, magistrates, and physicians), they have a legal influence on the public and form a special class of the intelligentsia, who are not free to make public use of their learning as they see fit, but are subject to the censorship of the faculties. So *the government must keep them under strict control, to prevent them from using judicial power*, which belongs to the faculties; *for they deal directly with the people*, who are incompetent (like the clergymen in relation to the laymen), and share in the executive, though certainly not the legislative, power in their field.[17]

What Kant is outlining here is the danger posed by this powerful new class in representing, participating, or "taking sides" in what he refers to elsewhere as "an illegal conflict of the faculties."[18] In this type of conflict, one side resorts to a means of coercion, threat, and bribery as a means to winning their argument against the opposing side. As pure "instruments of the government," this class becomes the very extension of state power over the "public," and can be used effectively by the government to achieve its end of influencing the people.

Elsewhere, Kant lists these ends in the following order (which he defines as government "incentives" for supporting the progress of knowledge in the corresponding fields), which also follows the rank and order he constructs for representing the division of the higher faculties into what could be called a "Holy Trinity": "*eternal* well-being" (theology), "*civil* well-being" (law), and "*physical* well-being" (the medical and biological sciences).[19] Here is a simple description of the logic at work in the Kantian division and ranking of the faculties between higher and lower. If the government invests itself most in the support and cultivation of the higher faculties with whom it deals directly and shares a common interest in knowledge, it is only in as much as it invests in the development of specialized knowledge and techniques that will further its own end — as any historical power would seek finer and more efficient tools to further its *absolute imperium*, as Spinoza also said.[20] Then as now, the lower faculties find themselves not only in a position of being less "funded," but also of being only indirectly instituted by this instrumental function and, thus, outside the circuit of state power.

However, this rhetoric of instrumentality works both ways, since Kant's intention here is to define the function that is proper to this specialized class (*qua* "tools") in such a way that he might cause the state to curb or restrain its influence both within the university and before the executive authority of the government itself. First of all, these technicians are bereft of any theoretical knowledge concerning the principles underlying their functions, since "it is enough that they retain empirical knowledge of the statutes relevant to their office (hence what has to do with practice)."[21] These businessmen, as the saying goes, "know only enough *theory* to make them dangerous" and should never be allowed to engage in a theoretical discussion in public concerning the principles of their field, a discussion which belongs only under the province of the faculties. Moreover, as pure instruments (or tools), their reason is limited to their function (or office) alone and is, therefore, defined by Kant as a "private use of reason": a use of reason that reflects only upon the means to an already assigned end. (This description of the "blindness" and "end-oriented" nature of private reason should recall the epigraph that appears at the beginning of this part, which is taken from Althusser's *Pour Marx*.)

The first strategic function of Kant's rhetoric of the tool immediately concerns the restraint of the class from having any "judicial power" (that is, the power of censorship) within the university itself. Kant is in effect asking the state to restrain its own judicial authority in university matters. Even more radically, he is appealing to the only true executive authority of the government ("Frederick William, by grace of God King of Prussia, etc., etc.," — the addressee and, perhaps, the only intended reader of *The Conflict of the Faculties*) to submit his own "agents" to the complete authority and censorship of the faculties, and to the censorship of the philosophy faculty in particular, who can exercise no power of their own, except a purely theoretical power which is identified with the power of reason itself.

The only possible motive that we might even conceive for King Frederick William II to acquiesce to Kant's appeal, which would amount to nothing less than submitting an organ or member of his own body to the control of another, constitutes the second aspect of Kant's rhetoric of the tool. This aspect can be phrased in the following way: An instrument can only be called such when it is completely surrendered to the command of a subject who uses it, thereby providing it with the energy necessary for it to "work" or to "function." Moreover, its function must be understood as the effect of a principle of reason, responsible for its determination as a "tool," which will regulate the knowledge and propriety of its usefulness (what it is for, how it works, and on which occasions it is useful). According to this analogy, as "pure instruments of the government," the members of this class can, by definition only, be said to be functioning properly when they further the ends assigned to them by the state. If they should begin to function according to another principle — for example, in their own interest — this would amount to the threat of "anarchy" (the loss of ruling principle), a word that Kant evokes several times in the text of *The Conflict of the Faculties*. This would potentially pose the greatest threat to an existing government because of the influence this class already exercises over the public, as well as the share of executive power it already enjoys.

*What better safeguard, Kant suggests, than to place the juridical authority over the principles that govern these instruments of state power in the hands of a faculty that has no direct influence upon the public and no practical means of exercising its own power — under the command of a faculty whose only function is in the interest of pure reason alone.*

In understanding Kant's argument around this point, we should be cautious of its rhetorical purpose by recalling that Kant was one of the first and perhaps the most vocal cheerleaders for "the lower faculty." Thus, Kant can be accused of being somewhat coy, and it is hard to imagine that a good statesman wouldn't be able to see right through the argument despite its subtlety. The rhetoric of Kant's argument can be interpreted on two levels: the first is intended as an appeal to the psychological state of the royal despot (i.e., a threat of anarchy); the second has to do with undermining, or at least inverting, the established hierarchy between the higher and lower faculties and appeals to a certain Christian sensibility in which the last will be first, and the lowest will be the highest.

As we might suspect, Kant does not press this allusion too strongly with regard to the position of the monarch himself; that is to say, he does not overtly argue, at least in this context, that the power of reason is a higher sovereignty than the wisdom of the despot or monarch, even though this is everywhere implied in the argument. Rather, Kant's strategy is to unseat the higher faculties by creating in the monarch's mind a bogey of the possible conflict caused by the dependence of the state on the knowledge and function of the higher faculties (law, medicine, theology), and consequently, the power that immediately accrues from this dependent relationship which demands that a class of intelligentsia produced by these faculties (such as lawyers, jurists, doctors, clergy) is properly subordinated to serve the ends of the state and not its own ends. (Thus, Kant's use of the term "businessmen" to describe this class of *intelligentsia* may have an additional meaning.)

As we know from the ensuing history, Kant's speculations concerning this class would be proven right, particularly as a greater number of students and intelligentsia emerged from the petty-bourgeoisie and would later use the instruments of their public offices to dismantle the monarchy and to tax the ruling aristocracy out of existence. Within a mere century of Kant's text, in *The Communist Manifesto* (1883) Marx would speak of this class precisely in terms of the successful campaign it waged against the nobility, as well as the emerging democratic states and the institutions of "civil society" (*bürgerliche Gesellschaft*) that were created to reflect and to secure the powerful interests of this new class. Thus, there is somewhat of an original historical irony we witness in Kant's argument to Fredrick the Great, especially in light of the following statement from *The Communist Manifesto* less than eighty years later — that "the executive of the modern State is simply a committee for managing the common affairs of the whole bourgeoisie."[22]

The second level of Kant's rhetoric does not concern the King as much as it does the position and importance of the disciplines gathered together under the lower faculty in the university of Kant's time. Since Frederick William saw the function of the university was primarily to train civil servants, it was mandated that all students must enroll in one of the higher faculties. (It is generally not known in which of the higher faculties Kant himself was enrolled, but it is traditionally assumed to have been medicine.) We might imagine from the simple description of the curriculum that the faculty of philosophy would have a nebulous position in terms of the power it exercised in the university. In addition to serving no apparent state-directed end and having no link to a professional body, under Frederick William's dictate students could only choose to dedicate themselves to the study of philosophy and related disciplines as a "minor." (In his argument, however, Kant will mirror the professional model of the higher faculties by assigning to philosophy the task of producing more faculties and doctorates to serve the state-sponsored end of the university.)

In fact, we might well imagine a situation that is very similar to the one faced by the Humanities in the university today with all the consequent difficulties this situation implies in terms of funding, enrollment and matriculation of majors, and demonstration of value or utility. Therefore, we must read Kant's appeal for a form of "government" to regulate "the conflict of faculties" with this imbalance of power and interest in mind; like other appeals of its kind, rhetorically it is the appeal to an outside judicial power (in this case, Frederick William) to regulate this imbalance in order to protect the weaker and more vulnerable party from the stronger one.

In one sense this form of appeal to "justice" bears a strong resemblance to a common judicial practice in which the court and its officers will be predisposed and even prejudiced in favor of the weaker party in a given suit as a manner of equalizing the conflict and "creating a level playing field," that is, by compensating for the inequality produced by powerful social or economic interests enjoyed by the other party. Although Kant frequently employs a judicial language as the source of his metaphors, the primary metaphor he employs for this conflict (*Streit*) is derived from the statecraft of war. Therefore, another analogy we might employ to get a better picture of what Kant is asking is the situation that occurs in the case of a civil war or conflict between internal warring factions when an outside party (a neighboring state, or imperial power) will furnish weapons to the weakest of the parties in order to equalize the conflict as well as to prevent the conflict from spreading outside the territory or region. As I have already argued above, implicit in Kant's use of this analogy (which Frederick William would have immediately recognized in conjunction with his own contemporaneous geo-political problems) is that more weapons must be provided to the philosophers in order to prevent this conflict from spreading outside the university and into society itself, even to the point of threatening the rule of the monarchy. Although the higher faculties enjoy a superiority that is derived from their intimate relationship to state power, Kant is asking for the power of "censorship" — the requirement of the higher faculties to submit their knowledge to the lower faculties, the faculty of philosophy, for an examination.

However, not satisfied with the discretion or the arbitrary disposition of "the Prince" as the sole remedy to the imbalance of power in the conflict between higher and lower faculties, Kant also employs another strategy, that of turning a weakness into a strength. As I said above, Kant is perhaps the first and most vocal proponent of the "lower faculty" in the modern university. It was during the eighteenth century, in particular, that the lower faculties were perhaps the most vital and innovative, as well as the most successful in accruing and applying new knowledge to the study of other fields and disciplines (for example, physics and biology, geography and anthropology; history, jurisprudence, hermeneutics and philology). It was precisely because of its relative autonomy, that is, its "freedom from" external professional and civil constraints, that, according to Kant's argument, the lower faculties were perhaps in the best position to emulate the "pure interest" of reason itself, the study of "knowledge for knowledge's sake," and therefore were best positioned to found the principle of reason that guides or steers the course of the university in society. In Kant's hands the term *lower* has been redefined and has been given a new architectonic value: as the ground, or the founding principle, of the whole.

Despite the bravado of this narrative as a compelling description of the nature of "pure reason," a description that would be consolidated and reproduced by philosophers as the natural image of reason over the course of two centuries, we must be more mindful than ever before that this image of "pure reason" is a rhetorical construction that is produced in an argument that favors the lower faculty, the faculty of philosophy. If we look at Kant's rhetoric more closely, therefore, we find that what he is arguing is the following. First, there is a contingent and historical organization of knowledge within a social institution of the university, all parts of which are ranked in value according to social utility, political interest, or the maintenance and reproduction of dominion, whether from the perspective of a dominant class or from the perspective of a current form of government power (such as the nation-state). Second, there exists an unintentional and accidental effect in this organization of a relatively free, autonomous, "pure" form of knowledge that also happens to be the best representative of the principle of knowledge itself as a *free, spontaneous, autonomous,* and above all, *transcendent* faculty. Kant is claiming that the purest representative of the faculty of knowledge is produced as the result of an accident or a design flaw in the organization of knowledge according to the dominant forms of social interest. Kant is simply capitalizing on the presence of a structural flaw in such an organization that has as its contingent effect the creation of a form of knowledge that expresses the degree-zero of interest, the negative and the negation of interest or immediate aim, and of a faculty that is freed from the constraints of social obligation either to a profession or in service to the State.

Of course, we know from Kant's other philosophical writings, and from the systematic presentation of the faculties outlined in the *Critique of Pure Reason*, that even though the creation of pure reason remains a structural effect of the finite or subjectively bound faculties, it is by no means merely accidental or contingent, but essentially belongs to the design of Nature herself. *In the final analysis, however, this is something that we have to take on faith—that there exists something like a transcendental contract between Nature and Reason.* I have highlighted the rhetorical occasion of this representation of the faculty of reason in order to mark the contradiction that is implicit in Kant's presentation, as well the possibility of self-interest and cunning behind Kant's image of pure reason. I will return to this question below in addressing the problem of dualism as the basis of modern critical knowledge: the problem of deriving a critical form of knowledge that is relatively autonomous or purified of dominant social interests.

One might notice that in Kant's list of "businessmen" he nowhere mentions the businessmen of the university itself. This fact marks the historical distance of the Kantian architecture of the university from our own. *It would never have occurred to him that there could be an administrative body of "businessmen" who would be charged not only with the practical functions of a university institution, but also with a theoretical knowledge of the idea of the university and, therefore, not only with a certain instrumentality with regard to the state, but also with a "juridical power" over the faculties themselves.* Of course, Kant's discourse can be determined as taking place during the incubation of the idea of the university; its historical realization as an institution which bears some resemblance to its current structure — whether I find a similar version of this structure at University of California or Syracuse University — did not take place until some years later, in Germany, particularly with the institution of the University of Berlin under the direction of Wilhelm von Humboldt between 1807 and 1810. Despite the historical and institutional distance between Kant's time and our own, a distance which makes the borders between intra-university and extra-university sectors difficult to trace using the map Kant provides, we might risk the following speculation.

Let us say we were gifted with the power to raise Kant from the dead tomorrow and we brought him to a modern university and asked him to survey and evaluate the current arrangement between the faculties, the legislative body of the state, and the present administrative class of university managers. Certainly, Kant would have grouped this class of administrators among the other "businessmen," as being pure instruments of the state even if their offices are now located within the university itself. He would have classified them as "state agents" for the following reasons: first, by the function of their office; second, in their role of communicating directly to the public (whether to parents and potential students in admission brochures and advertisements, to legislative bodies in mission statements and long-term planning reports, or to the media and ranking-agencies in statistics on admission scores, retention, diversity, and out-take interviews); third, by the executive power this class is holds in proxy for the state (in terms of budgetary performance and program review). Of course, this classification of present-day university administrators should cause us to interrogate more carefully the partitions drawn up in the Kantian discourse of the university between "inside" and "outside," or between "proper" and "improper" juridism, or what Kant had defined as the forms of "legal" and "illegal" conflict between different parties to the conflict of faculties.

With regard to our contemporary situation, what would probably cause Kant the greatest amount of concern would be the fact that the discourse over the principles of university reason rests primarily in the hands of these so-called "government agents," a fact which might force him to conclude that he had lost his "appeal" (in the juridical sense) a very long time ago. As I will take up below, this sign of failure is repeated in a lecture given by Jacques Derrida during a symposium in 1983 at the University of Alabama, "Our Academic Contract: *The Conflict of the Faculties* in America," toward the end of which the following interpolation appears:

> And yet, despite this parliamentary juridism, Kant is obliged to admit that the conflict 'can never end'; and the 'philosophy faculty is one which ought to be permanently armed for this purpose.' The truth under its protection will always be threatened because 'the higher faculties will never renounce the desire to govern' or to dominate (*Begierde zu herrschen*). *I break off brusquely, the university is about to be closed, it is very late, too late for this Kantian discourse, which is perhaps what I meant to say.*[23]

I want to be clear concerning my intentions at this point. With this little fable of Kant's second-coming, I am not necessarily privileging his point of view or performing a venerable return to the sources (much less to an original and natal site of the idea of a university for that matter). Kant's opinion in the present context may not be that relevant to the formation of the contemporary academic institution; his analysis is too limited and structurally primitive to account for the relationships that comprise the current institution. However, the difference may throw open the question for us as to how things got to be the way they are, as well as announce a task of historically grounded analysis of the modern institution which would trace, on the one hand, the emergence of this new class of technicians who could be seen as instruments in effecting the state's end of increasing the measures of a society of control in the name of higher education and; on the other hand, of marking precisely the institutional and historical narratives which would make an account of when and how the "discourse of principles" gradually passed out of the hands of the faculties and into the hands of this modern class of "businessmen."

Of course, the latter task must be approached in a preliminary and cautious manner since it would require a certain historical verification that this power had ever rested with the faculties, as if the university *once upon a time* existed as an autonomous social institution located within a given society yet external to rule of its positive laws. If so, then under what conditions? What were the limitations and positive restraints upon the exercise of this power of self-determination and auto-legitimation? Even if such an example of an historical institution were to be found, which is unlikely, it would betray the Kantian "idea" of the university and change the nature of the discourse of principles, thus being directed toward the past and concerned with a nostalgic recovery of an earlier incarnation conceived as being a more pure expression of its original ideals and objectives. Such a discourse of the university, for example, can be found in both humanist and postmodern representations of the modern university as a fallen (or in Bill Reading's word, "ruined") institution which is thoroughly contaminated by foreign principles or popular cultural sentiments on the one hand, or by "corporate values" and the evils of capitalism on the other.[24] Yet, such an hypothetical university did not exist even in the time of Kant. If it did, then there would be no need for an argument such as the one proposed by *The Conflict of the Faculties*. Kant would not have had the occasion to write it and, indeed, it would not exist as such.

Turning to the contemporary situation, perhaps the most plausible explanation concerning the emergence of this new administrative class of technicians is offered by Jürgen Habermas in *Legitimation Crisis*. Following the work of Niklas Luhmann on complexity and democracy, but within a more philosophical framework, Habermas suggests that the growing autonomy and dominance of an administrative "sub-system" in almost all social institutions (particularly in Germany at the time he was writing) is the result of the contingent nature of the political system itself in late-democratic societies.[25] "Reduced to a brief formula, it has to do with the fact that the political system can no longer derive its identity from the society if it is required by the society precisely as a contingent system which could possibly be otherwise."[26] Luhmann recasts the "old European" concept of freedom as "contingent-selectivity," and in turn, Habermas sees this as perhaps *the problem*, which has resulted in the growing autonomy of a political sub-system that is now the "differential steering mechanism" (Habermas) of many social institutions, particularly the contemporary university: the problem of the freedom to choose one method of social organization among all the different alternatives given that every possible choice will remain contingent *since there is no longer any "natural" organization of society.*

According to Habermas, it is the very idea of democratic freedom that can be determined negatively in the view that the current system could be otherwise or differently organized, that burdens the system with abstract possibilities of alternative methods of organization, and produces the autonomy of a subject who is in some way separate from the system itself and is pressured with the God-like problem of choosing, in a Leibnizian phrase, the "best of all possible worlds," that is, the possible manners of organizing the social bond. Thus, perhaps the current-day administrator is the modern avatar of a figure that Hegel once defined as the consciousness of *bad infinity*: a subject who is alienated from nature and, consequently, is burdened by its autonomy and its freedom in organizing its environment willy-nilly. Like Kafka's country doctor, this new organizer is struck dumb by the number of abstract possibilities as well as by the realization that any particular method of organization will immediately be haunted by all the others not selected (yet to be invented).

Perhaps the latent flaw in Habermas' analysis was its general application to any number of late-democratic societies in a global context without regard to specific differences in the forms of government or institutional contexts; however, in a very critical sense, his intuition concerning the growing problem of the autonomy of the administrative class directly addresses the situation of the contemporary university, as I have illustrated above in my commentary on the Report. It might allow us, for example, to understand one of the conditions of the problematic character of autonomy that now belongs to an administrative perspective we outlined above in the language of the Report, a perspective which seems strangely differentiated from other "intra-cultural" perspectives that populate the university, as if somehow approaching from a point that is external to the institution itself, a perspective that is often represented as the future of the university. Inevitably, the problem that this subject often encounters is the problem of adapting these cultures and these traditions to a new or alternative organization that is prescribed by the pressures of other systems on the university.

By far the greatest problem that this administrative subject faces is the problem of "what in fact a university is given the possibility that it can always be otherwise." We have evidence of the dilemma of "contingent-selectivity" in any number of the new administrative programs and initiatives that we see on a daily basis in the contemporary university, programs that are responsible for introducing new methods of organizing and "assessing" the historical structures and traditions that comprise a university. For example, we could refer to the influx of new models of organization (those mostly borrowed from other social institutions such as government or business); the aggressive promotion of new definitions of the existing social and moral relationships between subjects such as the pedagogical relationship between the students and the faculty according to a "consumer" or "client" model; the constant introduction of new assessment initiatives which ask academic units to evaluate themselves and their performance according to a set of criteria most often keyed to some performance or efficiency index that has been adopted from some other institution. Behind all of these initiatives, there is a tangible prejudice or bias that any existing structure should be viewed as fundamentally out-dated — simply, it seems, by virtue of the fact that it exists in the present — and must therefore be re-thought, changed, and re-configured.

Here we discover what is perhaps the most acute point of contradiction that structures the present system itself: on one hand, every part of the system is always being evaluated in terms of all the abstract possibilities of innovation, change, and adaptation; on the other hand, the aggressive drive or will to forget whatever method of organization exists in the present, there is a tangible prejudice toward any existing structure or tradition as necessarily being "out-dated" or "no longer in-step with the environmental context of constant change," and thus the urge to re-configure or to re-adapt every element in order to make room for the blind possibility of a new organization. As a result of this contradiction, any new method of organization, once it is fixed in place, will immediately become a candidate for "assessment" and "re-configuration," which only leads to a more accelerated pace of new reforms and assessment initiatives. All of these developments that are taking place in the university can be understood as "symptomatic" expressions of the problem of freedom articulated by Habermas above: the contingency of any structure or political form of organization in the context of all its abstract alternatives ("abstract" since we must also include here alternatives, or better yet "innovations," that have yet to be invented).

We should recall that the concept of freedom in a democratic organization is the ability and the spontaneous power of a "people" to self-select and organize itself without regard to precedent or to natural design. By contrast, earlier forms of government always established their form of hierarchy mimetically with an order of Nature. (We might remember all the poetic allusions that metaphorically established the identity of the monarch with the sun.) A democratic organization, on the other hand, is patently non-mimetic and even anti-mimetic. What is the nature of the authorization of a "people" (as distinct from species, race, or ethnicity) than the purely performative and mythic power of its founding enunciation? However, with this non-mimetic and purely historical nature, there comes the sense of arbitrariness and dizziness concerning the particular form of organization itself. The performative and arbitrary character of the enunciation itself haunts every manner of organization. Thus, the administrative power emerges as the "differential steering mechanism of the social bond," as that place and that subject where the question of organization and selection of method of organization comes to its most acute crisis.

In light of our discussion of some of these issues in Kant's historical document, let's return to our contemporary example and analyze a certain discourse of principles that can be read in the Report where "…participants reminded themselves of some of these values, and raised questions about how they […] might require redefinition and reformation in light of current and future changes."[27] As already cited above in the section of the passage, "Context for Change: Values in the University," the following principles emerge as both fundamental and in need of new redefinition:

1.   "The principle of the pursuit of knowledge irrespective of its immediate applications" (similar to Humboldt's earlier definition of "Pure Science," or "science for its own sake"); however, this principle may require redefinition in light of the great need for better economies in the university.
2.   "The principle of commitment to objectivity and dispassion in the search for knowledge" — a "cornerstone of the modern university"? — but one which may need periodic redefinition in the areas such as the "public nature of knowledge," "conflicts of interest," and in "limitations on stipulated conditions specified by external donors," etc.
3.   Finally, "the principle of academic freedom," a "valued tradition of academic life," but one which may need to be redefined in the context of departmental, campus, and university educational goals and policies.

I think that most would agree that these principles become most fragile and problematic when they appeal to a common sense understanding of the university in a very vague and amorphous manner. This appeal takes the form of a classical enthymeme. That is, in as much as our subject is "the university," we all must agree on these fundamental principles as cornerstones: the principle of an objective, universal, and *disinterested* reason; the principle of *objectivity* safeguarded from the passions, opinion, and other forms of private interest; the principle of *academic freedom* understood within certain social, political, and institutional conditions that are prior to and that legitimate its exercise. For the moment, I will suspend any commentary on the ideological nature of these principles in light of the criticism that philosophers and cultural critics have been engaged in for two decades concerning the purity or the political neutrality of these values. That is, I will not attempt to "deconstruct" the text in which these principles are articulated, forgetting or bracketing the fact that its discourse is neither rigorously philosophical (only pseudo-philosophical, an aspect I will return to in a moment), or necessarily scholarly and, therefore, should not be examined and exposed to the kind of scrutiny over minutiae that such a deconstruction would involve. At the same time, I do not want to over-look the implications that such principles of reason and the metaphorical language in which these principles are embedded might have for the discourse of the modern university. I do not want simply to take for granted the appearance of these foundational principles that are re-affirmed in the middle of an argument that proposes to radically transform, adapt, and streamline the historical and institutional position of the modern university. In what way does this discourse of principles provide its subject with the legitimation necessary to justify its self-assigned task of revising the institutional and disciplinary partitions that define its various knowledges, re-configuring the relationships between its internal (i.e., "cultural") and external (i.e., "public") sectors, and re-negotiating the interests between these various parties all in conflict around the modern determination of the university?

What I find particularly interesting is the very nature of the architectonic metaphors of "structure," "ground," and "cornerstone," which are innately speculative and metaphorical products of the historical imagination, and which Kant himself identified later on in *The Critique of Pure Judgment* as instances of what he calls "figurative hypotyposis."[28] Although the institutional narrative of the modern university, particularly in the United States, would recount the decline of the speculative language of the philosopher (who is no longer the transcendental or "universal" subject of a state or national spirit), we might at least discern within the discourse of the modern university those places where his "ghost" has returned, or even been invoked as in a séance, in order to prop up the language of the corporate body of technical managers that have replaced him. That is, as the above Report itself nicely illustrates, we can see the return of the speculative discourse of the philosopher as both a return of the dead, as well as the return of a dead and decaying language (cliché, metaphor), the remnants of a systematic architectonic of reason that is totally archaic and in disrepair. At this point, the modern discourse of the university — that is, the manner in which its subject represents to itself the *idea* of its social, historical, and transcendental mission, as well as the manner in which it speaks and talks about this mission to its "publics" out in the public, and to its "cultures" in private — becomes patently comic. This moment of comedy may be symptomatic of two things:

1. It might signal the fact that the historical and institutional "ground" of the modern university has changed so drastically that its classical language appears insupportable to justify its present form. This would mean that this language appears stale by the very fact that it no longer offers an adequate description (much less an authoritative prescription) of the social, economic, and corporate

principles upon which the modern university is grounded. (In French, by the way, "grounds" [*les fonds*] can also mean "funds.)

2. Despite the fact that the corporate body of these "technicians" and "institutional managers" have taken over the role of the speculative philosophy in assigning the social, cultural, and political ends of the university, we might notice that *they have no reason of their own* with which to protect the transcendental goals of reason, to employ the Kantian language, from becoming reduced to these more immediate and finite ends. Thus, in those moments when they feel the need to protect the university from becoming thoroughly determined by historical, economic, and political interests, they can only draw upon the archaic and now mythic appeal to the language of the philosopher to frame a transcendental employment of the idea of the university.

For us, this might imply that there is no contemporary discourse of the university, or that the modern subject of the university is split between an archaic and out-dated philosophical language, which now simply appears metaphorically descriptive rather than prescriptive and architectonic, and the various modern forms of interest, which appear without a systematic language, or synthetic presentation, from which one might be able to determine something like grounding principles.

I(c) *The subject at large: on Derrida's "position(s)"*

In the *Conflict of Faculties,* Kant argued that the university should be "governed" by an Idea of Reason, an idea that would immanently represent the whole of "what is presently teachable."[29] Yet, the current arrangement of knowledge that constitutes the partitions between schools, disciplines, and curricular programs is only an imperfect schema of this "totality" since, from the viewpoint of the present moment, such a comprehensive grasp of absolute knowledge is always impossible. Even according to Kant's early design, the architecture of the university is constantly threatened by the advent of a new configuration of knowledge, which always enters with the promise of complete renovation. As an institution, however, the university is quite resilient and not easily revolutionized; this is a lesson that can easily be illustrated by the history of the "critical subject" and of the subject of deconstruction in particular in American institutions of higher education over the past twenty years. In this section, therefore, I will review the rise of deconstruction and the writings of Jacques Derrida as a particular "case" of what I call *the return(s) of the philosopher.*

In *The Course of General Linguistics* (1915), Ferdinand de Saussure first compared social institutions to a language. This basic comparison or analogy has influenced how we conceive and "theorize" social institutions according to an earlier structuralist analogy.[30] One of the most productive aspects of this analogy was Saussure's comment on the "diachronic" nature of the structure of language, and his study of the manner in which languages historically evolve. (For example, Saussure was very interested in understanding the conditions in which a language could die.) As in the case of language, social institutions cannot undergo a change in nature, on a "synchronic level," since language is never entirely present on that level. Although the whole of language is virtually present in every instance of discourse, this synchronic presence is limited to the instance of discourse (*la parole*), and *a priori* to the time and place of locution. This is the condition of the consistency of sense and understanding in the medium of language—even more, the very condition of what we call *a structure.* If it were possible to introduce change on a synchronic axis — even just once — there would be nothing like language since the meaning of signs could undergo change from one instance of speech to the next. Applying this analogy, we might imagine that social institutions are organized in the same way, in as much as their structure is also linguistic or discursive in nature; this fact offers them incredible resilience and a very particular temporal rhythm in their historical evolution, as well as built-in resistance to sudden and sweeping change.

The university must, in some ways, be recognized as a non-localizable Structure (with a capital 'S') which is why I can travel from the University of California at

Irvine to Syracuse University and expect to experience a similar institutional organization of the faculties, even though the divisions between schools and colleges, and the disciplinary partitions are slightly modified by the particular institution's funding mechanism (e.g., public vs. private), as well as by intra-institutional factors that contribute to each university's local history. It is not simply by chance that faculty and administrators frequently move between different national and even international universities as if traveling through a sidereal space, implying that the considerations of locality, habitat, environment, specific culture, and even language do not fundamentally determine the constitutive architecture of the university or the subjects that can be found there. Even today, we must also recognize the modern university as the expression of a powerful social idea that cannot be determined by its physical architecture, its particular institutional locations, or its different institutional and disciplinary segments, borders, and territorial disputes. It is from this purely ideal point that the "idea" of the university participates in organizing and constructing social segments and ordering them in a relative system of social and cultural castes. Although this symbolic function may be less visible from the perspective of those who already inhabit the locale of the university itself, it becomes extremely apparent in secondary schools where this *idea* functions within a class narrative as the criteria of social discrimination, where individuals and entire groups are stigmatized for not meeting standards of achievement that have been historically defined by a relatively narrow class experience.

Leaving these considerations aside for now — I will return to them in the conclusion — and following Derrida's argument, I want to raise again the following question: Is the university today, in fact, governed by an "Idea of Reason"? My question is more philosophical and speculative, which I feel may be more to the point and already presumes a series of other preliminary questions: What is the "university" as distinct or distinguishable from the "cultures" (faculty, students, staff, administrators) that comprise it? As we have already noted, the language and rhetoric of the Report imply the presence of a distinct subject of the university, who defines its current role in the larger society, addresses this role by adapting or fundamentally changing the relations of power and autonomy among the various departments and divisions, and charges itself with addressing rigidities and resistance within and among the various cultures inhabiting the university. What is the authority of this subject? What is its legitimacy or "narrative of legitimation" (Lyotard)? What is this subject's relationship to the various disciplinary knowledges? Can these bodies, and the technical knowledge they represent, even be qualified under the Kantian definition of the "the Idea of Reason"? Finally, do these "technicians of learning" have any relationship to, or legitimate knowledge of, what Kant defined as "the totality of what is teachable"?

To help situate and discuss some of the more speculative and philosophical questions this new *subject of the university* raises, I wish now to turn to a more philosophical document that speaks to some of the principles that found, establish, and institute the modern university—Derrida's "The Principle of Reason: The University in the Eyes of its Pupils," a lecture that was originally delivered at Cornell in 1983 and was subsequently published in *diacritics* that year. I will provide a brief reading of this address as a kind of companion piece or commentary upon the above Report, noting both the similarity of problems concerning the "position" of the university and the context of its values or principles, even though the latter is different in its aims, its approach, as well as the texts and contexts (Kant, Nietzsche, Heidegger) that Derrida draws upon to question the place of these values in the modern university today (i.e., "professionalism," "utility," "autonomy").

In "The University in the Eyes of its Pupils," Derrida addresses the of reason at the basis of the modern university during the height of the Reagan era in American institutional history. Hence, Derrida expresses concern for what he calls "guided" or "directed" research can immediately be read in terms of the massive funding that research universities, and the hard sciences in particular, were receiving at this time in the forms of federal and corporate block grants directly (although, in many cases, contingently) related to the run-away defense spending that was the hallmark of this period. I say "contingently" here because the growth of the Humanities and, in particular, the massive funding that was responsible for the creation of Institutes and Research Centers was often the result of university by-laws which prevented donors from funding one department or program exclusively of other departments and schools of the University of California. It is ironic, therefore, that the corporate and federal matching grants by, say, Rockwell, General Electric, or Hewlett-Packard were re-distributed across disciplinary segments to the Humanities and were to a great degree — sometimes to the horror of the donors themselves — responsible for the creation and funding of "radical think tanks," "independent research units," and special academic programs dedicated to what has been defined in public discourse as the "over-turning of traditional Western values."

There is a certain cold-war rhetoric that guides Derrida's concerns over "end-oriented" research (which also includes research which Derrida will identify as seemingly free and undirected, but whose use-value for the State, if not immediately apparent, was at least immanent). We only need to remind ourselves around this point that the history of technological advancement in modern Western societies is partly the story of "pure," undirected research finding contingent (state sponsored, military-industrial) adaptations that have directed its ends or its generalized public deployment (e.g., the radio, the telephone, the automobile, interstate highway systems, atomic energy, the inter-net). Derrida's remarks, therefore, belong to an institutional context that has been taken up by social critics and philosophers over the last fifty years: the rise and the dominance of the hard sciences during the post-World War II years and the concentration in the study and invention of new technologies in the university that resulted from direct state or federal sponsorship.

We might also highlight, during the same period of roughly four decades up to the early 1990s, the incredible imbalance this introduced between the disciplines of the sciences and the humanities, so much so that in the late 1970s and early 1980s many humanities' faculties themselves abandoned an earlier liberal arts agenda and re-cast their knowledge as more scientific in form and methodology in order to compete with the "hard sciences." To take a very local or field-specific example, the entrance of structuralism into the fields of literary and cultural studies during this period gave the faculties in those fields the advantage of a highly specialized and technical vocabulary as new weapons for this very old conflict — a kind of SMART bomb with a French accent — even if this form of discourse was rejected by other disciplines, especially by scientists themselves, as unnecessarily obtuse and overly complicated. (As an anecdote of this, I remember a constant refrain uttered by literary critics during this period against those who charged theory as being obtuse: "You don't presume or expect a language of physics or molecular biology to be easy to comprehend, do you?") Whatever advancements this methodology brought to these disciplines — and I think it brought many — the form of specialization had a practical effect of making the knowledge of literature, for example, more of an object of expertise — a correlative of scientific specialization — than a discipline based on a subjective and aesthetic form of judgment.

European institutions could be said to have — at least, temporarily — averted a conflict similar to that which has taken place in the United States in two ways: first, in most cases by a different funding mechanism in relation to the State; second, by the resistance of the philosophical subject. This resistance first took the form of the advent of phenomenology, a movement that sought to complete the Cartesian representation of philosophy as a "pure science" (*La Science*), which presented, within the powerful concept of *phenomena* itself, the representation of the true object of knowledge as that which "shows itself in itself" and which was antagonistic to the knowledge of the object that appears to "ontic-consciousness" (Heidegger), where the object or entity is grasped in its ontic-horizon as "what shows itself *for*," or "in view of something else".[31] Second, I would argue that this resistance of the philosophical subject took the form of linguistics and structuralist theories, both of which emerged in the late 1950s and early 1960s to occupy the position abdicated by the classical position of philosophy by providing a "deep structure" (*mathesis univeralis*), a common trans-disciplinary grid upon which the human sciences could be reorganized and related to one another. In this connection, one can easily recall the importance of the work of Lévi-Strauss, or Foucault's earlier works such as *The Order of Things* (1966) and *The Archeology of Knowledge* (1971), as well as Derrida's vision of what he called "a general science of writing" in *Of Grammatology* (1967) and other writings before the 1970s.[32]

In the absence of both earlier structuralism and phenomenology as powerful disciplinary movements in the North American academy, I would argue that it is precisely the Derridean subject who emerges in the early 1970s to offer a certain philosophical resistance by discerning the "principle of reason" within a negative and critical methodology (deconstruction), whose disciplinary object, moreover, could not be represented by a specific discursive production of the text of knowledge, but rather with a general text, or system of writing (*L'Écriture*). The problem with this principle of reason, identified by academic opponents with deconstructive criticism and with the contemporary discourse of "theory" in general, is the emergence of a subject who speaks *of* and *for* the university, but whose knowledge cannot be legitimated within the framework of any single historical faculty, whose object of knowledge cannot be identified with any specific disciplinary object, and whose language and style of discourse was often hostile to a common sense understanding of the very idea of the university as part of a broader humanistic mission that has determined the philosophy of higher education in the United States. Because of this subject's disciplinary eccentricity, as well as the general inability of its earliest representatives to successfully defend its negative and critical image of reason within a dominant humanist discourse, we bear witness to a state of affairs when theory itself is often perceived as an uncanny guest, occupying a contingent and "a-historical" position with regard to the other disciplines.

The second reason that I find this article important is that it was delivered at a time when deconstruction was gaining enormous influence and even a certain hegemony in the Humanities, specifically in English and French departments, humanities programs, critical theory research institutes, and in the academic journals and presses. Derrida at several points makes a reference to the mobility and authority of his own position as an intellectual *"au large"* (which also contains a pun meaning, "Bear Off!" in nautical terminology) in response to the early signs of the reception of deconstruction by conservative public intellectuals, such as William Bennett (who is humorously and diminutively cited as "Willis [*sic*] J. Bennett," then Chairman of the National Endowment for the Humanities and author of "The Shattered Humanities").[33] Derrida situates the speculative and philosophical distinction between pure and applied knowledge, which underlies and structures the distinction between pure research faculties and "directed" or "end-oriented" faculties (such as the teaching of writing) and knowledges (such as the department of computer sciences) within the thematic and interrogative, critical force that Derrida sees in the deconstruction of the principles of reason at the ground [*Grund*] of the modern university.

Toward the end of this article, Derrida directly addresses the *position* of the university in sociological and psychological terms, and identifies its representation with the presence of a distinct subject who assumes the task and responsibility of the positioning the university vis-à-vis social and cultural ends. He writes:

> During more than eight centuries, 'university' has been the name given by society to a sort of supplementary body that at one and the same time it wanted to project outside itself and keep jealously to itself, to emancipate and to control. On this double basis, the university was supposed to represent society. And in a certain way it has done so: it has reproduced society's scenography, its views, conflicts, contradictions, its play and its differences, and also its desire for organic union in a total body.[34]

With this passage, one might immediately see that Derrida is positioning the university within the context of his own problematic concerning the question of *representation as such*. Thus, the site of "university" shares many of the vicissitudes with regard to its supposed function (i.e., a general system of writing, or representation) which Derrida has elucidated in his work under different names: supplement, *pharmakon*, crypt (*fors*), *double-bande*, *hymen*, or *tympan*; and in more recent writings Greek concepts such as *aporia* and *khora*. Its position, therefore, marks a kind of pseudo-organic unity (a "cryptic enclosure," or "body") that is, topologically speaking, both outside of and interior to society. On the one hand, the modern university is very remote and projected at a certain distance from society (a distance which is also characterized or discursively *remarked* by social representations of aversion, dissociation, rarefaction, parody, and eccentricity). On the other hand, the cultural and social site of the university is "jealously" guarded and maintained at the closest point to the origin of social, cultural, and national forms of identity and recognition. It provides the source of cultural values, forms of symbolic identification, narratives of cultural and national desire, subjective positions and potential subjectivities engaged in conflict over the proper "signs of history" (what the post-Hegelian Alexander Kojève described under the agonistics of "prestige," "recognition" or *fama*).[35]

We might recall here that the above Report also diagnosed a schism of sorts in the structure of the university between its internal cultures and its external publics; however, the force of this schism is what the "university technicians" want to mediate by making the schism more communicable and less caustic by translating the discourse of the university into a clear and unequivocal (i.e., "culture-bound") language. I will return in the third section to discuss the question of the university's "public perception." This is also the breach that many academics today are attempting to seal in their appeal to the position of the "public intellectual" whose arrival, speaking a language of the marketplace, of the media, a language that can be immediately understood in quotidian terms, is supposed to represent academic discourse as something more akin to "public" interests, and the academic herself as "familial" to the cultural values of recognition and prestige, by addressing an audience outside the narrow confines of the academic discursive community. In contrast to these other positions on the breach of university discourse, we should remark and clarify Derrida's concept of thinking as something distinctly modern, or postmodern, by situating the dynamics of this "dissociation" which is supposed to occasion its free-play, in relation to the psychoanalytic concept of "censorship" (repression, *Verdrängung*) which he had originally incorporated into his master philosopheme, *L'Écriture*.

The space and the function of the representation of society that takes place in the university is the result of an alienation of social-interest and, simultaneously, of the rebinding (or re-cathexis) of this interest in a symbolic form (or as Freud might have said, as the result of a certain "lifting [*Aufgehoben*] of repression"). We might see that this "lifting" of a normative command that belongs to social space is what accounts for the "time of discourse" of thinking as being precisely the "time for reflection that is also an other time."[36] This "other time" marks the specific form of ideation and signification with an heterogeneity and a formal alienation that is epistemologically productive. Simply illustrated, we might consider this heterogeneity as the manner in which the discourse of the thinker often appears eccentric, somewhat foreign, distant, even illogical and non-sensical to the general space of discourse that marks it off from a "common sense understanding" (*sensus communis logicus*). This eccentric appearance itself marks the phenomenal and social exteriority of the principle of knowledge, which in a certain sense produces the appearance of its *prior* nature. (The discourse of thinking simulates a position that is "before re-presentation" in every sense this preposition implies.) Maybe this is why we are often predisposed to find the thinker speaking a foreign dialect. The position that this heterogeneous textual instance of knowledge appeals to is a fundamental principle of the Indo-European formation of objective institutions (particularly evident in the discourse of law and the sciences), one that is socially co-aligned with the disinterested perspective of the stranger (i.e., the man of science, the judge, the philosopher).

By constructing the ground of the university as a general writing of culture, society, and politics, Derrida is portraying the topology of thinking itself as a certain form of alienation, or "dissociation," which is "relatively independent of social time and relaxes the urgency of its commands [to represent is "to mean," that is, to obey the prescriptions that define normative social space], ensuring for it the great and precious freedom of play."[37] This appeal to the purity and autonomy of what is called thinking — as opposed to technical reproduction of knowledges and professional competencies that Evan Watkins has defined by the term "credentialization"[38] — participates in a tradition which Derrida himself invokes under the concept of *Aufklärung* (i.e., the preparatory vigilance of a "negative, or critical, wisdom").

Derrida invokes this distinction by recalling that his discourse participates in a series of other general discussions, or academic addresses, on the subject of the "university" such as Kant's *Conflict of the Faculties* (which, once again, appeals to the philosophy department as the place for the production of a knowledge purified of a utility and/or "practical interest"); Nietzsche's *Lectures on the Future of Our Educational Establishments* (where Nietzsche first announces the distinction between "training and thinking," which appears again in *Schopenhauer as Educator*, a diatribe against a journalistic and utilitarian university culture in the service of State ends); and, finally, Heidegger's lecture *"What is Metaphysics?"* where Heidegger "violently condemns disciplinary compartmentalization and 'exterior training in view of a profession' as 'an idle and inauthentic Thing.'"[39] These are the texts from which Derrida draws many of the positions he articulates, simultaneously qualifying their historical usefulness in speaking for the principle of Reason that regulates the modern American university, and warning against too strict an association of these views with the representation of his own position toward this question.

The gesture of positioning his own representation in continuity with a certain modern tradition of European philosophy and, at the same time, claiming an eccentric and heterogeneous position from which he launches a critique of this very tradition, should be familiar to most of Derrida's readers. It is a gesture which reasserts the force of his pun on the position from which he addresses the American university — a "Professor-at-Large" (*au large*) — a post that is neither purely intra-institutional and disciplinary nor purely external and extra-disciplinary, but as if coming in from the high seas. It is the non-disciplinary nature of his subject, as well the suddenness of his arrival on the shores of America, that has also been used to characterize the subject of theory in general. I cite the passage in which Derrida introduces this pun in order to foreground some questions around the institutional and disciplinary position that this subject might represent within an American context:

> As I sought to encourage myself, daydreaming a bit, it occurred to me that I did'nt know how many meanings were conveyed by the phrase 'at large,' as in 'professor at large.' I wondered whether a professor at large, not belonging to any department, nor even to the university, was rather

like a person who in the old days was called *un ubiquiste*, a 'ubiquitist,' if you will, in the University of Paris. An ubiquitist was a doctor of theology not attached to any particular college. Outside that context, in French, an ubiquiste is someone who travels a lot and travels fast, giving the illusion of being everywhere at once. Perhaps a professor at large, while not necessarily an ubiquitist, is someone, having spent a long time on the high seas '*au large*,' occasionally comes ashore, after an absence which has cut him off from everything. He is unaware of the context, the proper rituals, and the changed environment. He is given to consider matters loftily, from afar. People indulgently close their eyes to the schematic, drastically selective views he has to express in the rhetoric proper to an academic lecture on the academy. But they may be sorry that he spends so much time in a prolonged and awkward attempt to capture the benevolence of his listeners.[40]

Implicit in these remarks, the daydreams of an ubiquitist, is both a confession and a warning — "*Bear off!*" With this pun, isn't Derrida also confessing to a certain "distance" and "dreadfully schematic" nature of a stranger's viewpoint? We also might read here the possibility that he may be somewhat overly concerned about his own status in view of the native audience in appealing to their "goodwill" and "welcome" (*bienvolance et bienvenue*). Consequently, the last sentence seems to hint that his "position" (and authority) may be derived from a certain indulgence on the part of his American audience, also from their hospitality and politeness (*politesse*) in analogy to what occurs, for example, when the good host patiently suffers his guest's self-serving and ill-mannered appropriation of the dinner conversation out of the sense of duty to make him feel welcome. Heeding both this warning and this confession, it would seem to fall to his American listeners, his hosts, to take more responsibility in how they *take* his representation. Such a responsibility would also include how they understand its pertinence to the American academy, how they appropriate his viewpoint, reproduce it, authorize and even institute its principles to guide their own understanding and point of view. In fact, Derrida admonishes his audience to take what he says concerning the American university with their "eyes wide open" to its "drastically schematic nature" as well as to the innate differences in viewpoints (cultural, historical, sociolinguistic, institutional, even national), thus playing upon the primary metaphor announced in his title, "in the eyes of its pupils."

The Derridean subject of the university embodies a kind of schematic knowledge that has been estranged by the distance of a cultural and institutional guest, having been "cut off from everything," "unaware of context," and "proper rituals." Thus, his discourse can be understood to be exemplary of both the ideational power and the positive weaknesses of an outsider's perspective (or position of objectivity in the affair). He offers a view toward things that could not be attained by anyone who was already thoroughly matriculated or socialized and whose view is conditioned by the internalization and subjectivication of the structure's specific intra-institutional and cultural site (i.e., a subject who could only see things from the inside). With regard to many matters, however, his view-point is one whose epistemological knowledge can be determined as theoretical or analogical, since it presupposes only a relative and limited familiarity with the actual state of affairs. Yet, I must stress emphatically, this view-point cannot be represented by an analogy to a colonizer's perspective, since it is deprived of any apparatus capable of installing and instituting this perspective: it bears no "Archimedean lever" that could raze existing institutions and cultural knowledges and reconstruct them according to the new principles set forth in his work.

In responding to the kind of objections made by Derrida's antagonists in the conflict over the institutional value of "deconstruction" — the name itself already betrays a specific mode of cultural production, like a manufacture's seal of authentication *made in America* — I want to draw a clearer distinction between the kind of epistemological and methodological renovation that Derrida's work often announces and performs, and the culturally divergent representation it receives when directly applied to specific institutional histories and arrangements of knowledge, or to particular disciplinary objects. The former, more programmatically announced in Derrida's earlier writings such as *Of Grammatology, Writing and Difference*, and *Margins of Philosophy*, can be more precisely understood as a critical renovation of general conceptual "schema" or what critic Fredric Jameson has called philosophemes (e.g., "writing," "speech," "nature," "history," "man," "animal," "reason," "presence," "sign," "system," "science") which establish the material conditions of knowledge across several historical fields and cannot, therefore, be represented by any single disciplinary object or institutional narrative, including that of philosophy itself.

In the context of a lecture on Kant's *Conflict of the Faculties*, the very use of the term "schematic" is an extremely significant and telling sign of Derrida's own self-consciousness concerning the empirical status of his representation (or view) in the North American university. With this word — as well as the mere mention of "daydreaming" in this context — Derrida is perhaps announcing the very determination and source of his perception is, in part, the supplemental function of the imagination which employs the verbal analogy, *figure* (or symbolic hypotyposis), association, and pun to schematize with the concepts of the understanding in order to explore the limits and the grounds of the subject's empirical knowledge. Consequently, the word "schema" can be understood according to the Kantian usage as the productive faculty of the human imagination that "schematizes a diversity in relation to the ideas"; its object does not consist in a particular "sensuous representation" according to Kant, but rather in spatio-temporal relations that are purely conceptual.[41] (And one must admit that Derrida's usage of the word "writing" has something purely conceptual about it, which is why it is so slippery when conceived as a particular sensuous appearance or genre of the written.) As the primary manner in which the ideas of reason first become historicized as "representations," which in turn become regulative with regard to other representations by the legislative function of the understanding which "judges by means of them," the objectives of a deconstructive critique can be understood most precisely as being directed at those types or species of representation, themselves products of an historical imagination, which become most regulative over time in the sense that they legislate (that is, pass judgment upon) the different forms of human experience.

At this point, we might want to classify those types or species of representation as having a certain institutional status, or as being identified with the generative power that belongs to historically established and organized kinds of representation identified with human institutions (a power that is not only legislative with regard to human experience, but also reproductive with regard to specific kinds of discursive agency and patterns of subjectivity). *After all, isn't the idea of the university that we have been discussing all along simply a species of representation that, in turn, becomes legislative of the very idea it represents?* Perhaps it is to point out precisely the contingent and historical nature of this kind of representation that Kant, in the preface to *The Conflict of the Faculties,* humorously recounts the origin of this idea with the anecdote of someone who, one day, in response to a particular need to find the best way to insure both the archiving and the continued progress in the areas of human invention and new knowledge, simply dreams up the university as being "a really good idea"! At its origin, a university is not that much different from a microwave, a personal computer, or any number of technological innovations. Moreover, just like other technological innovations that become instituted and habituated, like a telephone or electricity, the problem begins when this sudden and arbitrary origin is soon forgotten and we could not imagine a state of affairs without it. One can easily find other instances of these types of institutional representations. "English," for example, particularly as this idea is manifested in the institutional history of the American university, bears all the marks of a contingently conceived product of a certain era of our historical imagination, one which has grown so out-dated in its representation of "what is called literature," as a form of cultural and historical knowledge, as to lead many to wonder whether it can any longer be called *a good idea!*

It is true that Derrida's own writings both early and late are replete with instances of his intervention to "de-construct" precisely the types of representations that bear an institutional determination and auto-legitimation in the

French academic context. His preoccupation with the fate of his own institutional representation in France is especially evident in the writings that occur around the foundation of *GREPH* (in 1975) and The International College of Philosophy (in 1983). However, from his position in the United States I want to again emphasize the fact that the Derridean subject does not speak from within a particular instituted knowledge, or disciplinary community, but rather speaks from a more general, trans-disciplinary, even inter-national perspective of an *ubiquitiste,* a professor "*au large,*" which in a certain sense can also be identified with the position of the "text." To understand this last statement, we should recall that the Derridean subject is a subject of "writing" (*l'écriture*) and, as such, bears a transitive and proto-relationship to all disciplinary knowledges and historical fields in as much as the latter are constituted by their modes of inscription, particularly when one approaches the construction of knowledge in its institutional setting. The transitive status of this object, understood within the Heideggerian distinction between ontological and ontic-representation, legitimates a subject of knowledge and mode of inquiry that cannot itself be represented by a particular disciplinary classification (that of philosophy, for instance) or by what Derrida refers to elsewhere as "simple inter-disciplinarity" (which implies "identifiable proper identities").[42] Consequently, we can conclude that there is a certain seriousness behind Derrida's self-conscious puns on the position of a "*ubiquitiste*" in the classical French academy, or upon the position "*au large*" where he finds himself "positioned" in the American institution. Both of these positions bear some genealogical filiation with his own object of technical knowledge, which cannot find an easy disciplinary classification precisely because it forms the basis of all classification, understood as a general system of writing.

I also want to call attention to the fact that although this evokes the position of a Kantian first philosophy, or fundamental critique, there are also some significant differences that need to be remarked. First, the Kantian practice of a negative or critical wisdom also bore a practical task (or responsibility) of maintaining the historical structure of disciplinary knowledge and, at the same time, renovating this structure from the ground up, that is, exposing and working-over its supposed pure condition of knowledge and organization of faculties. The Kantian philosopher was also charged with providing, as we have already noted above, a teleological image of the total project of reason in which all its branches could be unified in a common task, and assembled in a common language represented by the philosopher and instituted in the very idea of the university whose material architecture was already implicitly a metaphor of its ideal perfection. On the contrary, in the Derridean representation of reason, one witnesses a hyperbolic criticism — perhaps even a figure of "absolute negativity," although still confined within a rigorous understanding of the implications this phrase would have in the history of Western Metaphysics (i.e., a "metaphysics of closure"). That is, although a Derridean practice accepts the responsibility of a certain "maintenance" or "repetition" of the metaphysical tradition, this responsibility and obligation for representation must be inscribed in a radically different manner, if not in an entirely different or new text. In all of Derrida's writings, therefore, one can bear witness to proclamations of a responsibility to represent. The object of this obligation is the "closure of metaphysics" and not its particular incarnation and historical configuration of disciplinary knowledges in the American institution. The purest expression of this responsibility is the deconstruction of this text, which also entails a "shaking up" (*soliciter*) within all its historical partitions. (And, of course, the deconstruction of the partition between speech and writing is fundamental to all other determinations of knowledge derived from representation).

The Derridean concept of "Writing" maintains a negative presentation of reason: an image of thought working-over and working-through the totality of its historical representations. Because of this critical operation, its form of reasoning is identified with a certain manner of writing that itself must be liberated from the constraints of a positivistic genre of the written, which enforces a certain distance (or alienation) between itself and the forms of reason that belong to the philosophical genre that has been contaminated or polluted by a transcendental and speculative employment. Consequently, the Derridean subject of representation can only be *topographically* situated from the position of *this text, here, at the very moment of its writing*, a position that can only be located from the perspective of what Derrida has called "the text of metaphysics" (the history of Western reason). I am using the word "topographical" (in the sense of a writing of or from a place, or *topos*) to, again, situate a difference in perspectives and to open this difference to its institutional and disciplinary coordinates. That is, how are we to represent the distinction between the "position" from which Derrida writes (here, at the very moment of writing, before a certain "text" of metaphysics) and the "position" from which he speaks to us, here, somewhere at large in America? A critical dilemma concerns us at this point since while the former could appear almost too singular and even too literal, the latter could appear too bloated and grandiose so that he appeared to be speaking to us from everywhere at once. Above all, it would be disastrous to mistake the two "positions"; otherwise, it would appear — at least, in "the eyes of his pupils," or in the ears of his publics — that Derrida had assumed the authority to assign himself a "position at large," to grant himself the power to cross all borders and pronounce himself on everything (rather than "receiving a position," or "accepting an invitation to speak" on such and such occasion).

Again, everything ultimately depends on how we take his position. We must also recognize that this is where a critical problem of representation can be situated, since the Derridean subject does not emerge from within a distinct and identifiable disciplinary field or faculty, but rather from a position "*au large*," which echoes the privilege and eccentricity of Derrida's own institutional definition as professor "at large" at Cornell, Johns Hopkins, Yale, and UC Irvine. He occupies a position that bears no affiliation or identification with any one discipline, but rather with the emergence of the institutional category of "theory" or "critical theory." Thus, while this position could bear some resemblance to the Kantian subject of the university, the resemblance is marked by an apparent difference in that the Derridean subject cannot be identified with any specific faculty or institutional representation of an historical discipline. We can only speculate on a number of possible divergences that might flow from this distinction; there must have been a reason why Kant sought to both privilege the representation of philosophical knowledge and, at the same time, to limit its transcendental status by situating it within the conflict of the faculties, a subject which bears a certain "practical interest" in the maintenance of its own position and interests within the historical configuration of the university.

The Kantian practice of critical wisdom was always situated within the tension and desire of a particular "faculty" (of knowledge) to maintain and authorize its object of knowledge, and would enter into the conflict of the faculties within the finite incarnation of reason in the philosopher, who remains anxious over his representation in relation to the "representation of all that is presently teachable." This might account for a difference with the Derridean subject of responsibility, since this responsibility is owed to a "general text"; consequently, the Derridean subject maintains and represents this "text" from a position that is "*au large*" — that is, outside and before any finite determination of this text by its institutional and historical configuration as disciplinary object, or within a particular institutional setting. Such a position might certainly be exposed to the accusation that it bears no practical interest in the historical representation of a discipline, but rather to a knowledge purified of all practical restraints of interest which only emerge in a certain anxiousness of the *subject of representation* (i.e., "faculty" in the secondary sense Kant employed to define this term, designating the historical subject who becomes "representative" of a specific mode of knowledge). By this I mean all the positive psychological and intra-institutional constraints of interest that limit the representative power of a "faculty," even to the point of contributing to the repression or censorship of new knowledge by the very fact of its "incarnation" in the person of the individual faculty member.

I would argue that the various instances of this repression and censorship — including self-censorship — happens when a pure "will-to-knowledge" (Foucault) is co-determined by the juridico-legal, economic, social, and psychological (or desiring) mechanisms that bind a particular form of knowledge to a subject who represents it. Anytime a particular topic or manner of reasoning is chosen over another in the interests of one or more of the following — "marketability," "promotion," "tenure," "happiness," "money," "power," "mobility," "popularity," "fame" — the force of such a repression can be localized within the body of the subject who, in principle, is supposed to represent a particular mode of knowledge (i.e., Philosophy, History, Biology, English). I do not mean to suggest that there could be anything like a pure representation, and repression here must be understood as formative and disciplinary rather than prohibitive; the history of institutional knowledges is also a history of such a repression. Its advances mark those points of rupture, lacunae, and conflict that occur between and within the two senses of the concept of "faculty" that Kant first defines in *The Conflict of the Faculties*. Consequently, even for Kant, the fundamental problem of the university is that the perspective toward pure reason must always be subjected to the institutional arrangements of interests that circulate within, among, and between particular faculties; this would extend and multiply the possible sources of conflict to also include the most private (idiomatic, or desiring) regions of the academic subject where the conflicting interests first come into view, often painfully, and where any resolution and mediation is always exposed to the charge of being highly idiosyncratic and subjectively motivated. Similar to the coordinates of the right and the left that he outlines in his *How to be Oriented in Thinking*, which Derrida himself cites toward the end of "*Mochlos*, or The Conflict of Faculties," such a perspective "does not arise from a conceptual or logical determination, but only from a sensory topology [a local position] that has to be referred to the subjective position of the human body."[43]

It should not have surprised us that traditional philosophy departments in America greeted Derrida's philosophy with both skepticism and hostility. In fact, were they not suspicious of an image of reason that proclaimed no "interest" (also meaning no affiliation, kinship, or identification) with the representation of philosophy, a "critical negativity" which evoked a certain metaphysical pretension to first philosophy? The image of a "text" that harbored within itself a language of metaphysics from which analytical philosophy has been trying to purify itself for nearly half a century? One of the greatest ironies, therefore, was that the Derridean subject found its entrance into the American university not through the department of philosophy, but rather through the department of English, when literary critics found in Derrida's image of knowledge of a general text a certain kinship and resemblance with their own disciplinary object. As we know, the results were mixed, as the position "*au large*" immediately installed itself in place of this finite text of literary history and immediately evacuated it of its content and, in a certain sense, of its specific institutional and disciplinary limits (including the modes of its institutional reproduction and legitimation). We only need to recall two early and influential developments from the late 1970s to establish this event. First, we might recall a passage that appears at the end of De Man's "Literary History and Literary Modernity" where we are presented with a certain privileged definition of "literature" which can be identified with a textual practice of reason that can be located as the condition of all knowledge, in as much as all knowledge is constructed by texts "whether these texts take on the guise of politics, history, or science."[44] De Man was implicitly announcing, with this statement, the priority of his own conception of rhetorical practice (a critical textual reflection combined with a technical procedure of close reading) over all other positively constructed disciplinary knowledge that either elided or suppressed their discipline's rhetorical construction of its object.[45]

The most troubling problem of representation occurred, however, when the literary critic began to occupy and speak from the position of the university in general, emulating the Kantian subject in assigning certain ends to the evolution of a critical reason in general, as well as justifying their own critical practices by representing these in terms of a discourse of ends (of culture, society, politics, etc.) This is because, even in the absence of a specific subject whose disciplinary discourse also could represent the discourse of the university, the classical language of the philosopher remains the dominant discourse with which the university represents itself, even though this language is often reduced to mere cliché and metaphor, as in the examples drawn from the Report above. Thus, while the discourse of the university remained, in the tradition of the Enlightenment, purely humanistic, literary and cultural critics have been hostile for some time to the language of humanism, and therefore represent an antagonistic and anti-humanist claim in positioning the ends and objectives of a post-Enlightenment *idea* of University. Second, we might recall the proliferation of other fields within literary study which advocated the transcendental employment of its own disciplinary practice and legitimated this employment to other fields by the transitive nature belonging to the object of its own disciplinary authority, the "text," and through its own empirical procedure of "close reading." Thus, literary critics gave themselves the right to accede to a position "*at large*," to proclaim a knowledge of any disciplinary field in as much as the knowledge of each field was constructed by texts and the literary critic took this "general textuality" as her object of specialized knowledge and mastery. Both of these developments can be understood to echo an appeal to the juridical disciplinary authority of the philosophy faculty who can, as Kant declared, require all other disciplines to submit their truth to an examination. This right is most strongly pronounced in the following passage from the first part of *The Conflict of the Faculties*, concerning the conflict between philosophy and the theology faculty:

The philosophy faculty can, therefore, lay claim to any teaching, in order to test its truth. The government cannot forbid it to do this without acting against its own proper and essential purpose; and the higher faculties must put up with objections and doubts it brings forward in public, though they may well find it irksome, since, were it not for such critics, they could rest undisturbed in possession of what they once occupied, by whatever title, and rule over it despotically.[46]

We might apply this principle to the present state of affairs. One can read the recent "Sokal Affair" as a challenge to this absolute pretension, as well as to the authority and legitimacy of the subject "*au large*" that can be found at the basis of "theory." As evidenced recently in the public debates around Sokal's unmasking the pretensions of this "illegitimate" and non-technical application of theory to other fields of knowledge production the subjects of other disciplines immediately accused literary critics of an illegitimate use of their own method of inquiry in application of other disciplinary objects; this resulted in the general charge of "irresponsibility," or what Kant would define as an illegitimate transcendental employment of reason. Although this event was often represented as Sokal's single-handed mission to unmask the Potempkin village of postmodernism, and some might even argue that he went too far in censoring any use of scientific knowledge by those who were not qualified as scientists, the real issue underlying this event was the question of "censorship" that determines and authorizes any academic knowledge.

We should remind ourselves that throughout the course of graduate study in any discipline that leads up to the Ph.D., the student apprentice must pass through a battery of censors, from individual judgments by supervising faculty to the series of qualifying examinations whose successful completion is required prior to entering the final phase (the dissertation or thesis). It was the philosophical pretence of critics who were not academically "censored" (evaluated, ranked or qualified) that created the conditions of Sokal's academic parody, the objective of which was to show that the disciplinary apparatus based on censorship was not operating in the case of many postmodern critiques of science and, as a result, any knowledge these critiques purported was ideologically-tainted (one interpretation that was offered by Sokal) or merely rhetoric and simulacra (which was another). In highly specialized or technical fields, it is often the character of some social apparatus of censorship that guarantees knowledge; any statement of knowledge must also present or embody the mark of a prior censorship in order to gain any authority (whether this mark is expressed in terms of the prestige of the journal or press, the rank of the affiliated institution or research body, etc.) Sokal's hoax, therefore, was not as much an attack on postmodern philosophy as on the apparatus of censorship that is responsible for authorizing such knowledge before the "public" who have no other criteria to judge matters of "truth and falsehood" than by deferring to the credibility of the censors themselves.

In a strange way, the whole event which unfurled throughout the academy both here and in France with a sound and fury that could only be matched by the De Man affair five years earlier, performed before the public a question posed by Lyotard more than twenty years ago in the opening of *The Postmodern Condition*: "Who decides what knowledge is and who knows what needs to be decided?"[47] Both questions, which I will return to address in the second part of this report, address the role of a *censor*, of the one who can evaluate and rank knowledges and, most importantly, who knows where such critical decisions concerning whether or not something counts as knowledge need to be made. In brief, the significance of the entire affair in question was that Sokal himself, a scientist, performed the role of censor: not only did he perform that he "knew" what legitimate scientific knowledge was (in this case by knowingly misrepresenting it in his parody), but more importantly that he knew the entire question of knowledge needed to be decided in the case of postmodern representations of science which, in a quasi-heroic light, subjectively motivated him to take upon himself this question and force it to a point of decision in a very public manner. As a result, the effectiveness of this censorship of "the subject at large," and of the modern-day philosopher or "theorist" in particular, has made itself felt in a series of subsequent decisions by editorial boards and presses concerning whether a humanistic or philosophical project on science is credible or whether it constitutes knowledge at all, and so a whole area of inquiry may have been effectively closed down as a result.[48]

As I will argue later, I believe that this whole question can be decided by referring back to Kant's earlier argument that the philosophy faculty, even today, has an absolute right to *lay claim* to the discourse of science as an object of its own specialization and critique. Here I am applying the same principle that I employed earlier in the case of the administrative discourse of the university. That is, the moment that modern physicists or mathematicians stop calculating and start speaking, they produce an object of discourse that can be examined both from the perspective of their own specialized practice, and also from the perspective of speech *qua* speech. As an object of discourse, the knowledge of science or mathematics falls under the jurisdiction of the philosopher and modern rhetorician, even the contemporary theorist. In a certain sense, I am arguing that Sokal's attempt to debunk and effectively to censor the philosophy faculty in all matters of pure science represents a return to the original conflict of faculties that Kant addressed, although it is interesting to note that in this contemporary conflict science now occupies a position in this conflict of the faculties that Kant originally addressed to the position of theology. Consequently, applying Kant's original argument, Sokal's entire campaign to *censor* (that is, to silence completely) the lower faculties of our time can be easily defeated by showing that it is ultimately based on a thoroughly contradictory and patently "unscientific" premise: that the knowledge of nature, in whatever form it takes including public discourse, is a closed affair, and is in possession of a few specialists who "can rest secure in their undisturbed possession [of it] and rule over it despotically."[49] Laying the "Sokal affair" to rest, therefore, we can say that he contradicted himself when, speaking as a modern scientist, he violated the first law of modern science itself: the freedom of scientific knowledge from any form of authoritarian censorship or despotic control. After all, nature is not so insecure as to need an official spokesperson or public relations officer to prevent it from being misunderstood.

## I(d) *On the university in the ears of its publics*

As we saw in the preceding section, Derrida defined the position of the university as being structurally "outside" society, forming a kind of "cryptic enclosure" (a pocket or fold) that is projected toward a position of critical distance and, at the same time, jealously "maintained" in a position of proximity at the heart of national, social, and cultural mechanisms of identification. This position both maintains and is maintained by a series of "apotropaic gestures" (some of which are discursive) that function to distinguish and remark the "position" of the university *vis-à-vis* society. Several of these discursive apotropaic gestures can be remarked in the examples of the recent attacks on the cultural position of the university in newspaper columns and in the various conservative diatribes that appear in mainstream journals, as well as in the lectures and books by "public-intellectuals" such as Bennett, Bloom, and De Souza. For example, each year the profession of English braces itself for another round of social parody as an object of derision and satire in the newspaper columns that appear around the time of the MLA convention in late December. Sandra Gilbert writes in her address that what results is an "acrimonious crescendo reflected in often absurdly exaggerated newspaper accounts about the organization's activities."[50] What often strikes me as odd is that, in their response to the parodic treatment the spectacle of the MLA convention often receives in the popular press, academic apologists like Gilbert do not read the social function of these representations as vivid contemporary examples of Bakhtinian "carnivalization," or Frederick Turner's "liminalization." From the perspective of the popular cultural subject or conservative representative of "Culture," the topics and subjectivities that are chosen to represent a carnival atmosphere of the MLA are the exotic corollaries to a grotesque procession of social and cultural oddities — freaks, queers, aliens, and primitives. Although academics often highlight the same subjectivities in popular culture, the difference is that in such representations these subjectivities retain their "transgressive" definition of liminality and subversion in the production of social and cultural value which serves the cultural sovereignty of the critic and academic cultural producer. The representation of liminality in mainstream popular culture maintains a certain identification with a modernist notion of culture, one which refers to the "critic" and "intellectual" as its agents and creators. In the hands of "journalists" and "columnists," however, this subject of culture loses all its rights of ownership and propriety and becomes itself an object of representation, no longer in a transgressive and ludic order of cultural appropriation, but as the comic character who belongs to the spectacle of cultural inversion and whose representation in mainstream journals and newspapers often serves to reinforce dominant (or normative) values.

In *Structural Transformation of the Public Sphere* (1962), Habermas traces this development, under the emergence of "non-public opinion" represented by new technologies and media (e.g., the poll, the pundit or talking head, the staged interview with the "man of the street"), as the power of regulating and institutionalizing the classical sphere of public opinion. This power concerns almost purely the power of the medium (e.g., newspaper column, television interview, documentary film, etc.) to convey a representation (an argument, a sign of authority, "reputation" or prestige) that bears the greatest intensity (energy) and the widest possible breadth (quantity). We might see, therefore, with the recent emergence of the academic in the public genre of the editorial, an attempt to encroach upon the authority of the dominant cultural producer: the editorialist, expert pundit, columnist, and intellectual personality. What this authority represents is the power of opinion. What measures the power of one opinion over another is not necessarily a criteria of adequation, but rather the appeal to a kind of "simulacrum" of common sense (*sensus communis*) which, in a postmodern media state, primarily concerns the power first to establish and determine the common sense of the public through a verisimilitude of the greatest possible consensus. In contemporary media societies, the sign of consensus is often mistaken for the amplitude or bandwidth of the signal that, in a certain manner, confirms McLuhan's earlier pronouncement that "the medium is the message." The power of the medium is often measured by its speed and its number of receivers. In the communications wars, for example, television has been determined as a more powerful medium than the newspaper or journal (which still require an analogue process of encoding, a large investment of time in de-coding, or reading, and whose semiotic system still involves too much indeterminacy and noise), and now the electronic medium is beginning to rival television in terms of speed and number of receivers.

What is most interesting in all this is the effect it is producing in the form of academic discourse. We can analyze this change almost under a series of physical laws: with an increase in velocity, the medium must be transformed and adapted in order to remain intact. It would not be an exaggeration to notice the effect that this greater velocity is having upon different styles of academic discourse. This is coupled with the conversion of academic publishing to market principles, which includes a swifter change of "topics" (the cultural logic of fashion) that adapt themselves to perceptions of new fields of knowledge, new trends or fads. These perceptions are speeding everything up considerably and, I would say, are causing an incredible instability in the structure of institutional disciplines (reinforced by the volatility of celebrity, status, and hiring trends). If we were to describe the rules of this new academic mode, we might recognize that the genre of academic criticism is beginning to emulate spoken discourse to a greater degree (the average conference presentation) and the criteria of "reading" is shifting from a text-based and "literary" rhetoric to one of ceremonial, deliberative, and forensic oration.

For example, we can discern that the many appeals from academics concerning the status and desirability of speaking as a "public intellectual" is an implicit appeal to the criteria of speed and quantity as powerful indicators of "public access." In the book, itself entitled *Public Access* (1994), Michael Bérubé underlines the distribution of a recent article in the *Voice Literary Supplement*, which carries a weekly circulation of 14,000.[51] Although his remark is intended as ironic, the reference to circulation is also a clear appeal to the medium's market-power, the index of modern persuasion, since it is by circulation that a journal sets its advertising rates and the industry rates its "prestige." The public, by definition, is reached only by the fastest and most powerful medium: the loudspeaker, the radio, the newspaper, the television; hence, quantity can also be understood as the intensity (or energy) of a signal. A journal with a weekly distribution of 14,000 bears a metaphorical equivalence to the mouth of the political organizer when it is attached to the speaking end of the megaphone.

Part of the recent appeal to "public access" therefore, such as in the argument of Bérubé, might easily be understood within the political claim for equal access (in the sense of political candidates who claim the "right" of equal access to the media), which also necessitates that opponents should always be able to compete in relatively equal mediums. Likewise, given the fact that conservative intellectual personalities and media pundits have traditionally enjoyed spontaneous access to the most powerful mediums, leftist academics are now appealing for equal treatment and equal access to represent their views in the public sphere — kind of *"you've had your say, George Will! Now its my turn at the mic!"* However, by framing this appeal implicitly in terms of the political right to fair representation, academics like Bérubé have often defined the political subjectivity and objectives of the "academic" in a too simplistic or allegorical fashion — academics on the left, conservatives on the right — often blurring the more fractured and "diagonal" lines which exist in each institution and within each faculty concerning the relationship between political activism and what the university defines as "public service." This disorientation becomes even more severe as more conservative academics utilize the "public intellectuals" to make their case within their department or college, often blurring the distinctions between left and right, inside and outside, between private and public use of reason. Here, we might even recognize in this type of persuasion the modern equivalent of what Kant called an "illegal conflict of faculties": the resolution through threat, bribery, and by recourse to the power implicit in dominant media.

As further example, I need only to recall one such confrontation over "legitimation" that took place between so-called journalistic practices and traditional disciplinary constraints. This is the series of confrontations between Derrida and "the journalists" that frequently took place in the newspapers and in his own occasional writings during the period of the late 1980s onward, particularly around the explosion of what would later be called "the De Man affair."[52] One constant refrain issued by Derrida and his adherents in this series of debates was that their opponents lacked the rigor of verification, or that they did not care to read primary texts. By itself, this complaint would seem to be self-evident, yet underlying its bravado was the implication that knowledge could pass without a careful evaluation of primary sources. Of course, this principle is axiomatic of the disciplinary constraints that exist within the university itself, and the significance of this debate which raged for several years was that there could be such a thing as a knowledge of De Man or of Heidegger without a careful weighing of primary sources, which could only be authenticated by a method of "close reading."

What is most interesting in this debate,however, was the use of the term "journalistic" to degrade the quality of the opponent's methodology in extracting knowledge from information. Now, we all know from many movies, especially *All the Presidents Men,* that journalists must verify their sources, assiduously, in order to establish the credibility that the story is also "true." At the same time, the public has no other guarantee that this principle is honored in every instance except to believe in the code of the journalist's own disciplinary order. ("Deep Throat" could be viewed as the ultimate instance of this professional code, which has no external apparatus of verification or legitimation other than the profession's own morality.) It is obvious, to verify a statement concerning a source, or to confirm the authority of a statement, is very different than the verification and responsibility that is demanded by the technical practice of "close reading." It is the basic difference between these two procedures of legitimation that was the basis of the conflict between Derrida and the journalists. This is because Derrida's major criticism was that those academic opponents who were described as "journalists" themselves only sought their information from secondary sources. Although this might obey a journalistic criterion, in which a statement made by an expert or witness can be used to validate the veracity of a claim, according to the different rigor or tradition of a scholarly perspective this form of legitimation is shallow and does not fully authorize the truth-claim of any statement, which must be supported by textual evidence. The very conflict between Derrida and "the journalists" announces different criteria of authorization, which departs from the traditional apparatus of philosophical and academic legitimation in a striking manner.

In *Secular Vocations* (1993), Bruce Robbins produced an interesting and, in my view, extremely accurate assessment of the concept of the "public" when he defined it as an imaginary construction of what he calls the "professional unconscious."[53] The criterion of "a larger audience" is nowadays often applied by academic presses (even where such an audience does not and will not ever become actualized in an increase of the book's distribution to a reading public), almost as if by unspoken consensus, or by a tacit assumption that such an appeal is a necessary good, and without much argument and debate concerning what this criterion might actually signify as a practice that determines the epistemological conditions of knowledge. Derrida has frequently addressed this phenomenon — although his statements are usually directed against Habermas — while reflecting on the possible cultural agency of censorship that the appeals for a more "homogenous medium" might represent in the space of a university. As Derrida writes,

> This can also happen through a *new university discourse*, and especially through a *philosophical discourse*. [I remind the reader that both these generic traits are present in the contemporary example of the "university discourse" discussed at the beginning of this part of the report.] Under the pretext of pleading for transparency (along with 'consensus,' 'transparency' is one of the master words of the 'cultural' discourse I just mentioned), for the univocity of democratic discussion, for communication in public space, for 'communicative action,' such a discourse tends to impose a model of language that is supposedly favorable to this communication. Claiming to speak in the name of intelligibility, good sense, common sense, or democratic ethic, this discourse tends, by means of these very things, and as if naturally, to discredit anything that complicates this model. It tends to suspect or repress anything that bends, over-determines, or even questions, in theory as in practice, this idea of language.[54]

However, the most troubling question is that such a criterion is applied as a disciplinary regime in academic discourse (in pedagogy, or in the censorship exercised by academic and editorial committees on possible topics and styles of academic writing), often without much discussion or reflection upon the possible censoring effects it may have upon other modes of writing and presentation, and thus, other styles of reason. What is most devastating is the incredible "mono-textuality" (using a term that was first coined by Russian linguist Yury Lotman) that the American academy seems to be driven by.[55] In some ways, I would also interpret this "mono-textuality" as the unconscious effect of our current form of "publicity" (which also regulates the univocity of media philosophies) as well as a political concept of "the people" as an organic, or ideal, unity. This is where my reading of "the professional unconscious" differs to a great degree from Robbins, since where he is still working with a modernist presentiment of the critic and intellectual as a cultural producer, he still sees the "public" as a product (albeit unconscious) of the academic. *On the contrary, I see the "public" as an effect of the political unconscious over which the academic not only has no authority and no relationship as a progenitor (even as an unconscious progenitor), but now is simply reproducing to a greater degree by identifying with the values of "publicity" and the political organs of persuasion that belong to public space. The form of the public, the* shape of "publicity," is generated by the most powerful medium; therefore, our image of the "public" is already instituted by the medium that generates it as a feedback loop.

Finally, we might ask why this process of identification (and the reproduction of the "professional unconscious") has only recently begun to change the shape of the "institution of literature," as well as the subjective regimens of prestige and recognition that are now looking for more exchange value with those public spheres that are supposedly exterior to the university. One possible explanation might be that, until recently, American academics were buffered from the pressures of "public access," not only by having little interest in spreading their work to a larger audience, but also by the fact that the concept of "literary culture" this subject worked with originated in European modernism, which was founded by a hostile relationship between its own moral sphere and form of publicity ("Literature," "High Culture") and the petty-bourgeois moral sphere of "vulgar" public opinion and common moral sentiment. This schism, I would argue, can even be understood as the quasi-religious conflict between two moral notions of "the Good" (Hegel) that, among other forms of cultural production, structured the modernist definition of "literature" as a sphere of publicity that was itself heterogeneous and necessarily alienated from the publicity identified with bourgeois civil society. Belonging instead to a "time that is an other time," the modernist notion of the avant-garde is itself the sign of this scandalous heterogeneity and "rupture" with any common and good sense, the appearance of which marks the pointed spearhead of a new world penetrating into the hermetically sealed interiors of the old.

The question of speed and politics, understood in terms of a certain vulgarization of the "publicity of thought," has a long European tradition. We have seen this conflict first hand in the public debates between Derrida and the American journalistic media discussed above. In every case, Derrida's response underlines a certain definition and privileging of "thinking" that also finds its place in slower media, and a certain image of reason (responsible argumentation) that privileges the incremental movement of hands across the pages of a printed book. The slowness of the preferred medium (the book, the text, the long and plodding duration of reading and re-reading, the meticulously careful argument, the uncertainty of all conclusions, the anxious citation of references, etc.) also expresses the privilege of a type of publicity that must be distinct from the speed, brevity, imprecision, of the public media, and newspapers in particular. (One has only to read Mallarmé's concept of the "Letter" to get a glimpse of *the hatred of the crowd* that motivates it.) However, we might propose that the homogenous concept of the "crowd" or "the masses" has found no historically analogous entity within cultural and political borders of the United States, which might explain why the politics of European modernism could never have existed here, or could exist only negatively as a kind of a "religion of art" (*Die Kunstreligion*) within the socio-political formation of American intellectuals as a class historically disenfranchised and alienated from having any authority over the production of values in the "political-public sphere." In this period we are now traversing, the question of the "public" as it has been phrased recently by public academics like Bérubé, Robbins, Graff, and others, remains preliminary to the determination and analysis of this entity (which is neither a "people," or a "mass") as an actual political *end* of a contemporary discourse of the university like the one above, a discourse of "the Good," which these academics reproduce as an object of the profession as well.

Concluding this section, I again cite the statement by Althusser that heads this part of the report and which functions, in a certain sense, as its interlocutor: "*A 'theory' which does not question the end whose by-product it is remains a prisoner of this end and of the 'realities' which have imposed it as an end.*" In my opinion, the first task of such a theory would be to separate the tradition of liberal and political values ascribed to this entity by a rhetoric of "public access," whether these values appear in an Anglo-Marxist representation of the function of criticism as a kind of "social-service" in the Welfare State, as in Robbins' account, or in a kind of coalitional representation of the profession (drawn from a kind of 1970s and early 1980s style "grass roots" model) and participatory rhetoric of "free-speech" and "equal-access" that underwrites Bérubé's account. The second task would be to situate and to interrogate these values in relationship to the actual function of "the public" (as what Fredric Jameson describes as a "media-object") within a postmodern organization of the transnational, socio-cultural sphere of a global *Cosmo-polis* (or "total media city"). Contrary to the image of "the public" as an elemental component of civil space, Jameson's analysis presupposes the disappearance of its "civil function," or at least its dissemination within the *simulacra* of public media images.[56] Speech, a fundamental component of "civil society," becomes a redundant and ciphered component of the medium in which it "appears"; it is robbed of its mythic power to "initiate," or "to inaugurate" a certain collective utterance, since all speech-acts are already citations of other speech-acts and, therefore, no one can be determined as founding. This might help to explain the feeling of nausea that surrounds spoken discourse, and which appears to underscore the representation of spoken dialogue in postmodern novels like those of Don Delillo and Thomas Pynchon, where all talk has been robbed *a priori* of the possibility of saying, that is, of an inaugurating or performative dimension that marks the priority given to certain speech-acts (philosophical, religious, poetic, or epic) in earlier eras.

Jameson's view would also be shared by French philosopher Gilles Deleuze, who sees the liberal and traditional values of "publicity" (*Öffentlichkeit*), a necessary good of a modern civil society, become more and more treacherous when, "at the same time the means of exploitation, control and surveillance become more subtle and diffuse, in a certain sense molecular."[57] In what Deleuze called a "Society of Control," which can be defined as an "abstraction" that has been super-imposed upon and has over-encoded the spatial concepts of civil society, what is identified as "public access" may be in fact the newest means of control. Thus, according to Deleuze's argument, we are passing out of an earlier arrangement of "disciplinary societies" (a term borrowed from Foucault) in which the *socius* is organized into a series of discrete "closures" (*les enfermements*) that can be identified with institutions such as the prison, the hospital, the secondary school, and the university. The sign of our departure from this organization of power is the character of the crisis that now grips each of these institutions and causes them to enter into variation with what Deleuze refers to as an "indeterminate outside" composed by the new formations of capital and new media technologies.

### Summary & transition

In the preceding section, I discuss some of the implications of the recent debates concerning the nature of the "public sphere," and how recent constructions of publicity vis-à-vis the specifically cultural mission of the university are contributing to the re-structuring not only of the idea of university, but also of the representation and authority of critical social and humanistic knowledge as well. As I will address in more detail below, the conflict within the modern university has always taken place between its purely archival and its various social or ideological functions, that is, between maintenance of archival history (of records, documents, and narratives) and the reproduction of dominant narratives of history, science, politics, and ideology. To put this somewhat schematically for now, the eighteenth century conversion of knowledge from the form of the encyclopedia to that of the university also marks a shift or transformation in what I will call *mnemonitechnics*. From this point onward knowledge is no longer organized and instituted in the form of the book, even a "Total" or "World Book," such as an encyclopedia, but rather can be conceived, in analogy to the relations between eighteenth century nation-states, as a distinct incarnation of the notion of the disciplines based on the model of demarcated territories of knowledge, each with their constituent faculties. Hereafter, there is the conception of a common site in which there are different fields of study that are interconnected, although physically remote, in addition to being isolated by "culture" and dialect; consequently, each discipline maintains a certain sovereignty with regard to its own procedures and methods, and each bears responsibility for legitimating and reproducing its own knowledge in the creation of new doctorates. Above all, no discipline could legitimate the knowledge of another without a charge of encroachment — without violating the sovereignty of another faculty and engaging in a dispute over the principles of knowledge and authority.

This development marks the heterogeneous condition of modern knowledge that replaces the earlier Platonic and Aristotelian metaphysical conceptions of absolute knowledge. It was perhaps Kant's genius to have first understood this shift systematically, and to have attempted to resolve this condition of heterogeneity by proposing a juridical model of government to regulate the "intercourse" (*Verkehre*) between faculties (a favorite term often employed by Kant to cover the *commercium*, the buying and selling of knowledge between one discipline and another).[58] As Kant noted, more often than not this "intercourse" takes the form of a "conflict" (*Streit*) over interests concerning issues of authority, property, and right; which is why some measure of regulation and mediation must be installed between the faculties in order to guard this field of conflict, or at least to insure that all conflicts are legal and no party resorts to an "illegal" form of overt threat or coercion to the disadvantage of the other.[59] (This is also one of the reasons why the question of *access* to universities became such a highly volatile and political question following the 1960s.) We might also see here a close relationship between the organization of knowledge and the polity of nation-states, and in particular the ecumenical association of bourgeois liberal states. This relationship still metaphorically determines the way we conceive or imagine the relations between different branches of knowledge in the university. At the same time, it is the very status of this metaphorical representation, the product of an eighteenth century imagination, that will allow us to ask whether, in view of the decline of an earlier notion of sovereignty based on territory, on the one hand, and the emergence of new technologies of writing and data-storage (i.e., computers, the internet), on the other, these developments would have a disorienting effect on the idea of a university. Witnessing at the various problems that have beset the university over the past few decades, we have many vivid examples of such disorientation. If what we call the "university" is nothing more than an imaginative picture of what various eighteenth century thinkers conceived and fixed into place as the historical embodiment of *absolute knowledge*, then this idea would naturally be vulnerable to the vicissitudes brought about by new arrangements between knowledge, power, new technologies, and new forms of government (or administration). Moreover, it will be important to place in question the territorial and geo-political metaphors that Kant uses to determine the nature of the conflict of faculties. Two possibilities arise from questioning Kant's figurative language. The first is that these metaphors do not essentially characterize or color the nature of the "conflict" that originates within and between the different faculties who, all at once, are seeking to preserve, cultivate, renew, and destroy knowledge (or rather, ideas). Rather, these metaphors of "borders," "territorial dispute or skirmish," "suing for peace," "violation of treaties" which occur throughout the Kantian argument are drawn from the geo-political conditions of the nation-state in Kant's time and, therefore, the nature of this conflict of the faculties would have to undergo rhetorical purification and historical revision for different ages.[60] Perhaps to characterize the nature of the relationships among the different present-day faculties by the term "war" is not only an inaccurate representation, but threatens to mischaracterize the causal connection these relationships have to the emergence of new knowledges. Second, there is the possibility that the structure of disciplinary knowledges and the polity that governs their day to day relationships are themselves based upon the formal divisions between nations and would, therefore, suffer an intense disciplinary crisis should the "nation-form" itself decline as a dominant form and the organization of states themselves would undergo a global re-arrangement according to a new principle of market-alliances (as many have argued lately). The university would begin to be reshaped by the principles of a new arrangement and this would have an effect upon disciplinary knowledges as well.

Following the analysis of Habermas and Luhmann, one thesis I will explore in the next part is that the emergence of this new administrative model in the university is no longer premised on the classical principle of autonomy (neither the autonomy of the university vis-à-vis the larger society, nor the autonomy of the faculties from the pressures of end-oriented assessment). In turn, this *change of government* would effect the institution of the public sphere itself as the medium of knowledge and information becomes more porous and multiple, such that the earlier grand or "meta-narratives" of "History," "Reason," and "Universal Cosmopolitanism" no longer seem adequate to the form of the contemporary social institution. As I will discuss below, we might be witnessing a transformation in the form of knowledge, with the advent of computerization and virtual technologies such as the Internet, as important as that effected by the earlier conversion into the form of the university itself.

## Part II  *The Postmodern Condition Y2K*

*Abstract*

*Much of my discussion in this part is informed by the earlier "report on knowledge" made by Lyotard in* The Postmodern Condition *(1979/ 1984). As indicated by the above title, in many ways I see this report as a reappraisal and even "upgrading" of Lyotard's original document according to the terms of the current situation. I would argue that much of the critical significance of Lyotard's report, made more than twenty years ago, was misunderstood and, therefore, I re-visit and explicate many of his most provocative arguments: the decline of, or incredulity toward "universal meta-narratives," the rise of "performativity," and the post-modern character of what he calls "de-legitimation" (i.e., nihilism). In the following sections I return to emphasize the two guiding questions of Lyotard's report, which I take up and attempt to address in my own argu-ment: "who decides what knowledge is and who knows what needs to be decided [concerning knowledge]"? I show how Lyotard's thesis concerning the nature of "performativity" represents an extreme development of Kant's original concern over the power held by the higher faculties and refers to a situation in which the conflict of the faculties today is often resolved by what he called "illegal means" (coercion, overt pressure, intimidation, or threat). In an institution ruled by the performative criteria of evalu-ation, an institution which conforms to the standards and values of a late-capitalist society, all conflict is "managed" and "highly regulated" and the possibility of any real dispute (or differend) is met with a threat of isolation and gradual exclusion, which Lyotard defines very succinctly as the aspect of "terror" underlying the current social bond.*

## II(a) *Assessing Lyotard's* Report on Knowledge *twenty years later*

In 1979 Jean-François Lyotard published *The Postmodern Condition: A Report on Knowledge* (*La Condition postmoderne: rapport sur le savoir*) in which he first presented, at the request of the *Conseil des Universités* of the government of Quebec, an original thesis addressing the state of "knowledge in modern computerized societies."[1] It represents, to my knowledge, one of the few occasions in the contemporary period that a state-bureaucracy commissioned what is purely a speculative narrative, that is, the opinion of a philosopher, as part of an ongoing assessment of its institutions of higher education. Read in this context, it is also one of the most strange expositions of its kind. First, unlike its philosophical predecessors (for example, earlier expositions by Hegel, Humboldt, Kant, Schelling and Schleiermacher, just to name a few of the most well-known) we find absolutely no attempt to persuade, or to appeal to, the subject of the State; in fact, for reasons I will give below, I'm not sure that the State can even be called "an addressee" (in Lyotardese). Second, although it would be a humorous exercise, it would be nearly impossible to imagine any concrete policy following this report. In short, it is not a very practical document, which only highlights the anachronism of both the occasion and the genre announced by the subtitle — *A Report on Knowledge*.

Given our incredulity concerning its official purpose, we might therefore be tempted to read Lyotard's document as a "parody." A parody of what exactly? Perhaps of the discursive occasion itself as well as its supposed genre: "a report" written by "an expert" on a subject which pertains to the writer's field of expertise — everyone knows that a philosopher's field of expertise is knowledge *qua* knowledge — with the explicit expectation that the information contained in the presentation will assist some government body (in this case, a committee on higher education) in establishing policy that will guide and shape the future of higher education as a social institution. Of course, all of these presuppositions will be placed in question by the arguments contained in the report itself. In fact, it is this occasion that will become Lyotard's primary subject.

*A philosopher has been asked to give his expert opinion on the state of knowledge in higher education. He responds by declaring that, as a philosopher, he cannot be qualified as an expert in the usual sense this term is employed today (primarily in the areas where knowledge becomes "useful" information), and that his subject perhaps has no legitimate position from which to render an authoritative opinion.*

Because the philosopher is no longer a recognized player in the social game of knowledge, the request itself could be considered somewhat anachronistic to the current rules that belong to this game today. Lyotard argues that in such a situation of speaking to the State and its representatives and in order to remain up-to-date, the subject of a speculative or humanistic philosophy must renounce any pretension to assume such legitimation duties. This is why philosophy itself has been facing a crisis and has responded by arrogating its duties to the study of logical systems or to the history of ideas when it has been realistic enough to relinquish its former role.[2]

Nevertheless, Lyotard does respond to the invitation and does provide something that could be used as "information" concerning the social condition of knowledge in late-capitalist societies. In the introduction, Lyotard states that one of his objectives was to combine both "language games," the speculative language of the philosopher and the positivistic language of the expert, in order to show in what way both languages fail for different reasons to describe the current state of knowledge. The report he issues to the committee on higher education (*conseil des universites*) proposes the following arguments:

1.  A system has gradually emerged which no longer requires what the author defines as "grand narrative." (I will return to clarify this notion below.) The default or the "failure" of the grand narrative means that the nature of the social bond has evolved within late-capitalist societies in such a way that it no longer requires the classical function of *consensus*. In point of fact, a certain form of consensus already occurs in the "performativity" of the kind of "language-games" promoted by the system itself.

2.  This system has gone under the name of "capitalism" for the last century, since Marx, but has evolved to a degree that the historical materialist concept may no longer adequately describe its reality, and as a consequence may have fallen into confusion as an analytical category. Therefore the decrepitude of an earlier critical meta-language, specifically Marxist discourse, and the accompanying incredulity toward meta-narratives in general, especially philosophical or speculative narratives, are posited as major developments and form the context of the current state of knowledge.

3.  According to the author, the task that falls to us now is the invention of new language-games — or, to use an earlier and perhaps now out of date term, new "critical knowledges" — that correspond to the heterogeneous condition of knowledge in society today.

These hypotheses, now over twenty years old, will form the subject of my commentary in this section. With these arguments in mind we might revise our understanding of the occasion of Lyotard's report, if only to emphasize a further degree of irony. According to the first thesis, if the current system no longer requires a "grand-narrative" in order to effect the social bond in contemporary society, then the authority of the "State," or what Etienne Balibar has re-defined as the "nation-form" (i.e., the historical meta-narrative of the social bond of a "nation," or "a people"), can be effectively called into question.[3] In response to its query the State ultimately receives information concerning its own obsolescence. As Lyotard suggests:

> The notion that learning falls within the purview of the State, as the brain or mind of society, will become more and more outdated with the increasing strength of the opposing principle, according to which society exists and progresses only if the messages circulating within it are rich in information and easy to decode.[4]

Under the second aspect of Lyotard's thesis, if the form of narrative is no longer a crucial element in the performance of the social bond effected by "late-capitalism," then the social institution whose primary task was the social reproduction of "competencies" in various kinds of narratives (civil, juridical, moral, political) can also be placed in question. The university no longer authorizes the kind of knowledge that currently *performs* the social bond in "computerized societies," and does not store or reproduce information on the basis of which the most critical decisions concerning society are made today. Hence, the linkage between knowledge and society that was traditionally located in the social institution of the modern university would need to undergo a period of intense re-evaluation. As Lyotard writes, "[t]o the obsolescence of the meta-narrative apparatus of legitimation corresponds, most notably, the crisis of metaphysical philosophy and the university institution which in the past relied on it."[5]

Accordingly, Lyotard's report is less a theory of knowledge (an epistemology) than a series of working hypotheses which are intended to have a strategic value in relation to the guiding questions of the report: "What kind of knowledge is necessary for society today?" "Who decides what knowledge is, and who knows what needs to be decided?"[6] Again, we must imagine the concrete situation in which these questions are posed: the agent of the State asks this of the philosopher. In order to understand the philosopher's reply — "Where, after the age of meta-narratives, can legitimacy reside?" — we may have to abandon our predilection for a certain nineteenth century "heroic narrative" in which the philosopher is necessarily opposed to the "Man of the State." Ultimately, such a narrative must presuppose that the "subject who decides" can, in the last instance, be identified today with either party. Lyotard himself points to the fading of these old coordinates in the following statement:

> [S]uffice it to say that functions of regulation, and therefore of repro-duction, will be further withdrawn from administrators and entrusted to machines [...] What is new in all of this is that the old poles of attraction represented by nation-states, parties, professions, institutions and historical

traditions are losing their attraction. And it does not look like they will be replaced, at least not on their former scale.[7]

Given the situation outlined above, how is this possible? The crisis that concerns both subjects equally is what Lyotard calls "the blind positivity of delegitimation." In an earlier philosophical terminology this would simply be called "nihilism," which is more visible in "advanced technological societies," and can be registered in the area of the State in terms of cynicism toward all representative or "public" functions of democratic institutions and the transformation of the social bond into a patchwork of narrowly defined and heterogeneous "interest-groups." In the area of knowledge (and the university, in particular, which traditionally adapted knowledge to correspond to the form of the social bond), what Lyotard calls de-legitimation has taken on a primarily negative or critical form, which may be equally blind, in the sense that the new "subject-groups" this form has created, in actuality, might be the most suited and easily adaptable to the new social bond described above under the term "late-capitalism," the dominant mode of production and exchange in contemporary first-world post-industrial societies. In other words, perhaps the "conservative" interests of philosophy have much more in common with the interests of the state than ever before. (I realize that this statement may seem incredible to some, and goes against more orthodox views of agonistics.) After all, the state still believes in the principle of "justice," however impractical it is to realize within the current historical moment, just as the philosopher still believes in the principle of "truth," however arbitrary and hard to defend this principle has become. Yet, both are facing or struggling with a power that has little use for either of these old values for optimizing its performance. For example, the textile industry does not ask whether or not it is "just" to relocate their operations in the under-developed world where labor is cheaper, just whether it is "good business" and the relocation is cost efficient. The advertising company does not ask whether it is "true" that there is really a relationship between shampoo and a female orgasm, just whether the association is pleasing for the consumer and whether the whole question of pleasure can be an associative factor the next time the consumer buys shampoo.

By taking the discursive occasion of Lyotard's report somewhat paradigmatically, therefore, we might be able to clarify the nature of the crisis that causes the above question to be raised with some sense of urgency for both parties: who will have control over the social determination of knowledge, if this power no longer falls to the state? Who decides — "Who will know?"[8] In the following sections, I will show how this crisis, in as much as it concerns the legitimation of the subject who will appear in society as "knower" and of the procedure by which knowledges are ranked and gathered together, can be defined as the crisis at the origin of philosophy itself.

## II(b) *The university in cyberspace*

I begin by recalling again the anecdote by Kant which inaugurates *The Conflict of Faculties,* where the university is presented as an innovative idea initially created to solve two problems: data-storage and the maintenance or reproduction of knowledge. According to Kant's fable, the idea of a university occurred to someone whose own identity was longer ago forgotten, perhaps in a state of fitful sleeplessness, who worried about these social needs and finally arrived at a brilliant solution to the problem: a place, or centralized location, an artificial brain where all knowledge is gathered together, and to insure its maintenance and perpetuation, where an assortment of "faculties" who represent, in a patently allegorical manner, the particular mental capacity that corresponds to each kind of knowledge, can be reproduced for the future benefit of society. Like other fables of this kind, which were popular in the eighteenth and nineteenth centuries (for example, the fable of the social bond itself as a "contract" in Rousseau, or of labor as a "muscle" or "machine" in Marx), Kant reduces the corporate nature of a social institution to an organic metaphor, in this case, the brain. The university, in principle, is a giant brain (i.e., the mind of society itself); the faculties are like the different lobes of the brain and represent its mental activity. The university is a primitive, or at least, an early prototype of artificial intelligence. It is, very simply, an archaic computer and the faculties are software.

This cybernetic metaphor is not specious or trivial, but addresses the heart of Lyotard's report on knowledge *"in computerized societies."* As Lyotard writes, "the scenario of computerization of the most highly developed societies allows us to spotlight (though with the risk of excessive magnification) certain aspects of the transformation of knowledge and its effects on public power and civil institutions — effects it would be difficult to perceive from other points of view."[9] To demonstrate the pertinence of cybernetic technologies and the transforming effect these could have on the status of knowledge in society, and on the status of the knowledge that is stored and maintained in the university in particular, is to recall that the modern-day personal computer is an invention that responds to the very same social needs — data-storage and the reproduction of information. At the same time, we might also perceive that the user of a modern personal computer, linked to other users over a vast network configuration, solves this social need far more efficiently than a centralized and "land-locked" (i.e., geographically located) data-base that users can only access on-site, and whose information is only publicly available by means of a very slow and now very expensive medium of printed material, usually mediated by an even slower and cumbersome apparatus of historical gatekeepers or mediators (e.g., editors, expert-readers, publishing institutions, distribution channels, canons or authorized lists, etc.). Therefore, we might recognize the principle of the historical university's obsolescence according to the same process that occurs through the successive improvements in second- and third-generation machines.

In light of the above, it is important to reflect upon the causes behind the "technological revolution" that has been taking place in universities and colleges for many years, precisely in order to up-date and improve its programs and earlier technologies for knowledge reproduction. These initiatives are extremely aggressive, ear-marked for capital investment and a high priority for institutions of every rank and level, and have translated into lucrative incentives to faculty for incorporating new technologies into the classroom, as well as new computer facilities and programs to make computerization an intricate part of all aspects of university life. (This includes setting up e-mail accounts for all incoming students and faculty, the provision of computer and networking equipment as a standard clause in all new faculty contracts, the "hard-wiring" (networking) of all offices, dorm-rooms, and classrooms; the increasing use of list-servs as sites of political and cultural activity on campus, the use of web-pages as distribution points for class materials and reading, the increase of web-based journals and publications for professional and academic distribution of new knowledge, etc.) The above list only covers a few of the more prominent changes that have take place in the last decade in the university.

What is most critical to emphasize in the increasing number and the rapidity of these new programs is that they all implicitly, if not overtly, correspond to the form of a social mandate. Consequently, there is always a meta-narrative that accompanies their implementation that runs according to the following set of prescriptions: *We must improve our technological capabilities. It is urgent, if not vital to the survival of the institution that we invest in this area of its capital growth. We must overcome all resistance on the part of existing cultures and practices and insure that, by the year 2000, every aspect of the university is thoroughly digitized for the coming era of knowledge production and exchange.* All these statements — which many faculty have heard if not themselves made at crucial moments concerning where a large portion of annual investment should be concentrated (usually, weighed against the priority of salary increases for faculty and staff) — appeal explicitly to the presence of a *de facto* consensus concerning the state of knowledge in society. It is a form of consensus, moreover, that does not often appear to be questioned on political or so-called "ideological" grounds. In fact, some of those who locate themselves ideologically on the left have also been among the biggest cheerleaders for the new technology, as if the question of the nature of the forum of publicity appears as politically neutral or, amazingly, bereft of ideological implications. (And this last belief seems quite fantastic in my view.)

At the same time, we might speculate that these endeavors may also signal, on the part of the university, a frantic attempt to up-date its understanding of skills and competencies, which now include computer training and literacy, in order to repair its fragile bond with society.

What is the form of knowledge today? The answer is all too evident: all *critical* knowledge is solid state, which is to say, "computerized." The most pressing question concerning the current state of knowledge today is whether it is digital or analog, and if the latter, can it be converted and brought up to date. (In this context, it is often interesting to observe that the fields that are most threatened with obsolescence, such as the study of Medieval Literature or Languages, are often the quickest to convert their knowledge base into a hyper-text or cybernetic format.) In those cases where it cannot, then an investigation and assessment of the social "legitimacy" of this kind of knowledge will immediately ensue. At the same time, we can assess the predominance of this situation today by observing that within the most traditionally resistant and fiscally remote disciplines of the Humanities, where a new professional model has become dominant, there is a visible and growing divide between form and content where the process of learning and acquiring knowledge is assessed in terms of potential "markets." On a formal level, English departments are beginning to define their practices in the same terms as other culture industries; no matter how radical the content, the representation of new knowledge in particular has taken on the form of a commodity. The implementation of new computer technologies into the historically defined practices and forums of university knowledge, therefore, is precisely the place where the question of the current state of knowledge needs to be situated, as Lyotard himself announced nearly two decades ago when he wrote the following:

> It is only in the context of the grand narratives of legitimation — the life of the spirit and/or emancipation of humanity — that the partial replacement of teachers may seem inadequate or even intolerable. But it is possible that these narratives are no longer the principal driving force behind the interest in acquiring knowledge. If the motivation is power, then this aspect of classical didactics ceases to be relevant. The question (overt or implied) now asked by the professionalist student, the State, or the institutions of higher education is no longer 'is it true' but 'What use is it?' In the context of the mercantilization of knowledge, more often than not this question is equivalent to: 'Is it saleable?' And in the context of power-growth: 'Is it efficient?' [...] This creates the prospect for a vast market for competence in operational skills. Those who possess this kind of knowledge will be the object of offers and seduction policies. Seen in this light, what we are approaching is not the end of knowledge — quite the contrary. Data banks are the Encyclopedias of tomorrow. They transcend the capacity of each of their users. They are 'nature' for the postmodern man.[10]

When Lyotard wrote these words, the idea of a global data base that was accessible from any user with a computer terminal was not yet a reality; only governments could afford such technology, which nevertheless was still in a fairly primitive state. Today things are much different. Although Lyotard rejects the idea that his speculations on the advancement of "computerization" will have any predictive value (rather than a "strategic value" in the context of the guiding questions outlined above), looking back from our vantage point in the Y2K I think we would have to admit that on this issue his predictive powers were somewhat uncanny. As an example of his predictive powers, I quote the following passage concerning the transformation of the role of the state in an era of globalized capitalism and ask the reader to keep in mind that these observations were first made in 1979:

> The opening of the world market, a return to vigorous economic competition, the breakdown of the hegemony of American capitalism, the decline of the socialist alternative, *a probable opening of the Chinese market* — these and other factors are already, at the end of the 1970s, preparing States for a serious reappraisal of the role they have been accustomed to playing since the 1930s: that of guiding or even directing investments. In this light, the new technologies can only increase the urgency of such a reexamination, since they make the information used in decision-making (and therefore the means of control) even more mobile and *subject to piracy*.[11][my emphasis]

At this point, let us return to the guiding questions in light of these observations: "What kind of knowledge is necessary for society today?" "Who decides what knowledge is, and who knows what needs to be decided?"[12] From the above discussion we can come to the following conclusion, confirming Lyotard's thesis concerning the decline of "grand narratives": it is a fact that the most transformative effects on the current state of knowledge in the university as well as in society at large do not originate from the traditional forces of society (despite what idealists of both sides today continue to argue in terms of the power of critical or grand narratives), but rather from the incremental and gradual conversion of the materiality of knowledge itself into bites of data that can endure endless permutation, compression, distribution, and storage. The change in materiality is necessarily accompanied by a change in form of "publicity," as I have argued in I(d).

Yet, this observation does not clarify the cause behind the current stage of crisis that these transformative effects are inflicting social institutions, and on the university in particular. Rather, the crisis occurs when we recognize that the "place" or "site" where knowledge is stored and can be accessed is no longer centrally located, a situation in which access to knowledge can be easily regulated and controlled (even distributed according to the calculated interest of social or class prejudice), but is dispersed in virtual space that can be accessed from any terminal without regard to its physical location. And it is precisely this "virtual space" where knowledge is stored that marks the occasion of the crisis, since this space exceeds its previous locations and the authorities that belonged to them, and exposes the question of the control and dissemination of knowledge to the most dizzying potential for de-regulation, or what Lyotard has calls "de-legitimation."

The question of the "subject who decides," which opened our commentary on the discursive occasion of Lyotard's report, can be raised again in the context of the transformative effects of technological innovations in data-storage and the public availability of "knowledge" (over networked computers on the Internet or World Wide Web). The question indicates a crisis of "authority" or "authorization" which occurs when the form of knowledge undergoes a kind of general de-regulation and becomes unbounded from the traditional locations and social relationships that discipline and control its transmission and reproduction according to a highly determinate criteria of exclusions, qualifications, and social controls. For example, the traditional relationship between a teacher (as the sender) and a student (as the receiver) reinforces a determinate social paradigm which always conditions the transmission of knowledge. Regardless of the content, the real object of the lesson is the imperative that the transmission of knowledge conform to the form of a social bond that is invested with a certain authority; thus, what will count as "knowledge" must either conform to this procedure of legitimation, or it will appear as "non-public opinion" (which is Habermas' term for the modern version of Plato's *doxa*, or Hegel's *Meinung*). It is because this notion of discipline is central to the kind of "knowledge" that occurs within legitimate sites where learning occurs, that one finds an array of illegitimate and unauthorized knowledge populating the perimeter of any major campus, from the activist passing out leaflets to the local coffee shop guru or sage who teaches the subject of Life to anyone who wants to submit to his teachings.

We might see the relevance of how the change of the "site" where knowledge is stored and reproduced will have concrete effects on traditional procedures of legitimation, or upon the modern alliance between the university and the state. As a social institution, the university traditionally performed a number of crucial functions of authorization that were critical to the state, comprising what we might call the *homologies of citizenship*. Because the university is a *place*, moreover, the question of "who has access to knowledge" could be highly regulated and controlled; inversely, the very question of "who has access" can become politicized since all the factors that will determine eligibility are by definition political. Only those who receive admission and are properly matriculated can gain entry to locations where knowledge is transmitted, or can pursue programs of study leading to a public license or degree. Moreover, because the university is located at a particular site, questions of access will also be determined by considerations of region, travel, language, nationality.

As I noted above, because of the expense involved in earlier technologies of data-storage and reproduction, only the government had enough capital resources to afford a data-base (a library) which was usually located at the center of the nation (e.g., The Library of Congress, or the *Biliotheque Nationale*) or at the university site where the right of access is strictly controlled (leaving to the side the creation of public libraries which belong to a more socially progressive form of data-base). Even today, this principle governs the question of access to the university's data bank, so that only matriculated students, faculty, staff and other authorized personnel have a *visa* to cross into the "mind of society." The critic Roland Barthes had earlier emphasized that the library is one of the two socially repressive forces that determine the procedure of reading (the other being "pertinence," which results from the education of the discriminating reader, or the one who knows what materials are not worth reading, which are usually found in more public venues such as check-out stands at the grocery store).[13] From this observation of the procedures of identification and authorized entry that continue to be enforced in university libraries — moreover, by gatekeepers who are sometimes dressed as police or border guards — we might discern the a notion of the "public availability of knowledge" according to the same model of *territory* employed by the historical institution of nation states. (I have already argued that the disciplines correspond to this same model.)

There is a "right of access," to be sure, but only under a series of very strictly observed conditions of proper identification and legal rights which are only extended to "citizens" of the university community, reinforcing the partition between the private sphere and civil society (or more accurately, "the political public sphere"). As in their larger juridical framework, these rights may be revoked under specific infringements, which include non-payment of fees, tuition, and fines for late or outstanding property of the university (i.e., the universal obligation to pay your debts in a timely fashion). It is this last criteria, in particular, that demonstrates that the "rights of access" are still very much determined by the historical institution of the bourgeois public sphere, for which education and respect of private property were prerequisites for the admission to the political public sphere.[14]

On the basis of this example (perhaps this anecdote) let us try and imagine the manner in which the nature of the public access to knowledge has changed today. With the advent of a vast configuration of networked databases, the organic metaphor employed by Kant (i.e., the university "the brain" usually located in a central location of the state or nation, such as a capital, or the center of a large metropolitan city) must be revised to account for the virtual space that this new database occupies. Today, knowledge is *out there*, constantly circulating. Discrete quantities of data are constantly undergoing new combinations, permutations, and "arrangements." Take, for example, the invention of more and more powerful search engines: a basic query that would have formerly taken an "expert" several years of research to answer can now be performed in a few key-strokes. This is becoming a volatile factor in assessing the nature of expertise, which before had been determined by the difficulty of access, conditioned by the time involved in gathering and in extracting knowledge from raw data; however, today the criteria for determining expertise is modulating into what Lyotard defines as the creativity of manipulating and arranging quantities of readily accessible data into new and unexpected combinations. In the academy, this might address the expertise of the "theorist" who has emerged as a new kind of knowledge expert in the genre of philosophy; who, in a certain sense, has replaced the subject of the modern (idealist) philosopher. The difference between the contemporary "theorist" and the contemporary academic philosopher (that is, the analytic philosopher who populates most philosophy departments in the United States) simply corresponds to Lyotard's injunction at the beginning of this section: the theorist or critical theorist has not renounced his or her role vis-à-vis "the State" (i.e., the duty of legitimation albeit in a negative or critical form), while the analytic philosopher has renounced this power which *he* has determined to be metaphysical pretension, at least an illusion, and has instead focused his energies on addressing pure philosophical problems — of logic, language, the brain, etc.

As I raised the question in the beginning of my remarks on Lyotard, perhaps the analytical philosopher is right and we might see the theorist as holding on to a nostalgic and unrealistic, even self-important, view of the efficacy of his or her discourse with regard to the medium of power. Again, this question goes to the heart of Lyotard's argument concerning the kind of knowledge that is promoted by the contemporary social bond. If society no longer sutures itself to a world-view (*Weltanschaung*) or some order of totality by the thread of a "grand narrative" (History, Nation, Empire, Race, etc.), then the subject whose former role was the creation, maintenance, and even the critique of grand narratives will sooner than later be out of work. (This is one possible explanation for the vocational crisis now confronted by would-be philosophers and theorists who have been relegated for the most part to English Departments, that is, when they can find a job at all.) It is interesting to note that the above split between the role of the analytic philosopher and the theorist might address the split in the subject of philosophy itself, whereby a certain speculative and even metaphysical discourse that formerly belonged to the genre has been separated out and today is most likely to be found, not in the department of philosophy (or if so, then only in the ghettoized zone of "Continental Philosophy"), but in the Department of English where the questions of legitimation and power still persist to a degree that has even eclipsed the former object of the discipline, what was once called "literature."

As an aside, in response to those who might see this as an aberrant or improper development in the disciplinary coordinates of "English," I would point out two factors that may indicate more of a continuity than a break with the traditional tasks of the literary critic. First, despite the change in topics, the methodology employed by contemporary critics continues to privilege some form of "narrative analysis," even if this is no longer defined by earlier formalist or "new critical" principles of close-reading. Second, and most important in my view, the one underlying problem one finds in almost all critical theories that populate the university today (whether ideology-critique premised on Marxist axiomatics, critical expositions of racial ideologies, or feminist and queer constructions of gender identity) concerns what Kant first revealed in *The Critique of Judgment* as the "subjective conditions of all judgment" which, I would argue, has always been the province of *criticism*. Although this problem is certainly most relevant to the political sphere, especially concerning the legitimation of those judgments which are given power "to rule," we need only to recall that it was Kant who shifted the study of this problem to the aesthetic sphere, where the formal qualities of judgment itself could be systematically analyzed within what he called "a critique of taste." Thus, today the object of this critique continues to be judgment, or rather narratives of judgment (dominant or minor, historical or contemporary), although it is no longer concerned with literary narrative exclusively, but more generically, narratives of the subject (of race or ethnicity, gender, queer or trans-sexual identity, etc.), or narratives of power (marginal or class-based, nation and empire, colonial and post-colonial, trans-national or trans-cultural). Moreover, the "theorist" is a subject of knowledge who is capable of generating new paradigms for arranging already existent knowledge, and of being able to draw on several different fields of disciplinary knowledge that were formerly accessible to only the subjects trained and "qualified" in those disciplines. As the recent "Sokal affair" demonstrated very well, this situation has created a certain anxiety around the question of the "authorized user of knowledge."

Nevertheless, the most critical change has occurred around the question of general "access." When the database was centralized and "landlocked," this issue could be regulated or controlled. Those naturally excluded might not have enough money, time, basic skills or knowledge of the system itself; others would be excluded *a priori*, since "knowing" did not have any real interest for them. (This is a nineteenth century characterization of the interest of the "rabble" or the "masses.") With the advent of large public institutions of higher education, along with the democratic principle of granting access to a wider population no longer defined homogeneously or narrowly by class or regional affiliation, the question of "authorization" enters into the period of crisis whose lasting effects are still very much at the center of current discussions. Today, the database can be accessed from any location with a terminal and a modem, by anyone who "has any interest," for any reason whatsoever. From this fact, and all the possibilities it implies, it is fairly easy to picture the occasion we began with, when the man of the state asks the philosopher, "who decides what knowledge is, and who knows what needs to be decided?"

The subject being addressed is not another avatar of the grand subject (of a super-state, or of a dominant class ideology), but rather the inchoate mass of isolated and faceless "users," each with their own intent, or research project (as common or frivolous as it may seem). This class of users is not a "public" in the classical sense, which is an entity that belongs to a demarcated site or sphere of civil society and more specifically designates the type of interests and social relationships that are located there. From the Greek and Roman origin, as Habermas presented in his study of this institution, the notions of public and publicity in fact referred to a sphere of the *polis* which was common to all citizens, and strictly separated from the sphere of the *oikos*, where each individual is in his own realm, or *idia*.[15] However, it is well known that the history of this institution was always mediated by other institutions (e.g., slavery, private property, the institutions of class and gender) that regulated who had access to this common sphere.

The most critical problem emerges when we realize that there are no criteria to determine access, no identity card or passport to verify "legitimate users" from the illegitimate or spurious. A "password" is all that is required, and this only requires access to an account (which is a latent political factor of access I will address below), and enough basic knowledge or training to qualify as a "user." Lyotard poses this crisis in the legitimation of access in the strongest of terms when he suggests, as a result of this new technology, even "the state may only simply be one user among others."[16] Humorously, the university's solution to this problem has often been to install computers within the library so that the same identification requirements can be enforced concerning authorized access. This solution, however, demonstrates the anachronism of this archive. The situation that is being addressed by the name *the postmodern condition* is the dispersion and general deregulation of knowledge, its overflowing of earlier channels of legitimation and authorization; in short, the entire question of the control and the rarity of information in society. It is primarily through its rarity and the difficulty in attainment that knowledge has been historically controlled, either by the creation of an educated class or through the creation of expertise which presupposes a certain discrimination and prejudice concerning "who" can have access. In fact, we might easily imagine that the political question of access will gradually shift from the university, no longer the location of knowledges that are critical to society, to other sectors and, in particular, to the access and use of the Internet.

We can already see this most dramatically in the gradual shift of the political question of "access" from the site of the university, where it has been located since the 1960s, to the Internet. For example, a recent government report announced with some concern that there is a growing divide between poor minority households that have a personal computer with Internet access and white households that are so equipped in the United States.[17] Thus emerges the political question of "equity" in the distribution of technology across economic and racial boundaries and the effects this will have on the social and economic opportunities of those children who come from these households, but who do not have the skills and the knowledge to compete, either in school or in the marketplace. The importance of this example is that it demonstrates how the question of justice that is implied in acquisition of knowledge is no longer posed in the context of the university's position and role as a civil institution, but rather in the context of general access to new technologies by disadvantaged groups and economic minorities. With this example, we might also point out the powerful "myth" of global access to new technology, which seems to be endemic to the idea of a "World Wide Web," since one can easily imagine on the basis of this technological gap that exists in the United States, that the relative wealth or poverty of countries will be determined by the level of computer skills of entire populations. I imagine that within ten years the most critical question of social and economic justice will in some way be centered on the control and distribution of computer technologies, even though today this question does not seem to inspire much political enthusiasm among first-world intellectuals.[18]

And, at the same time, this shift certainly does not explain why this crisis emerges in its current form. For example, we couldn't imagine that the state (understood as an institution determined by dominant ideology or class interest according to the classical Marxist understanding) would have ever let knowledge get so out of hand and out into the public, unless it is due to what Hegel called the kernel of "Non-Reason inherent in Reason itself." The public availability of information on the Internet concerning how to build your very own atomic bomb, or a complete list of all British spies past and present; the general dispersion or deregulation of all kinds of sensitive knowledge, including state secrets — certainly this is not in the best interest of the authority of the modern state, which in the nuclear age has been based upon the exclusive control and domination of access to technology, as well as the creation and maintenance of various restricted databases. As we will discuss next, perhaps we find in all the above examples, all of which concern the current problems of "de-legitimation" (Lyotard), that there is a tendency in knowledge itself to be dispersed and out of control.

**II(c)** *How philosophy originally solved the problem of legitimation.*

So far, our discussion has only concerned one aspect of the university's function, data storage and public availability of knowledge, which in no way implies that there are other functions that the university still performs for society. I will now turn to show how what Lyotard describes as the postmodern crisis in knowledge is actually endemic to the question of philosophy and even, in some ways, repeats its foundation. For practical reasons I have chosen not to raise the question of the distinction between "knowledge" and "information," or between what can be saved as data and what cannot, including the creation of new knowledge. In part, Lyotard himself performs the reduction of knowledge to information throughout his argument, and thus abandons strategically the question of epistemology — i.e., *what, in fact, counts for knowledge?* —due to his rejection of the dualism upon which the critical distinction between knowledge and information rests: in short, the distinction between a positivistic function and a more transcendental, or critical function of knowledge.

Although we have highlighted, by means of cybernetic metaphor, the nature of the university as a tool or instrument for gathering together all existing knowledges, this instrumental determination (which I would say is purely functional or positivistic) does not address the different ideological, civil or moral functions that have also accrued to the function of the university as a modern social institution. According to this view, the university is reduced to its positive function, and can be seen in terms of what Heidegger called a "standing-reserve" of information, techniques, skills and languages that fulfill, in some aspect or another, a current social need. However, this still does not clarify the principle reason why the university fulfills this function in society, why it is important for society to have a place to gather knowledge together, and how is this defined as a social problem that the idea of the university historically solves. In order to clarify this fundamental principle, we will have to turn to the speculative narrative of knowledge on which the original idea of the university was founded, that is, the "master-narrative" that historically instituted the idea of the university.

A good place to turn in order to clarify Lyotard's notion of a "meta-narrative" occurs in the "Memorandum on Legitimation" in *The Postmodern Explained*.[19] In this text Lyotard distinguishes between two basic types of "grand narrative procedures": the mythic and the emancipatory. He writes:

> [b]oth of these procedures make recourse to narration; that is, they both disperse this absence [i.e., the "logical aporia of authorization"], spreading the theoretical problem along a diachronic axis. But that is the only thing they have is common.

For while one procedure directs this dispersion upstream, toward an origin, the other directs it downstream, toward an end.[20]

Here the difference between mythic and emancipatory narratives is presented as the difference between their *sens unique* (or "one-way direction"). Following Lyotard's own metaphor at this point, narratives can be likened to salmon: returning to the origin (in order to spawn), or swimming to a destination (the open ocean). Personally, I have always liked this metaphor of Lyotard's and have often used it to clarify, pedagogically, the distinction between the two kinds of narrative, however rigorously applied, we would have to question whether, like the salmon, one species of narrative could undergo modulation, so that the same narrative could at different phases move in one direction or another, or, in a stage of decline or obsolescence reverse its original course. There is a certain weakness in Lyotard's classification of narrative procedures, therefore, since he fails to account for the fact that certain narratives behave in some ways as mythic, and at the same time, in other ways as emancipatory. Certainly, the state or "nation-form" behaves this way, which is to say that it is inconsistent in its procedure of "legitimation" from one moment to the next.

The master-narrative that is pertinent for our discussion is the "speculative" narrative, the genre of which is the philosophical, but whose unique historical embodiment is the university itself. The speculative narrative is the narrative of "spirit" or "mind" (*Geist*). I will turn to address the definition of Spirit in a moment, but first we need to understand the nature of "speculation." The primary function of speculation is "totalization," the creation of "a Big Picture." On the one hand, this first aspect of the speculative function accounts for the encyclopedic impulse, which is the condition of the existence of a University. This encyclopedic impulse (or drive) might also be discovered to be behind the interconnection of computers over a network configuration, or "World Wide Web" — as Lyotard says, "[d]ata banks are the Encyclopedias of tomorrow" — if one begins to ask the question concerning why centralization or inter-connectivity (i.e. the tendency of data-banks to link together to form one total memory) seems to be an endemic trait of knowledge. However, it is important to note that both these forms of organizing knowledge in some "total configuration" are in no way a natural tendency with the *form of knowledge* itself. Knowledge is not self-organizing, as Hegel argued early on, since left to itself knowledge tends to become separated and dispersed.

To counteract this centrifugal tendency, a manner of unifying every kind of knowledge into one central form must be artificially introduced in order to prevent the various knowledges upon which a society depends from getting too dispersed, and possibly even from getting lost, either as a result of rarity and eventual extinction, or from becoming too dependent upon the individual knower. It is this last danger that might account for a fundamental axiom of all knowledge, that it must be reproducible. This could even be said to constitute a social obligation or command for its essential gregarious nature, which found its most acute historical expression in the Enlightenment in the public character of reason. According to the Enlightenment Principle, all knowledge must, in as much as it has the character of knowledge, essentially belong to 'the people.' This is the basic principle of reason, which Kant called its "*Öffentlichkeit*," its openness. It is also for this reason that any knowledge that appeared obscurantist in form, or privatized and non-transferable in content, could be charged with violating a fundamental law of reason, which is its public character. (Thus, the "irrational" character of certain private forms of reasoning, including in the modern period the religious revelation and mysticism, and forms of madness.)

This is one of the meanings that can be ascribed to Kant's understanding of the "tribunal of reason" which, rather than depicting a kind of authoritarian or despotic impulse as this phrase has been interpreted so often, in actuality refers to a determination of the absolute right of the people or the 'public' to all knowledge, which must be protected from any private appropriation or control (especially by the church or the state and any of their agents). From this observation, we might also want to underline that this "public" character of knowledge does not refer to any actual entity, but rather refers to the essential trait of knowledge, its transmissibility, or its tendency to seek a state of more and more "openness" (*Öffentlichkeit*).

Knowledge reproduces itself and proliferates in the form of a virus, which is why the forms of secrecy and obscurantist knowledge must be reinforced with supplemental sanctions, since under Kant's description, there is no form of knowledge that is also not determined by this moral obligation of transmission or reproduction. Consequently, there is no such thing as "private knowledge," which is why everything that is known by anyone at any time is destined for the public, in the sense that it bears within it the seeds of its dissemination or becoming- "Universal." It is on the basis of this law that the Kantian "tribunal of Reason" could judge any instance where knowledge is repressed or maintained in a state of secrecy as a violation of the principle of Reason. In the appendix to "The Essay on Perpetual Peace," for example, he spends a great deal of time outlining the special conditions and criteria by which states can conduct themselves through secret treaties or pacts and still obey the Enlightenment principle of reason.

The Kantian practical prescription (or "categorical imperative") has an essential relationship with this public character of reason. It requires that the maxim that can be derived from any action must be capable of communication and this, in effect, forbids the realization of certain actions whose discursive representation cannot be formulated and publicly communicated. For Kant, the statement that all actions must be universally valid means nothing less than their principle must stand up to verification and legitimation by a language situation. Those actions that cannot pass such a test would be declared illegitimate and illegal. Yet, both Marxism and Freudianism have launched powerful critiques of precisely this principle and, thus, have both shown why the Kantian universal is impossible to realize. They have shown that that maxim of the subject's action is not directly communicable, but rather always takes place "in another scene" than consciousness, and in effect can describe the position of consciousness that is occupied by another subject, whether this is rendered as the subject of ideology, as in Marx, or as the subject of the Unconscious (*Das Unbewust*), as in Freud.

This last observation immediately leads us to formulate another aspect of the "speculative spirit," which is its critical function. Classically, the faculty for speculation is linked to the psychological states of "wonder" and "curiosity" before the Whole, as Aristotle first observed. (Here, we need to remind ourselves that the earliest meanings of "spirit" corresponded more to the definitions of the psychological meaning of "the soul" or "mood" than to the modern sense that was provided by German idealism.) As Schleiermacher said, "there is no creative scientific capacity without a speculative spirit." We understand by this that without a sense of curiosity that is sparked by "wonderment" or "amazement" before the whole, there would be no motive for knowledge, no "will-to-knowledge." To these basic sensibilities of wonder and amazement, Kant in *The Critique of Judgment,* added a third, "terror." By doing so, Kant basically modernized the Aristotelian conception of the speculative spirit, which was until this point far too pacific or "theoretical." Before the whole, one of the psychological responses of the human being is fear and dread, which characterizes one of the states of the sublime. Thus, Kant's revision of the speculative mode effectively changed what could be called the mood of the speculative faculty.

His revision speaks less to the creative capacity than to the incapacity at the basis of the scientific spirit (governed by the faculty of the understanding) by underlining the conditions for its weakness and failure. Kant's *Critique of Judgment* installed a dynamic tension in the state of knowledge itself which henceforth is no longer completely motivated by curiosity and by the wish to know everything; knowledge is guided or directed by an equal wish *not to know*, or to repress those experiences that provoke in it a feeling of uncertainty, anxiousness, and finally, terror. It is because of this discovery, as many of Kant's commentators have already noted, that Kant fundamentally revised the hegemony that the faculty of understanding enjoyed over the imagination and reason in *The Critique of Pure Reason.* The power of understanding and imagination pale and even falter before the awesome power of the "whole" to provoke a response and even a "spontaneous accord" within the subject (even though Kant would, by sleight of hand, come to identify this power with the nature of reason itself). Regardless of whether this identification is true, or was simply Kant's attempt to salvage something from the ruins of his earlier philosophical system based on the spontaneous arrangement of the faculties into a trinity (as many have argued, beginning with Heidegger) the effect this revision had on the power of understanding and imagination would be the same. As forms of synthesizing a given presentation to concepts, or a given immediacy to a presentation, they become secondary and even "reactive" powers in relation to a primary power that is identified with the apprehension of the "whole."

Another way of putting this is that Kant detected a basic interest of self-preservation in the faculty of understanding, which is to limit its curiosity to only those things that it can know with some degree of certainty, and to exclude the rest. This "exclusion" is not simple. By this I mean that it is not simply a pacific, Heideggerian "letting be" of the unknown at the borders of what can be known. Rather, as Freud later argued, this exclusion takes on an active and constant force of repression in the life of the knowing subject, the repression proper that constitutes the region of psychic life he calls the "Unconscious" (*Das Unbewuste*). With this concept, Freud completes Kant's earlier revision of the relationship between the faculties.

At this juncture, I may be accused of simplifying Kant, but I am doing so in order to underline the critical conditions for the dominant critique of modern science as guided by a subject of certainty, on the one hand, and by a desire to repress or control the unknown, on the other. This is the critique of the Cartesian subject that has been carried out several times over the course of the last century, a tradition of critique that is fully developed in Heidegger and Derrida, but also in Lacan where the "subject of certainty" is submitted to the most intensive scrutiny as a subject of "desire." The significance (one might be tempted to say, "the greatness") of Kant's earlier intervention into this matter is as follows: first, by attaching a self-preservative instinct to understanding, he underlined the conservative impulse at the basis of knowledge; second, by including the state of terror as one of the speculative moods, he established the conditions for a kind of permanent conflict between speculation and understanding, a conflict by which all understanding must be forced beyond its limits (beyond its own natural inclinations to confine its knowledge to that which can be known with some degree of certainty), to confront its own state of uncertainty and blindness. In short, Kant created the conditions by which knowledge can become "critical" of its own conditions, and changed the fundamental mood of the speculative spirit into a highly critical spirit.[21]

The above observations on these dual aspects of the speculative faculty, a tendency toward totalization counter-balanced by a subjective pathos of terror or dread before "the whole" (which underlines an essentially conservative impulse of understanding and "common sense"), may give us insight into one of the instituting principles of the modern university. The first aspect is explicitly articulated in every founding statement that corresponds to the command of reason, such as Humboldt's instituting statement of the University of Berlin, "to lay open the whole body of learning," or the Kantian description of the university in *The Conflict of the Faculties* as the concentration of "everything that is presently teachable," and even in Ezra Cornell's statement describing the mission of Cornell University as "to make available to anyone all areas of study." All of these statements can be understood to respond essentially to the command issued by reason itself, which might be phrased "render to the people that which is already theirs." In actuality this is a speculative illusion, since we know that this image of reason is historically very recent and did not exist in this form before the eighteenth century.

Each of these statements is reflexive, which echoes the formal structure of self-legislation. To recall Lyotard's manner of phrasing this reflexive mode of reason, in each statement "the subject" occupies both the sender and receiver poles of the address. While the emphasis is placed upon instituting a social form (the university) according to an already avowed principle of reason, what in fact is taking place is the institution of the principle of reason itself. The instance of founding is simply represented as having already taken place, as already authorizing the claim to universal knowledge by the subject of the university. This is a vivid illustration of what Lyotard had earlier referred to as the "aporia of authorization," which the form of narrative diachronically disperses either toward an origin or toward an end.

This last observation leads us to the third aspect of the speculative, which is properly historical in the sense that we can identify the nature of speculation with the various philosophies that have emerged to ground the above "aporia of authorization" in a particular narrative, or "meta-narrative," that establishes the principle of reason. I will not dwell at length on these narratives, since they are well known. Lyotard recounts several of the most significant narratives by Schelling, Fichte, Hegel and Kant. For example, in the Kantian narrative, the authorization of the image of reason (as public in character) and its mode of enunciation (reflexive) is referred to the end of the process in the figure of a free and self-legislative subject ("Humanity"); this, in turn, serves to legitimate an image of reason based on the principle of self-legislation and, most importantly, to authorize as its practical subject the philosopher as "the best" contemporaneous representative of an enlightened Humanity.

In the Hegelian narrative, on the other hand, the "aporia of authorization" is projected both forwards and backwards, which is why Hegel's system is partly mythic (or cosmological) and partly historical (or dialectical) in narrative procedure. Hegel's picture of the original state of knowledge, dispersed not only through time but space as well, refers to a stage when Spirit is alienated and separated from itself. The process by which knowledge is able to gather itself together" (that is, in the form of an encyclopedia) is also the process by which it "lifts itself up" (*aufgehoben*) to a higher state of perfection. This process will lead all the way to an absolute state when Spirit (or the Subject) returns to itself and thus is no longer alienated in an external object. From the beginning of its long "Error," therefore, Spirit was already for itself (*Fur Sich*). Consequently, what Lyotard calls Hegel's "(hi)story of the life-subject" resolves the problem of authorization by positing its origin as its end or goal; moreover, it revises the classical procedure of the dialectic by incorporating within a purely syllogistic or logical procedure the proto-modern epic form of narrative. With Hegel the speculative spirit achieves the modern form of the novel, specifically, the *Bildungsroman.* One might locate here, in the Hegelian image of the dialectic, a critical turn to "narrative procedures" in the game of legitimation, one which grounds the materialist conception of "History" as a certain *true narrative* that has been won dialectically from all false narratives (of ideology, class consciousness, and heroic narratives of science and religion), such as we find in Lukács as well as in Jameson's hermeneutic conception of materialist analysis of culture. At the same time, we might also locate in Hegel the conditions for Lyotard's own arguments concerning "narrative legitimation" and the "decline of all master narratives" (the end-game of the "age of Hegel" which marks the moment of our "postmodern condition").

But here we must interrupt our account of these speculative narratives of reason for a moment to again pose the same question we took up with Kant: In whose interest is the representation of Reason? Who benefits in having knowledge accessible in this manner? That is, what are the real forms of interest that determine this principle of Reason, on the one hand, and the university as the institution that houses and perpetuates this principle, on the other? From among the various speculative narratives that have been offered, including the Kantian and Hegelian outlined above, one might assess Hume's narrative as perhaps the most realistic and practical explanation. In the essay "Of the Refinement of the Arts," Hume writes that "*industry, knowledge,* and *humanity* are linked together, by an indissoluble chain, and are found, from experience as well as reason, to be peculiar to the more polished, what are commonly denominated, the more luxurious ages."[22]

> However, industry, knowledge, and humanity are not advantageous in private life alone; they diffuse their beneficial influence on the *public,* and render the government as great and flourishing as they make individuals happy and prosperous. The increase and consumption of all commodities, which serve to ornament and pleasure of life, are advantages to society; because, at the same time, they multiply those innocent gratifications to

individuals, they are a kind of *storehouse* of labor, which, in the exigencies of state, may be turned to the public service.[23]

The principles articulated in the passage could be called Hume's "trickle-down theory of Culture" Thus, the question of "culture," in the sense of refinement of pleasure and the accumulation of knowledge, particularly in the manner that these experiences are not dispersed within the natural state but concentrated and highly disciplined and rarified, is a form of expenditure that must be measured by its collateral effects; however, all these effects will ultimately be an increase of power and wealth — the manner in which the processes and forms of cultural refinement release certain energies that serve generally to stimulate industry, knowledge, and technical mastery of the environment. "In a nation where there is no demand for such superfluities, men sink into indolence, lose all enjoyment in life, and are useless to the public, which cannot maintain or support its fleets and armies from the industry of such slothful members."[24]

Accordingly, it would be in the best interest of the State to have a place where all knowledge, and the techniques associated with cultural refinement (or the fine arts and taste, or the knowledge of luxuries), can be stored, like a national reserve, from which it could at any time immediately draw in a time of war, including wars of commerce or trade in which the study of new technologies would have an integral place. Thus, "industry," Hume argues, "is promoted by the knowledges inseparable from art and refinement; as, on the other hand, this knowledge enables the public to make the best advantage of the industry of its subjects."[25] Therefore, all knowledge (including cultural knowledge) can be determined under the principle of accumulated wealth, as a latent form of capital that belongs to the State. However, it only belongs to the State in as much as the university is created and sanctioned by the State.

Here is the original sleight of hand. In effect, the State only provides a space and a mechanism for gathering all knowledges and skills together in one social institution that remains under its ultimate command and disposition. However, this would in effect make it appear as if all knowledge first originated under the tutelage of the State, instead of being just gathered together and administered by a State-sponsored mechanism, as if the State was the origin and the creative principle of knowledge itself. If the state represents itself as the ultimate principle in the creation of knowledge, then it also bestows upon itself the rightful authority to dispose of all knowledge it has supposedly sanctioned, and this might give a more strategic character to the principle of public reason discussed above, since the State at all times controls the apparatus of the courts for policing the division between public and private property, including intellectual property and technological innovation — i.e., forms of intellectual capital that are critical to the State's authority. This principle can be vividly illustrated even today by the Justice Department's recent suit against Microsoft Corp.

Hume's description of the function of "culture" in relationship to the State also recalls the essential relationship of universal knowledge to an earlier form of "central organization," the city. We might recall in Plato (as well as later in Marx's *Grundrisse* and *The German Ideology*) that the city represents the totality of knowledge for the simple reason that it is the nexus of trade and exchange; as a result, all skills, techniques, and knowledges are aggregated there. This reveals the original motivation of the speculative genre of the philosopher, which takes the form of a distinctive "problem." The problem is how to evaluate, rank, measure, and to apply the increasing quantity of knowledges that are the result of the city-form's tendency to function as a center of attraction for new techniques and goods, as well as alien *idias* (family gods, moral precepts, etc.). This can be determined as the first crisis of knowledge, which gave birth to philosophy proper in the West, and to the first procedure invented to solve this problem, the *dialectic*. We might recall the figure of Socrates strolling through the market and interrogating all the techniques and skills that comprise the *agora* (the open space at the center of the city). If we traced the steps of Socrates around the entire circumference of the *agora*, we would find an early form of "totalization" that corresponds to the technical meaning of the Greek term *census*.

In Hellenic culture, the *census* was a ritual procedure of "illumination," in which the high priest would circumnavigate the entire city once a year to signify the completion of a temporal cycle, as well as the circumference of the *polis* or demonstration of a privileged location of "totality." As Indo-Europeanist Émile Benveniste writes concerning the transformation of this religious notion into a function of political and civil institutions, "we could content ourselves in translating *censeo* by 'judge, think, estimate…,' but as sociologist Georges Dumézil has argued, [t]he technical sense of *censor* and *census* must not be a secondary sense but must preserve what is essential in the primary meaning: To site (a man or an act or an opinion, etc.) in its correct place in a hierarchy, with all the practical consequences of this situation, and to do so by just public assessment …."[26] What is important to remark in this argument is that the generic meaning of "assessment," which continues to have this meaning today, particularly in the university, must be linked to the functions of the *censor* and *census*, described as a "situation within a hierarchy." Thus, dialectic was the procedure whereby the totality of knowledge and techniques were unified under one measure, a measure (*med*, or *mensus*) that in effect submitted everything that could qualify as knowledge to the rule of the Socratic method. As Heidegger writes concerning the function of the dialectic, "the proposition (λε´γειη) proceeds back and forth for itself within its own domain, goes through it (διαλε´γεςθαι), and so covers it to the end. Thought now is dialectical."[27]

With the invention of this procedure the crisis of knowledge that was caused by the city-form itself — its openness to a diverse and often heterogeneous mix of ideas, techniques, and specialized knowledges (or what Lyotard calls "language-games") — was averted by a method of:

1. conducting a regular *census* of everything that is currently known or could be qualified as knowledge and;
2. submitting all knowledge to an order of rank and hierarchy which descended from those knowledges and skills that were critical to the life of the city to those other knowledges that were judged to be the least critical, "private," and too idiosyncratic to justify the social investment involved in their maintenance and reproduction.

It is easy to detect in the above description the earliest principles for both the encyclopedic form of knowledge and for the speculative spirit, or what Lyotard calls "the speculative meta-narrative," since the early dialectic submits all knowledges that belong to the city to a common measure, or "language-game" performed by the philosopher. What is important to remark about this early form of "meta-narrative" is the transparency between society and the subject of knowledge, in response to Lyotard's guiding questions concerning this relationship: "Who decides what knowledge is, and who knows what needs to be decided?"

Several other remarks could be made at this point. The first concerns the critical immediacy of this relationship to the "mode of production," which functions as its cause. It is the nature of the market that first creates the conditions of a crisis, the crisis being the spontaneous aggregation of different techniques, products, languages, cultures, and gods in a common place at the center of the city. The conflict between different "language-games" and the potential failure of the city to find a means, a common measure, by which to evaluate these different forms and to discriminate (or to separate out) its own interests from other forms of interest that could be generally determined either as "private" (belonging to the realm of the household or house economy which is outside the common sphere or the city proper "*oikos*", or are deemed alien ("*barbaros*"), that is, interests that are determined not to belong to the city at all). Finally, it is the need of a procedure for determining which knowledges and skills are critical and, therefore, must be placed under the rule of government in order to regulate their use and their reproduction.

Taking this early example of the dialectical relationship between the society and knowledge, we can also discern in this example the critical interests for the creation of the modern university, which is the form of this dialectic that belongs to a later form of the mode of production, from the eighteenth century onward.

Thus, when Clark Kerr, in *The Uses of the University*, compared the university to a factory, many thought that he was introducing an alien idea imported from the influence of capitalism on modern societies.[28] In fact, he was simply articulating the classical dialectical function of the university also articulated by Kant, who described the University as a manner of resolving the above crisis of knowledge by means of "*mass production.*" Here again, in both its formal relationship to the dominant organization of social needs, on the one hand, and to the technologies and knowledges that comprise a dominant mode of production, on the other, the university becomes the means of resolving the same problems of heterogeneity that the dialectic had been designed to solve for the Greek city-form. This relationship is firmly established in Wilhelm von Humboldt's plan for the founding of the University of Berlin, where it is stated that the two-fold function of the university is:

a.  "to lay open the whole body of learning and to expound both the principles and the foundations of all knowledge;
b.  "to orient its constituent element, science, to the spiritual and moral training of the nation."[29]

As Lyotard quickly points out, these two tasks would appear to be contradictory. The first would demand a lack of interest in "training" much in the same way that the interests of pure research continue even today to be opposed to the interests of pedagogy. Yet, this contradiction is real, and Humboldt may have even intended it as a constituent part of the design of knowledge, which is always pulled in two opposing directions. Thus, either pure speculation or pure application would be balanced by constant conflict, which might explain why this conflict continues to perpetuate itself. Just when one side seems to have enough power to end it — in favor of pure research as in the 1980s, or in the favor of pedagogy and service-learning as in the 1990s — the balance of power swings the other way.

A different understanding of this split or tension (even conflict) in the faculty of knowledge was introduced by Cardinal Newman as Jaroslav Pelikan has discussed in *The Idea of the University: A Reexamination*.[30] Although Newman promoted or reproduced the principle of "knowledge its own end," he did not consider the faculty of knowledge to be necessarily suited to carry out both "advancement" and "extension" (teaching) duties at once, since "he…who spends his day dispensing his existing knowledge to all comers is unlikely to have either leisure or energy to acquire new knowledge."[31] Thus, according to Newman, "[t]o discover and to teach are distinct [one might read exclusive] gifts, and are not commonly found united in the same person."[32] Unlike Humboldt, who saw the possibility of such a combination, and even demanded one talent or gift as the condition of the other, Newman argued that, although not impossible, their combination in one person would at least be infrequent enough not to build an institution that seems to contradict the natural disposition of these gifts to entirely separate individuals. In short, such an institution that openly contradicts nature would likely create the conditions for carrying out both activities badly.

Newman's observations were fairly prophetic, and we might judge the problems concerning the conflict that surrounds the division of "research" and "teaching," and the mediocrity that generally undermines both activities in major research-institutions today, to be the result of adopting a German model of higher learning rather than heeding Newman's advice.

*I am arguing that policies that presuppose and even enforce an equal distribution of talent within the same individual faculty (as most current tenure policies do) are based on an unrealistic criteria that effectively promotes more cases of failure than success, and may even inflict a greater damage to the whole enterprise of knowledge in the sense that it ultimately prevents rather than encourages both gifted extension (teaching) and brilliant research (advancement).* This has resulted from the somewhat contradictory and often unfulfilled doctrine that structures the history of the idea of the university in the twentieth century, which Pelikan describes as follows:

> [O]n the one hand, the advancement of knowledge should be pursued even if the results turn out not to be capable of being translated, now or ever, into the diffusion and extension of knowledge to students; but on the other hand, that such diffusion and extension is infinitely more rich and profound when in the hands of professors who were and still are engaged in the advancement of knowledge through research, even though there appears to be at any given time a small pool of candidates who can carry out both assignments.[33]

As we saw with Kant earlier concerning a different matter, which was the historical embodiment of "pure reason" in the lower faculties, the principle that seems to underline the success or failure of this doctrine is based on a wager — that nature would be so disposed to provide some proportion of faculty who can carry out both assignments, even though at any given time the pool of likely candidates would be small. However, most of the time and for the greater part of the university population, one is likely to have good researchers who make miserable teachers, and good teachers who make shoddy researchers. Most often, however, we have miserable teachers who also happen to be shoddy researchers. In any proportion, the faculty who belong to this last category would contribute nothing to either the extension or the advancement of knowledge, but rather its obscurity and retreat.

Contrary to such a doctrine, Newman advanced the more extreme position that the sole objective of a university is "the diffusion and extension" of existing knowledge rather than the creation of new knowledge or the advancement of knowledge, which would be the objective of free-standing intellectuals, academies, and learned societies. Although Newman's division was not exclusively adopted in the United States, his "dialectic of the faculty of knowledge" was put into place in the current separation of research universities (where the faculties would be expected to combine research with some form of teaching or extension-duties) and liberal arts colleges and various community-colleges where the faculty are not expected to advance knowledge as one of their primary duties.

Concluding my discussion of the philosophical dialectic that has grounded the function of the modern university, allow me to digress concerning one qualification that could be made to the above presentation. My qualification concerns the form of teleology this history often takes, a teleology that corresponds most directly to Marxist theory: the progression of different modes of production and their consonant social institutions leading up to late-capitalistic societies and the dominant narratives of knowledge that are consistent with each stage. Here, I could be accused of "economism," or "technologism." Nevertheless, I have used this teleological narrative above, primarily out of convenience, in order to relate a form of knowledge consistent with the mode of production embodied in the city; another with the state or nation form; and now, to suggest another that is coming into view, one that belongs to the most recent stage of "global market capitalism." In some sense, this evolution may be true, but only because the narratives of history are written according to the most dominant interests that authorize them.

We must remind ourselves that all the above narratives are themselves inherently speculative, in the sense that they more or less represent the various historical attempts to produce a coherent and teleological narrative concerning "the state of current knowledge" and to explain where it is going and in what manner it can best achieve its true form. These explanations function as long as they produce consensus (or agreement), not only between things and their representation (words and things), or events and their description, but also a consensus of "minds" — that is, the practical agreement between subjects and their real practices, or in a more Kantian diction, between the subject of representation and the subject of will or action. In reminding ourselves of this fact, we might apply this insight to the narrative that recounts the history of the University itself as the simple and teleological progression from one grand narrative to the next. In order to correct or to subtract a teleological understanding of this institution, it would be necessary to no longer speak of "the University" (which still subscribes to the idea of "Universal History," or to the encyclopedia as the historical incarnation of Absolute Knowledge), but rather of "universities," in the plural, and of specific universities which were founded upon different and potentially conflicting understandings of the dialectical relationship between knowledge and society.

Two recent examples that come immediately to mind are the University of Chicago and the University of California. The University of Chicago was the first university created to house the knowledge and the faculties fitted to the social and cultural life of an industrialized modern city, which significantly diverged from the European influenced models based to a large degree on the nation-state. As Chicago emeritus Charles H. Long writes concerning this incarnation of the university (which can be understood as a return of an earlier organization of knowledge that corresponds with the city-form):

> It is significant to note that…from the very beginning of the University [of Chicago], the public service languages and those departments and schools related in a direct manner to sociological aspects of culture were to the fore. […] Significantly, the first university building ever dedicated to the study of society as a scientific endeavor was the Social Science Building at [the] University of Chicago.[34]

On the other hand, the University of California was created as part of then Governor Pat Brown's "master plan" of education, which had both an economic and democratic purpose. By reserving a desk for any state resident who qualifies by graduating from high school for one of the three tiers, the state provided an economic resource for the period of intensive capital growth in the state that lasted up until the recession in the late 1980s, and an incentive for upward mobility to a largely immigrant population. (Since the state itself is not much more than a hundred years old, the majority of the population could be classified as immigrants, which is a factor that continues to shape the history of racial politics in California as a question of ethnic or racial hegemony.)

Of course, not all immigrants were given equal access, and discrimination was built into the system at the level of preparation children would receive at primary and secondary levels of education and this would be depend on the location of their district, which ultimately led to the urban and racial cycle of poverty in Oakland, Los Angeles, and in the poor white and Hispanic ghettoes of San Bernadino and Riverside (which were a kind of dumping ground for the poor classes of L.A. and Orange County), or the ethnic ghettoes of Alameda and Contra Costa counties (which has a similar function for the upper-class areas of Marin and San Francisco). Even progressives and liberals in California would continue to compound this discrimination by focusing all democratization and affirmative action efforts at the University level, the highest tier of the education system, which would mostly benefit those racial groups that comprised the middle classes. One of the most ironic results of the reactionary attack on Affirmative Action programs at the university level in Proposition 187 was that it forced progressives in schools like

Berkeley and UCLA to finally begin to re-target their efforts at the primary and secondary levels, primarily in the inner-city areas, in order to raise the standards of quality in these education sectors enough to allow high-school graduates to compete "on a level playing field" with other middle-class districts in the state.

Finally, at the lowest tier, the community or junior colleges, the state provided a resource for the technical re-training and re-education of transitional workers who would be the necessary fall-out of the intensive process of capital growth, thus supplementing the state welfare system. Of course, this more or less progressive plan came to a grinding halt during the first term of Governor Pete Wilson's administration when a greater and greater portion of the budget went to the building and staffing of new prison facilities, which occupied the same category in the general fund as higher education.

Returning to our discussion, it would appear that I am laying the groundwork to argue for an essentially positivistic or seamless view of the university's historical relationship to a dominant form of social interest. Recalling the above example, which I cite as the very origin of philosophy proper in the West, the crisis of knowledge introduced by the agora ("the openness") of the marketplace, we could argue that the crisis of legitimation that philosophy attempts to resolve by method must address the interest of the dominant social form. Since it is grounded upon the same principle, by extension we could say that there has never been a "university" that did not respond to this obligation in as much as its emergence has always been confluent with a dominant mode of production. In point of fact, what I am trying to do by a kind of resumé of different historical arrangements is to return to Lyotard's guiding question: what is the relationship between knowledge and modern society? More importantly, how does the current arrangement legitimate "critical" knowledges, that is, those kinds of knowledges that resist an easy assimilation to serve the means of production? From the above observations, however, we might come to the following tentative conclusions:

1.  It goes without saying that the maintenance and reproduction (even the creation or invention) of knowledge is critical to society. In order to highlight the importance of this fact, we must think of this in the most common or quotidian of terms. For example, imagine a society in which from one day to the next, certain knowledges upon which the life of the society depends would undergo periodic lapses or disappear entirely. One day perhaps the knowledge of making shoes may become extinct; the next day the knowledge associated with a whole area of manufacture or agriculture could be lost. This can be defined as the fundamental problem of knowledge.

2.  According to the second aspect, since information (or knowledge) has no intrinsic form of organization, it requires that one be invented. Actually, this

aspect has two sub-features: first, "discrimination" (or selection) and, second, storage and reproduction. In this section, I have outlined the manner in which philosophy comes to fulfill the duty of the first by inventing criteria for "censoring" knowledge and choosing those that are critical enough to society to warrant the expense of storage and reproduction. I have also highlighted in what way the invention of the university was a manner of solving both tasks simultaneously: a place, or centralized location that is easily accessible for society, where all knowledge is stored and, at the same time, where the assessment of which knowledges are critical to society and which are not is a constant enterprise that takes place in every one of its faculties. To put it another way, to forget is just as much a principle of disciplinary knowledge as to remember.

3. Finally, in as much as society is dependent on knowledge that is not intrinsically organized, the university, as a form of organization, is dependant on a prior "openness" where these knowledges circulate and where the whole question of "discrimination" and "selection" is first posed as a critical problem for society itself. Thus, the university is dependant on another form of organization that provides it with the "energy," so to speak, to perform its critical social function, whether this organization takes the form of the city or the state, and whether this energy is understood in terms of dollars or drachmas, it takes the form of Capital. The problem that concerns us at this point is the confusion between the mode of organizing knowledge and the mode of organizing capital, which in the current period has gone under the term "ideology," but whose most succinct mechanism is defined by the term "performativity."

## II(d)  *The rise of the performativity principle and the crisis of "de-legitimation" (nihilism)*

Concluding our assessment of Lyotard's report, let us return to examine the primary argument concerning the current power that determines the nature of social bond — what Lyotard calls "performativity." The first characteristic of performativity is that it no longer requires a form of consensus in order to function effectively since, in actuality, this consensus occurs automatically in the performance of the system itself. Lyotard's supporting thesis is that the nature of consensus no longer takes its earlier route via "grand narrative," but appears *de facto* in a certain aspect of performance or performativity as a new procedure of legitimation. It may not have been the best word that Lyotard could have chosen to describe this new regime, since the relation of this form to the linguistic notion of performativity is somewhat misleading. Nevertheless, what is performativity and how does it appear to us today, in a manner that is distinctly separate from earlier forms of legitimation? By *de facto* consensus, Lyotard refers to an *a priori* agreement, that is, to a form of consensus that appears as already decided. Performativity appears concretely as a statement or action that is most consistent with "reality"; in short, it agrees with a certain reality that appears *a priori* most real, it expresses the same intensity. As Kant defined it, "the real" in actuality refers to the *quale*, or the quality of an intensity. When we refer to "reality," it is not a representation, but rather the strength or intensity of a "presentation" (*Darstellung*, which bears a stronger sense of "exhibition," or a presentation that performs its correspondence with "the real").[35]

Strictly speaking, what we call "reality" refers to the quality of the presentation; it does not require proof in order to be "true," since truth (*adequatio*) is already implied in the notion of "the real." Here, we should underline the fact that the question of agreement or consensus is presented as having been already decided, as self-evident in the presentation. In the failure of the narrative of reason, "performativity" can be defined as the autonomous realization of a practical subject (the subject of will) that functions, without an idea of reason. (Three such modern practical subjects are the subject of the unconscious in the psychoanalytic sense, the subject of ideology, and that of technology.) I am simplifying things a great deal, but my intention is to underline the major premise of Lyotard's argument. When he describes a state of affairs in which a practical subject (that of technology, or capital) is capable of organizing things without a form of narrative legitimation, he ultimately is addressing the conditions of "nihilism" in which the classical narrative of reason has no legitimate control over the social powers of interest and desire. "Performativity" is just the name of this new practical subject that appears to be truly autonomous — running on automatic.

The second characteristic that belongs to the concept of performativity is the notion of power (or *torte*). In a concrete social situation performativity is the expression of a practical subject who appears as the most realistic and powerful operator of the contemporary social bond. Thus, there is a direct relationship between performativity and power that can be detected in many social institutions today. An increase of power, today, also means *de facto* and *de jure* an increase of performativity, whether this takes the form of relevance, efficiency, wealth, fame or charisma. Here, one can detect how the system rewards certain social perspectives with a greater degree of amplitude and reproducibility. Moreover, upon encountering the subjects who occupy these perspectives we can usually perceive a tangible expression of power: a chauvinistic or arrogant character underlying an expression of de facto legitimation of opinion or viewpoint in most matters, a tendency to express his or her opinions (or advice) to others as a "moral duty" in the belief that this subject's statements are in their very nature prescriptive; finally, a severe critical perspective toward viewpoints that do not conform or "obey" the subject's own prescriptions concerning "the way things really work," and the tendency to ridicule or dismiss any statements that are not consistent with the subject's own enunciation. Again, I am using the term "subject" in a more structural sense, since this personality or character is not individual, but rather appears as an instance or expression of the system itself. This factor might help to explain the aspect of "force" (*torte*) or "social pressure" one feels when confronted by this subject, since this force derives from the immediacy of the system this subject actualizes in a language-situation. Lyotard addresses this aspect of force that is present in the legitimation by performativity under the name of "terror," the threat of annihilation or the potential destruction of the social bond itself, which often appears as a stark alternative to conformity or adaptation.

A third characteristic of the rise of the performativity principle is that performativity is often considered as an end in itself; improvements or changes to make the system more efficient are not considered in terms of whether they will "improve" the social bond or even create a "just society" (two criteria that belong to what Lyotard defines as the narrative of emancipation). This subscribes to Lyotard's basic view that all forms of consensus are essentially false, since they fail to account for or represent the possibility of "terror" that lies at the basis of all agreements. This observation can be applied to the current understanding of capitalism as a dominant form of the social bond. Marx clearly showed capitalism is not a "social institution" which originates based on a contract, at least, not for and between all parties. Rather, it is a form of extortion. It is the process of extracting or extorting "surplus value" from production, and specifically from labor or the worker who is defined as a class by the process of production (and, here, I am following Immanuel Wallerstein's most succinct formulation that historically "capitalism is the *only* mode of production in which the *maximization of surplus-creation is rewarded per se*").[36] Thus, it refers to a technology that has undergone a certain, undeniable improvement, and even perfection over several centuries. At the same time, no social institution can be based on extortion, just as extortion cannot originate by the instrument of a legal contract between parties, since the party who is being extorted would never willingly agree to such terms. This is why, according to Marx's classical analysis, the very notion of a social contract always comes later on and is used to legalize (or "rationalize") the state of affairs between the parties that had originated in extortion. Thus, it is ironic to hear those today who extol the beatitude of Capital, and who are in actuality praising the technological perfection of the systematic *extortion* of wealth from the process of production, the efficiency of its extraction and conversion; and, finally, the manner in which this process works so that it is no longer centralized or managed, but rather seems to happen all by itself, like a new natural order which has replaced an earlier, mechanical view of the universe.

What is odd to note in Lyotard's account of the performativity principle is his extreme Kantianism. We might even go so far as to say that in his effort to describe the failure of narrative as a means of legitimation Lyotard effectively *out-Kants Kant.* In the first two critiques Kant outlines the a priori principles that govern the possibility of knowledge in the first critique and the possibility of the moral will (or more simply, desire) in the second. He comes to an impasse that the third critique is supposed to resolve, since neither condition can be grounded by the other without resorting to a form of what he defines as "transcendental illusion." The third critique, *The Critique of Judgment,* grounds the *a priori* and spontaneous accord between nature and reason on the form of judgment *as such.* On the other hand, Lyotard resolves these two functions by assigning them to different phrase universes, as he calls them: the cognitive and the prescriptive. He even removes the usual *pathos* and *mysterium tremendum* which has heretofore been associated with the "terrifying abyss" that separates understanding and action, knowledge and desire, reason and will. Perhaps this "abyss," as the division between theoretical cognition and practical reason (i.e., the faculty of desire) in the Kantian system, produced a "dead-end." Even the word "abyss" already signals the approach of a "sublime view" and, thus, already foreshadows the form of the presentation that will emerge to fill the gap which suddenly appeared at the end of the *Critique of Practical Reason.* Lyotard writes:

> We see no reason to grant a 'mystical' profundity to the abyss that separates cognitives and prescriptives. (Kant is sometimes drawn into this, as is Witt-

genstein. Pascal, because he is closest to the sophists, is in the last analysis more 'reasonable,' even with his tears of joy.) Incommensurability, in the sense of heterogeneity of phrase regimens and the impossibility of subjecting them to a single law (except by neutralizing them) also marks the relation between either cognitives or prescriptives and interrogatives, performatives, exclamatives... For each of these regimes, there corresponds a mode of presenting a universe, and one mode is not translatable into another.[37]

Lyotard's account, therefore, returns to the moment before the third critique and denies Kant's solution: the bridge between theoretical and ethical phrasing. Without the aesthetic presentation to suture the two ends together, there appears an irreparable and gaping wound between what Lyotard calls the two phrase universes, or between the two modes (denotative and performative), which can only be resolved by force, in short, by "terror." Therefore, the division between theoretical and practical is purely analytical, descriptive, and takes the form of an axiom — that is, one must not translate one mode into another. They are, for all intensive purposes, incommensurable.

Lyotard's subsequent writings increasingly emphasize this division since it is the manner by which he attacks the nature of the dualism that underlines modern critical knowledges (and Marxism, in particular.) He argues there is no synthetic relationship between these two phrase universes and no possibility of mediation, except by means of narratives, which are essentially "fables." The separation between a denotative statement and a prescriptive statement is a ditch one cannot cross except by a kind of magical leap that sutures these two modes together within one genre, thus "dispersing the *aporia* of authorization" to either the end (or goal) or to some origin. To provide an example of this in the most quotidian manner, today it is an accepted scientific statement that smoking is bad for the health, and there is a statistical degree of probably that regular smoking will lead to some form of lung disease; however, we also witness the fact that this knowledge does not, as a result, become prescriptive immediately. It requires narratives, which are composed of addressor and addressee instances that are socially reproducible and enforce a certain pressure (or *torte*) to make this knowledge a *de facto* performative.

Lyotard's manner of representing the two phrases of knowledge is completely consistent with the Enlightenment, which he boils down into its simplest parts. The problem of the Enlightenment, as Kant phrased it, was two-fold: how to transform prescriptive statements into denotative ones (i.e., freedom from tutelage); second, how to verify which prescriptive statements are true and therefore *ought to* be legitimately denotative (i.e., the primacy of reason). Lyotard's theory of performativity is essentially based upon the qualitative difference between two classes of statements, the denotative and the prescriptive, and the widening gap that separates them during the period of de-legitimation (i.e., the postmodern period). In a very elliptic but interesting argument, Lyotard shows that the contemporary character of "nihilism" occurs when this separation, first installed by science to create the "autonomy" of scientific knowledge from prescriptive or didactic power, gradually turns back against science itself. Under this very same autonomy, there is no criteria by which a denotative statement that is endowed with being "true" can become effectively prescriptive (transformative of reality), that is, without a supplementary "mechanism" that gives it a prescriptive power. Thus, power is the deciding principle as to which statements are given a "performative" value in which they become prescriptive in that they transform "reality." The brief step to nihilism occurs when it is realized that the means of controlling the force of a prescriptive mechanism can effectively establish a determinant reality, whether or not it is "true," or "just," or "the best one" — the old criteria of a speculative or philosophical evaluation of a social system. Lyotard writes:

> [S]ince "reality" is what provides the evidence used as proof in scientific argu-mentation, and also provides prescriptions and promises of a juridical, ethical, and political nature with results, one can master all these games by mastering "reality." That is precisely what technology can do. By reinforcing technology, one "reinforces" reality, and one's chances of being just and right increase accordingly. Reciprocally, technology is reinforced all the more effectively if one has access to scientific knowledge and decision-making authority.[38]

The original schism between the criteria of truth and the criteria of performa-tivity emerges most starkly in the nineteenth century in the theories of Marx and Freud, both of whom address the problem of this gap in the concepts of truth and knowledge in the notion of science itself. Marx, in the notion of ideology (as "false consciousness"), shows a separation of truth from consciousness; Freud, with the notion of the unconscious, shows the separation of truth from instinctual representatives. Both critical systems are founded on the principle that something "true" is not for that reason alone also endowed with the quality of being *real*, as well as on the notion of an agency that obscures the subject's true *reality*, which remains hidden from view. That is, what prevents the "truth" of the subject from becoming real is a form of power. Science has no power of its own, but always requires the *consensus* of a social apparatus, a form of "consensus" that itself must also exhibit a performative sign of social investment. Hence, the basic rise to performativity occurs when knowledge is linked directly to the increase of wealth, in other words, to the advent of technology. As Lyotard argues, this occurs at the critical juncture when the hierarchy between pure scientific knowledge and technology is reversed. Henceforth, the advancement of knowledge is directed (even selectively stimulated) by the introduction of capital into the relationship between "the owners of the means of production" and the "methods of legitimation."[39] According to Lyotard, this happened at the end of the eighteenth century, with the first industrial revolution, when the reciprocity of the following equation was discovered: no technology without wealth, but no wealth without technology. A technical apparatus requires investment. However, since it optimizes the efficiency of the task, it also optimizes the surplus value derived from this improved performance. "It is at this precise moment that science becomes a force of production, a moment in the circulation of capital."[40]

In the above description of the "nihilism" implicit in the principle of the scientific genre, we might also detect the conditions for the current failure of the discourse of the faculties (specifically the old philosophy faculty) in the university. Similar to the inability of science to resist certain technological applications, we might conclude that the famous autonomy of the faculties has been turned against the faculties themselves — as exemplified by their current inability to *censor* the various applications of knowledge (as Kant had originally hoped). Many critical theorists in the Humanities today continue to play according to the old games of legitimation, believing that their statements will have some effect in the system. At the same time, one can feel the effects of "performativity" and "de-legitimation" in the growing irrelevance of critical knowledge to the society at large, simply by noting a decrease in capital investment, or the selective shrinking of certain knowledges and departments. Thus, like science, the faculties of other disciplines today are seen to be playing their own private language-games, and this has contributed to the derogatory sense that now determines the meaning of "academic knowledge." In many cases, academic knowledge is not seen to be practical, and thus, under the regime of performativity, could also be assessed to be illegitimate and not authorized as a result. It would only be a brief step for society (basically, other social institutions) to begin to question this legitimacy, demand its justification and proof. But here again, the decks are often stacked against the current critical faculties since the criteria of evaluation are performative and not academic (i.e., speculative), as Kant had originally thought.

The nihilism that was present in the concept of autonomy itself can be summarized along the following lines. Taking the classical notion of philosophical or speculative autonomy that was first championed by Kant, the philosophical subject must assume a position of purely theoretical or speculative interest. If this subject's discourse is framed by practical motives, then it becomes prescriptive and no longer qualifies as purely philosophical. The problem occurs when the philosopher's truth is then dependant on other phrase regimes to give it a performative function (by technology, the state, social or class interests). Both

Habermas and Lyotard have highlighted this problem in the philosophical notion of autonomy. Habermas studied the evolution of this notion of autonomy in the institution of the bourgeois public sphere and the decline of this institution in the modern day "non-public character of opinion." Lyotard simply highlighted the flaw at the basis of autonomy in its most extreme form, by absolutely dividing theoretical or denotative phrasing from obligatory or prescriptive phrasing, which in turn, makes denotative statements dependent upon a supplemental instance to make them truly descriptive of a reality. Simply put, this very autonomy which was invented to safeguard the objectivity of truth, or to purify philosophy of any form of interest other than "reason itself," is also the condition of nihilism at the heart of the concept of truth promoted by this "move," since it establishes no necessary relationship between truth and its realization as a descriptive or performative reality. Nihilism then is the arbitrariness of certain truths being selected for realization under other criteria — "power," that most ambiguous and perhaps yet to be defined of modern concepts, being the ultimate modern representative of a generic criteria of selection according to a dominant social interest.

I have suggested throughout the course of this part that nineteenth century critical knowledges (in particular those offered by Freud, Nietzsche, and Marx) all develop the crisis of legitimation to an extreme formulation (which I will argue in the final part has been surpassed only by Lyotard). All are based on a common premise: what is represented as truth in consciousness has no necessary relationship to its real determination. The subject in each case is split, between the real forms of interest that are determinate of his or her life and their conscious representatives, which are like the false or inverted idols of these forms of interest. This led to the "loss of credibility" in the great conscious representatives — "autonomy" or "freedom," "the good" or "virtue," and "the truth." For example, the classical autonomy or freedom of the bourgeois subject is revealed is based upon several prior exclusions and limitations of which the subject is not conscious (exclusions of race, sex, nationality, class or economic identity). For each thinker, therefore, "consciousness" itself is the entire problem. It is a symptomatic or imaginary construction. Thus, any form of knowledge that takes representations that belong to consciousness as its literal approximation of truth is unfounded, since truth does not belong to consciousness or its representatives — rather error and falsehood. In this instance, the concept of truth becomes unequal to its conscious representation; it does not resemble itself, and this principle of dis-similarity is the principle upon which most, if not all, modern critical knowledge is founded.

What is implicit in Lyotard's categorical rejection of "meta-narrative" — although this statement must immediately be qualified to address only "universal" meta-narrative — is an experience that has been shaped by the 20th century, particularly by the experience of Stalinism. Lyotard's position on this point is not far removed from that of Adorno and Horkheimer, in the belief that all "universal" meta-narratives necessarily contain the seed of "terror" as a possible means of their realization. This was the lynchpin of their entire critique of Enlightenment reason as a form of "instrumental rationality" and a new myth of totality. In principle, the cause of consensus is good; however, in practice we have witnessed certain historically limited and imperfect notions of consensus (that of a particular "people," a "nation," or "race"). The problem occurs when these notions of consensus are attached to the instruments of technology which, in fact, realize the abstract ideal of universal agreement by means of "terror": from the modern instrumentation of surveillance and control to the removal, isolation, and even the gradual annihilation of heterogeneous and non-adaptive social elements.

This is the legacy we have inherited from the historical coupling of the narrative of universal emancipation (the politics of the state-form) to the new technologies. In this context, the practical application of the narrative of emancipation to society (i.e., the regularization of 'moves' under the axiom that all moves must belong to the same narrative) becomes something very different and is capable of terror as one of the means of realizing its end. The step is all too brief between a speculative spirit of agreement and the actual creation of agreement by technological innovations that, in certain historical moments, have effectively solved the problem of consensus. Strictly defined, the notion of consensus can never be determined by race or "blood," by "class ideology" or by "linguistic community." These would be impure conceptions of the consensus of free minds or wills first posited by the speculative or philosophical definition of consensus in Enlightenment reason. However, in order to insure their purification and proper usage, one would have to violate, as we have said many times, a fundamental condition of the "power of reason," and of scientific knowledge in general, which is its freedom from the interest of prescription that it leaves to other *powers*.

The modern philosopher has no power but "reason" with which to censor the social application of concepts and ideas. Neither the philosopher nor the scientist has any administrative or executive role in the communication of concepts to the practical subject, no ability to extract fines and penalties (*penuria*) for the impure and improper adaptations of the principle of reason, other than the self-elected submission of free will to the philosopher's censorship or jurisdiction. We recall here that such authority only exists in the university in a very brief historical period, or rather in the Kantian ideal authority of the university, in which all the disciplines must submit their knowledge to the philosopher for a proper examination. At the same time, as I have argued above, it is this very principle that contains the seed of the crisis of philosophy in the modern period, the crisis of the de-legitimation, which limits or restricts philosophical authority by subordinating the speculative spirit to the criteria of performativity, to "what works in the present." As we have seen in the first part concerning the authority of the subject "who decides" (the *censor*), anyone who assumes the task of establishing the criteria of what is the best manner of organizing the social bond, whether this subject assumes the form of the classical philosopher or the modern day administrator, immediately confronts the critical problem of consensus itself. Consequently, in the next part I will attempt to address this problem in more detail.

### *Summary and transition*

In this part I have reviewed the critical argument advanced twenty years ago in *The Postmodern Condition*, which was first published in France in 1979, and appeared five years later in the influential University of Minnesota Press series "Theory and History of Literature" (i.e., three years after Derrida's talk at Cornell). Lyotard's earlier report concerns what he calls "the crisis of legitimation in the period of postmodernism," or the failure of philosophical (speculative) authority according to his now famous and contested thesis concerning the decline in the credibility of "meta-narratives."[41] Two such meta-narratives form the primary subjects of Lyotard's argument: the first is the narrative of the Nation-State, and the second is the narrative of "the University." In my reading of Lyotard's report, I show how both are integrally related, even necessarily connected, and that the loss of "meta-narrative" must be understood historically in terms of the "crisis of philosophy" whose speculative role since the time of Kant, Hegel, and even Hume has been indispensable to the rise of the "Nation-Form" (that is, the ideational form of the state). It is also central to the social and cultural function of the modern university as the institution which houses the civilizing functions of state or national memory.

The nature of dominant or grand institutions that define the "public sphere" is a critical question that has been taken up many times in studies by philosophers and social scientists from Habermas and Niklas Luhmann to Alain Touraine.[42] Yet, even as early as Marx's arguments in *The German Ideology* there is an explicit recognition of the correspondence between the emergence of a dominant class perspective and the formation of massive social institutions like the modern university that establish, as a mode of legitimation and reproduction of civil society, or the "bourgeois public sphere" (*bürgerliche Gesellschaft*), narratives that prominently recite as well as reproduce certain names, titles, and legends, as well as civil codes and moral values.[43]

As I have argued above, what Lyotard intends by the term "narrative" is not defined as a genre of discourse or fable, but rather by a *mode* of reproduction in which proper names and narrative events (or "legends") are set within a socially discursive and institutional form that itself constitutes the primary medium of memory and its socialization along a chain of "addressees" (Lyotard). The term "narrative," therefore, would also include as one of its moments the reproduction of a text that occurs in the act of reading, or in successive readings that are distributed across an institutional network made up of authorized readers (professors) and novice or apprentice readers (students), as well as through various media such as books, journals, and syllabi (or curricula). Consequently, the narrative form is very much dependent upon the transmission of knowledge and modes of authorization that this network requires in order to function, and also upon the apparatus (or "meta-narrative") by which this reproduction takes on the specific form of a social institution. The social institution of the university can be understood from this perspective as the invention of an apparatus which houses these functions of memory and reproduction (i.e., transmission), but in a highly selective and determinant form which bears close affinity with other "grand institutions" (a term first coined by Michel Foucault) that mark both early- and late-democratic societies.

In Fredric Jameson's forward to *The Postmodern Condition*, we find a confirmation of the earliest conditions of the "crisis of legitimation" that now grips many of the disciplines of the Humanities, even though it is not yet addressed explicitly in those terms. His forward was written in 1984, at a point when this crisis was not yet pronounced. (Although ever-present, it was hidden beneath the sound and the fury that critical theory and discursive analysis represented for many faculty in those fields; today, one can easily detect a certain premature *kudos* in the rhetoric that surrounded the major proclamations that belong to the 1970s and 1980s.) Jameson refers to this crisis himself at a certain moment in the foreword, where his own analysis of this "legitimation crisis" in the discourse of science diverges from Lyotard's own strategy of *narrative analysis*. According to Jameson, because the disciplines of the Humanities are based upon the study of narratives, the epistemological condition for any knowledge derived from the privilege of this medium is the belief that narrative itself is a "form of primitive data storage or of social reproduction."[44] However, Jameson also argues that the cultural authority of narrative knowledge would depend upon the current performativity of this form for the purpose of social reproduction — that is, on the transmission of codes for normative morality, class consciousness and national characteristics of the public sphere.

What particularly marks the postmodern period are two developments concerning narrative. The first is the gradual emergence of a greater and greater degree of *non-performativity* in the medium of narrative, which can be registered in terms of the increase of "noise," feed-back, and the loss of transparency in reading technologies as the result of the creation of new determinations of the narrative mode (for example, determinations of different levels of meaning established by new critical hermeneutic theories, psychoanalysis, "deconstruction," feminist and Marxist interpretation). As the complexity of the narrative mode has increased, we might surmise that it has become less suited or adaptable as a medium of "social reproduction." Here again, I am following Lyotard's definition of narrative as something more than genre, which must also include the form of a social institution, apparatus, or convention (as, for example, when we speak of a literary culture). We might suspect, therefore, that these codes of social reproduction are now being transmitted outside their earlier institutions of culture and writing (such as the Bible, eighteenth century didactic novel, or the institutions of canon) and narrative itself as a "primitive data storage" — what Jameson here and elsewhere defines as the early vestibule of "the political unconscious" — has been superseded by information technologies that are no longer dependent on earlier narrative forms and reading technologies as a primary means of reproducing social and cultural "values."

It is also possible to think that the decline in the centrality of the narrative itself is the fundamental condition for those knowledges based on narrative (history, culture, language and literature, for example); therefore, the loss of transparency of this form was the underlying condition for the creation of new critical knowledges remarked by the *redundancy* of the narrative mode itself for the purposes of social reproduction — and specifically, the reproduction of the dominant values consonant with "civil society." Contrary to what critics and specialists of this form continue to assert today, the current decline of narrative knowledge can be understood as the result of a certain *relaxing* of the goal of social reproduction as a *modus essendi*, on the one hand, and by the progression of new techniques and strategies of social reproduction beyond this primitive form, on the other. As Jameson wrote in 1984, we might be witnessing in the current moment

> the radical differentiation between the consumption of the past in narrative and its storage, hoarding, and capitalization in 'science' and scientific thought: a mode of understanding that, like the first surplus on an economic level, will little by little determine a whole range of ever more complex and extensive institutional objectifications — first, in writing; then in libraries, universities, museums; with the breakthrough in our own period to micro-storage, computerized data, and data banks of hitherto unimaginable proportions, whose control or ownership is … one of the most crucial *political* questions of our own time.[45]

In addition to the possible archaism of narrative, and the consequent decline of social investment in the disciplinary knowledge that defines narrative as both a "field" and as a primary object of analysis, a second development can be inferred from Jameson's description of an evolution in the "institutional objectifications" of the mode of production that belongs to late-capitalist societies. Here, Jameson is suggesting, along with Lyotard, that the "institutional objectification" of the activities of "writing" and "data-storage" has evolved beyond what is basically an eighteenth century understanding of the university's central importance for housing and reproducing those knowledges deemed important or critical to society. As a result, either the university becomes more removed from *the political* question of "ownership" and "control" of critical social knowledge, or, the institution itself must evolve in order to adapt to a new form of objectification so that these questions can again become central to its function in contemporary societies.

I think there is enough evidence to accept both as working hypotheses for the purposes of this report. As I have already suggested, the latter development can be detected in the efforts of what I call a *new* faculty, represented by the administrative class I discussed in part one, to adapt the university to a new set of institutional objectives that directly correspond to new technological advancements in the distribution and control of information, as well as to new political constituencies, patrons, and "publics" that have emerged along with these advancements. The former can be inferred from the pattern of decline experienced by certain historical disciplines (mostly located in the former Humanities), a pattern which might signal that these knowledges are no longer "assessed" to be critical to the political question of knowledge as I have outlined (following Jameson's earlier argument). We might also refer this question to the rise of the status and function of the advanced media, which have taken over many of the cultural and national functions that were previously located in the university. The very disciplinary conditions of knowledge within the academy, by which discourse is highly regulated and controlled by standards and practices that determine *what counts for knowledge* and *who is authorized to claim knowledge* may no longer be definitive for establishing credibility for the surrounding society.

The situation just described points to one of the principle characteristics of what Lyotard calls "the postmodern condition": an incredulity toward meta-narratives, and the narrative of a consensual spirit formerly believed to be the underlying principle of late-democratic institutions. According to Lyotard, this has been replaced by a spirit of "universal functionalism" (from the concept first coined by Niklas Luhmann) that is believed to be the "prime mover" of the contemporary social bond in all its aspects (political, cultural, religious or moral, etc.) Ironically, this incredulity has also been performed by critical theories of the left over the past several decades, and in the criticism of Enlightenment principles in particular, as the result of which any historical representation of consensus (including the consensual mechanisms that form the basis of social institutions) is suspected of being essentially false, of secretly harboring an ideological expression of bad faith or malevolent design. By contrast "the right" can be said to have capitalized on this situation by turning this intuition into a universal rule. They have just taken it a step further and have fashioned this intuition according to the following maxim: "act in such a way that the rule of performativity is, for all practical purposes, the universal criterion of decision." In both positions we might discern a latent spirit of nihilism that both subjects could be said to share, a nihilism based upon the common incredulity concerning the Enlightenment meta-narrative of reason: the arbitrariness of principles, or more classically phrased, the belief that ruling ideas are really only the expressions of ruling interests (i.e., the partially of reason, or ideology). The only difference is that while the left continues to represent this as a theoretical problem (i.e., the problem of truth, or of the representation in general), the right approaches it as a practical problem (i.e., the problem of conforming or adapting the social bond to the rule of performativity as the "universal" criteria of decision).

# Part III  *Lyotard's War*

*"Let us wage war on totality!*

— Lyotard, *The Postmodern Condition*[1]

## Abstract

The third part explicates Lyotard's major statements concerning the myth of consensus, particularly the form of consensus that is implied by major theories of language in the twentieth century, and comments on the series of historical debates between Lyotard, Habermas, and Jameson (or Marxian critical thought in general). With the above arguments in mind, I turn to assess the major "genres" of the critical that exist in the university today (primarily Marxist and postmodern, or deconstructive) and test them against Lyotard's hypothesis that earlier critical genres, which are premised on a dualistic model of knowledge and an understanding of conflict as opposition, are now out-moded and are no longer capable of effectively "moving the social bond" (Lyotard). In the final section, "On the 'Ethical Turn'," I address the perceptible change that is taking place in critical discourse today: the replacement of an earlier concern with "universal meta-narrative" (such as "History" in the Marxist theory) with a concern for "justice" or "doing justice," which I describe as a turn to ethical discourse. In part, this argument corresponds to Lyotard's own observations concerning a shift to "small narratives" that no longer take the form of the universal as their horizon; however, I interrogate this statement by investigating the concept of justice itself and its relationship to the failure of consensus, that is, to the perceived arbitrariness of principles or the partiality of reason(i.e. ideology).

### III(a) *The trouble with consensus (homologia)*

The above sub-title is an allusion to an early film by Hitchcock, *The Trouble with Harry*. In watching the film one soon learns that the trouble with Harry is, simply put, he is dead, and throughout the entire course of the film the characters undergo a series of comic reversals concerning the problem of how to dispose of his corpse. (It is buried and then exhumed, only to be buried again no less than three times.) I wonder if the same could be said of the fate of *consensus* in the postmodern period. First, the trouble with consensus, simply put, is that it is dead. Second, one doesn't know what to do with its corpse, that is, with the critical or grand narratives that still depend on a certain image of consensus (even, as we noted above, in its negative form) in order to function. Like the nineteenth century pronouncement "God is Dead!" before it, the statement that belief in consensus is dead is a revelation that will probably not occur all at once, but rather in jerks and fits of gradual realization, most of all, in the realization of new discursive and technical practices of "knowledge production" that already occur outside the rule of consensus, as well as social and particularly administrative narratives that already operate well beyond its earlier conventions, turning the very idea of consensus either into an "empty sign" that can be employed strategically to "move the social bond," or into a pitiful sign of nostalgia and "hope."[2]

This idea is not new, of course. Marx, in *The German Ideology*, already charged that the spirit of consensus was essentially a fiction of a certain state-form (democracy) that was itself the creation of one class, the bourgeoisie. The "idea" of consensus as a strictly ideological notion was, for the Marx of this earlier period, the product of the practical and real exclusions of various social subjects from the political or consensual mechanisms of society. In short, consensus is easy to attain or to produce when the possibility of any real dissent (or *differend*) was already excluded from the dominant political and cultural institutions, a fact which resulted in the false appearance of an *a priori* agreement or *sensus communis*. Most modern critical theories have been built upon this fairly direct and simple intuition, including critical theories that have championed the viewpoints of social minorities in late-democratic societies, and women in particular, by calling attention to the homogeneity of the consensual institutions in society and the *a priori* "exclusion" of certain subjects from decision-making positions that play a crucial role in determining how power is distributed throughout the social bond.

It is for this reason that the question of access to these instruments of consensus (schools, the media, politics, the courts, etc.) has been a fundamental site of politicization in many sectors of late-democratic societies, but is mostly concentrated in institutions that historically presuppose a consensual ideology as the basis of their social function. (The history of affirmative action and the politicization of curricula and academic programs in the modern university are primary examples of this aspect.) In light of the above observations, however, we might ask the following: given the fundamental change in the "speculative spirit," how has this change played itself out in the university which is supposed to function as the historical embodiment of the speculative or critical faculty of knowledge? If, according to Lyotard's thesis, the current state of knowledge no longer requires consensus, then what would the image of the critical knowledge be, since it cannot be founded effectively on a form of conflict that is authorized by "disagreement," that is, on *dis-sensus* which would appear more like noise in a cybernetic program? *If* this thesis were accurate, there would be no effective *resistance* offered by a critical model that is still based on the premise of a consensual function believed to be at the center of the social bond.

Today, it is clear that there is enough evidence to at least to throw this question into sharp relief — perhaps as *the question* that needs to be taken up prior to going about our usual business as "critics of the current society." Of course, Lyotard's argument in *The Postmodern Condition* is only the most extreme articulation of this thesis and itself takes the form of another meta-narrative, that of *the postmodern* itself. However, this fact should not disqualify his argument entirely, since it has enough credibility at least to become a working hypothesis for examining the state of knowledge in late-capitalistic societies, and particularly, the state or function of critical knowledge in the university within these societies in particular. Despite the numerous books that have been published in recent years which continue to take up the questions that Lyotard first raised twenty years ago — for example, Bill Reading's *The University in Ruins*, Michael Bérubé's *Public Access,* John Guillory's *Cultural Capital,* and more recently, Stanley Fish's *Professional Correctness* — it is remarkable that no one has followed Lyotard's lead and taken up his most important questions concerning the relationship between knowledge and society with a view to clarifying or fundamentally revising the social function of critical knowledge today.

The basic question that concerns us is why earlier forms and genres of the "critical" (and by this I mean the various discursive genres of conflict, what Lyotard calls "agonistics") seem somewhat hollow or anemic today, as pure forms of representation. Their very appearance as *genres of discourse* — in short, as "narratives" or what Lyotard calls "language games" — might imply that they have been robbed *a priori* of any performative power "to move the social bond."[3] If "the principle of consensus as a criterion of validation now seems to be inadequate," according to Lyotard, perhaps this is because the notion of consensus itself can be formulated in two somewhat contradictory manners.

1.  According to the first model, consensus is the agreement between subjects, defined as knowing intellects and free wills, and is obtained through dialogue. This is the classical and philosophical form of consensus elaborated by Habermas, but his conception is based on what Lyotard defines as *homologia,* that is, the harmony or identity between two phrases.
2.  According to the second model, consensus is simply *an object* of administrative procedures or techniques. It is a component of a system, which is manipulated or engineered in order to maintain and improve the system's performance.

Under the second definition, the ideal of consensus is often addressed directly to the subject of desire or will without the intermediary of "narrative" (that is, rational explanation, education, learning, etc.) and addresses more the "agreement" attained between a desired outcome and a subject's action or behavior. If narrative is employed at all, we might suspect that it is often only as a surface that misrepresents or distorts what is really going on or intended. This is the classical Marxist definition of "ideology." We have found this "philosophy" of the performative (i.e., *de facto* nature of consensus) operating in the language of the long-term planning report. Here, we can define the notion of consensus that operates as a component of technical discourse as essentially a *simulacrum,* which explains why those who misunderstand its "phrasing" (to use Lyotard's term) and seek to enter into argument and dis-agreement miss the point entirely. For example, those who seek to link the sign of a *de facto* (or "performative") expression of consensus ("It is agreed that…") to the mode of a "question" ("Is it, in fact, agreed that…?"), according to a now out-of-date genre of the philosophical dialectic, are likely to appear somewhat disingenuous, almost as if they were violating the rule of this new genre of dialogue. Even though there are subjects determined to occupy a point of "error" or of being "ill-informed," which is the cause of their disagreement, there is no attempt made to "educate" them or to engage them in a dialectic until consensus can be reached through the process of learning, but only to *deal with them* in some way to minimize their effect on the program.

This is the form of "terror" that lurks at every level of the contemporary social bond and is governed by the performativity principle. As Lyotard cautions in his argument, "education" and "learning" are no longer alternatives used to treat the states of error or misunderstanding that belong to the system; rather, "exclusion" and "alienation" from the social bond itself are the methods used to *deal with* what the system determines to be its "bad subjects" (to borrow a term from Althusser). Therefore, to engage in dispute or conflict in order to arrive at consensus or agreement is not what is being sought; rather, consensus (or agreement) is simply the expected response of the addressee, which is not directed to a cognitive faculty, but rather to the faculty of desire or will via the intermediary of some mechanism of *torte*. The narrative form of reason itself often functions as a "lure" to trap the subject into believing that he or she is free to choose, even while he or she is already adapting or conforming (his or her behavior) to the underlying objectives. As for the classical notion of *consensus*, it becomes an instrument to be used toward achieving the real goals — power, efficiency, and wealth — that unify the entire system in all of its occasions.[4]

To be fair to Habermas, much of Lyotard's diagnosis of the default of master-narratives and the increasing dependency on performativity-languages can also be found in Habermas' work. Especially in *The Structural Transformation of the Public Sphere* (1962) and in *Legitimation Crisis* (1973), Habermas addresses these factors as part of "the de-politicization of the bourgeois public sphere." In fact, in the conclusion of this study, Habermas poses the same problem as the one I just outlined above. He frames this question as follows:

> With the methodical choice between the universal-functionalist and the critical-reconstructive approaches, the question [...] is already decided: whether…the reproduction of social life is still bound to reason and, especially, whether the generation of motives is still bound to internalization of norms that have need of justification. If this is not longer the case, reconstruction of historically developed institutions [*including, I might add here, the university as I have been arguing*] and interpretive systems [*including, according to Lyotard, the interpretive systems based on narrative procedures*] in accordance with a normative-genetic procedure [*i.e. consensus*] has lost its object, and crisis theorems can no longer be contructed.[5]

Given the above statement, along with my interpolations made to bring the above passage in line with Lyotard's argument, it is odd that, despite their published arguments against each other's position, both Habermas and Lyotard appear to be arguing the same thing, even though they come to different conclusions concerning the second Kantian ideal of reason: *What must we do?* The problem for both thinkers can be defined in its simplest terms as the increasing complexity of social systems, and the concomitant transformation of the idea of rationality into something akin to universal functionalism (i.e., performativity) as the necessary result of this complexity. (The philosopher Alfred North Whitehead, some 50 years earlier, had already reached this conclusion concerning the complexity of organic and inorganic systems in *Process and Reality* [1929], although because of the difficulty of his metaphysical system, few have attempted to apply this philosophy to current social and technological processes.) The difference, however, is the conclusion that each philosopher draws from this situation.

In response to the situation of complexity described in *Legitimation Crisis*, Habermas remains strictly Kantian and continues to pose *the question of the political as a question* precisely at a time when this notion designates more of an economic and administrative function that has become one of the component expressions of the system itself in an overall effort to maintain that precarious balance in the face of its own complexity. The question that follows from Habermas' study is whether this new function is, in fact, a creative and emancipatory development, or rather, "a symptom" of the problem of complexity itself that cannot be resolved by what he calls "Old European Concepts."[6] That is, as we highlighted this question earlier on in this report, we are asking whether the administrative subject (acting as "the differential steering mechanism" of late-democratic societies) is actually creating any new synthetic languages that will eventually replace the blind ineffectualness of out-moded concepts of a self-legislative or consensus-based model of the social bond, or whether these new programming languages and alternative models of self-organization only serve to make an already too complex system more burdened and over-wrought, dooming the social bond itself to repeated episodes of failure and breakdown in much the same way that in the nineteenth century the "individual" (that now out-moded elementary unit of the social bond) was earlier doomed to frequent neurotic or even psychotic episodes.

Following Kant, Habermas defines this question as one that must be addressed to the rational subject of desire: *what should we hope for?* He writes:

> The fundamental question of the continued existence of a truth-dependent mode of socialization constitutive of society is, as one can see, not easy to answer. This could lead one to think that it is not at all a theoretically resoluble question, but a practical question: should we rationally desire that social identity through the minds of socially related individuals or should it be sacrificed to the problem — real or imagined — of complexity? To pose the question in this way is, of course, to answer it.[7]

Of course, the question posed is already answered by the fact that Habermas addresses it from the position of a subject identified as "We" — for example, "a people," or "a Universal Humanity." In the spirit of Lyotard's argument, one might respond that to raise this question in this way is to remain old-fashioned, to cling to the nostalgic belief "in the dignity of that good old European humanity" (which is actually Habermas' self-descriptive phrase).[8]

According to Lyotard's analysis, one of the most pressing and urgent problems faced by any form of rationality that will emerge after the collapse of the old rationality is precisely the way in which this question itself is strangely always already decided. That is, what Lyotard defines as "performativity" is the manner in which the problem of consensus is resolved before the moment of rationality (thus, it appears as a new naturalism), prior to the subject's election (or not) to agree. This is compounded by the fact that the notions of "individual" or "individual reason" have been disqualified as chimera by many postmodern critical theories as well. Thus, the moment of rationality always appears secondary and contingent to the determination which appears in the form of a "structure" or a "system" that is remote from the position of the subject's consciousness — or as the psychoanalyst Jacques Lacan has remarked, its position is always deferred to "another scene" (than the one of conscious self-reflection).[9]

As Habermas writes: "While critical social theory can founder on a changed reality, universal functionalism must suppose — that is, prejudge at the analytical level — that this change in the mode of socialization and the 'end of the individual' have already come to pass."[10] Any theory that suspends or forecloses the subject's own reality could be seen as an effect of this universal functionalism, rather than a critical response to it. This could be regarded as Habermas' implicit critique of Lyotard's position, although in this context, it is more explicitly directed against Luhmann's "system theory," which he regards as a rational model that has abandoned the classical formulation of reason and has subordinated itself "to a fundamentally opportunistic life-process" (which I take here to refer to the economic opportunistic spirit of late-capitalism).[11] Thus, functionalism solves the problem of consensus by foreclosing the possibility of freedom at an individual or even social or collective level of "totality" — in short, it forecloses the very space of the political.

## III(b)  *The phrase "there is a language (logos)"*

In the conclusion to *The Postmodern Condition,* Lyotard poses two major objections to Habermas's ideal of "communicative action": first, "transparency" in the medium of dialogue as well as in the notion of the ideal subject who corresponds to "communicative actions"; second, the belief that all statements and actions ultimately flow in one direction toward one great ocean of emancipated humanity. The latter is the belief in a universal meta-narrative of emancipation, one that assumes that speakers could ever come to a possible agreement concerning the rules that will govern *all* language games for every occasion. The former is Habermas' assumption that the goal of dialogue is, or has ever been, *consensus.* On the contrary, Lyotard argues that the goal has always been what he calls "paralogy," the search for instabilities. The idea being presented here is that every instance of dialogue can, in fact, be reduced to logistics or strategy. That is, the principle of dialogue is the performative goal of the "winning move." The speaker merely seeks out instabilities in the opponent's discourse, and attempts to make a "move" based on the strategy of winning a game.

Perhaps Lyotard has been too influenced here by the analytical philosophers he refers to in this context, where this statement is more or less an accurate description of the goals of an average conversation. But, do all "language games" function according to the same rules as the game of chess? If the rules that function in dialogue can be reduced to the rules of a game, then the "speaker" responds to the discourse of his or her opponent by seeking out instabilities in the previous statement in order to discover the move that ends the game when the other player tips his piece in recognition of "agreement"(consensus). It remains a question whether all conversations can be submitted to this principle of power. On the other hand, if one accepts this principle of agonistics, then the position of the speaker who recognizes the importance of strategy will be the speaker most likely to be realistic, to attain an advantage in the *agon* (or conflict) of discourse. Accordingly, critical theories themselves can also be evaluated according to the same principle: a) who makes the "best" move, and b) which are most likely to succeed in winning an argument concerning the contemporary social bond. (This has certainly been the *modus operandi* of "neo-pragmatists" like Stanley Fish.) However, winning is only evidenced by the complete surrender of the opponent under the axiom of performativity. There is no room here for the old, nostalgic beliefs in an original accord — the Leibnizian *Harmonia Praestabilita,* or the Kantian "transcendental subject" — upon which all subsequent agreements (linguistic, cultural, political) are based. It is no wonder that Lyotard sees Habermas' notion of consensus as naïve and "false," when he understands that consensus never occurs in the mutual concordance of minds, but only through "a strategy." Therefore, the "silence" of consensus, or the sense of mutual understanding and agreement is, for Lyotard, simply a repressed or extinguished *differend*.

And yet, this is Lyotard's strongest thesis, one which concerns the nature of *logos* itself. In *The Differend*, he writes:

> At bottom, one in general presupposes *a* language, a language naturally at peace with itself, "communicational" and perturbed for instance only by wills, passions, and intentions of humans. Anthropocentricism. In the matter of language, the revolution of relativity and quantum theory needs to be made.[12]

Here, we have a sense of *Lyotard's war* against the very principle of consensus that defines language as a total unity, "at peace with itself," at the point of nearest identity with itself as a whole in the linguistic performance of agreement which functions like a "final causality." In the Saussurian model, the whole of language is immanent within each instance of a statement or phrase (*la parole*) and constitutes the condition of the possibility of *a* phrase, or *a* statement. It is, to use a more archaic philosophical concept, the "univocity" of language in the statement, the consensus or agreement that is performed by the relation: *langue / parole*.

However, we also need to recall that even for Saussure the power of agreement always remains on the side of language. Although Saussure originally employs the metaphor of "the contract" to characterize the agreement that belongs to the understanding of speech, he later retracts this analogy, "for language furnishes the best proof that a law accepted by a community is something tolerated as an expedient and not a rule to which everyone freely consents."[13] Therefore, the form of consensus or agreement that is performative in every language-situation, including this sentence, is an impure or false image of the consensus that actually *performs* sense and meaning in language. It is the *retrogressive image of the understanding* that is projected backwards, so to speak, as the condition of the possibility of the enunciation itself. In this way, its function resembles myth as we defined above. Similar to Marx's critique of the social contract, Saussure reveals the character of extortion or *torte* (what Lyotard calls the innate possibility of "terror") that always underwrites the linguistic contract between speakers, or rather, between a community of speakers and *a* language. Saussure writes:

> This fact, which seems to embody a contradiction, might be called colloquially 'the stacked deck.' We say: 'Choose! But we add: 'It must be this sign and no other.' No individual, even if he willed it, could modify in any way at all the choice that has been made; and what's more, the community itself cannot control so much as a single word; it is bound to the existing language.[14]

Taking this last observation by Saussure as our cue, it might help us to understand Lyotard's enmity toward any image of consensus or agreement as the principle of language, and his characterization of its true principle as something closer to a game between opposing players: the principle of agonistics that is determined by "paralogy." Even in Saussure's own description we find a confirmation of this notion of a language-game, one in which language always plays with a "stacked deck" and thus is predisposed to winning every move. According to Saussure's rather grim description, which is only pushed to a further degree by Lyotard — and partly, I think, for strategic purposes — for the individual as well as the collective community of speakers there is no winning move, no way to win in the game *against* language.

But what kind of game is that? For example, if I knew beforehand that, each time I played an opponent in a hand of poker, I would lose all my money, and not because of the skill of the other player, but simply because he holds all the cards and the deck is stacked so that each hand wins, I would sooner or later avoid the game altogether, since it would no longer be a game but something more like a con. Yet, this is precisely Saussure's original point: even though language is a differential chain of signifiers whose genesis and structure closely resembles that of a game (meaning that the rules of linking phrases and the choice of individual signifiers are arbitrary in principle), sooner or later one comes to believe or chooses not to see it that way, since everything depends on getting it right, that is, on winning! As Lyotard writes, "You don't play around with language … And in this sense, there are no language-games."[15] Thus, as was also true for Wittgenstein, the analogy of language to a game is genetic, and not merely a metaphor.

Like Saussure before him, Lyotard is fundamentally revising the image of the "natural contract" at the basis of language. If *logos* is represented as most identical to itself in the event of understanding, at peace with itself, where it comes to a "form" by which we understand what *a* language is, this severely distorts the real event of a language situation or speech-event. On the contrary, when viewed from the perspective of discrete linguistic situations (so-called "phrases"), the social side of language becomes heterogeneous, fraught with danger and violence, and not at all in a state of *being at peace*. This is what happens when *logos* is opened to the question of power, which is not distributed evenly across all speech-events, phrases, identities and genres of discourse in the manner of a grammatical form, or "structure," but rather functions like a quantum field surrounding and shaping various speech events like a nebulous force.

*Consensus*, therefore, is the foundational myth of language that hides or eclipses *the real* in every instance of discourse (*parole*); the image of *a* language as a total or unified system is like a field of battle on the morning after a conflict. *War, polemos, conflict* — perhaps these are the natural states between each genre of discourse or phrase regime. Seen from the perspective of "phrasing" and not from *a* language, when "I speaks," it does not want the consensus of the other party; rather, it wants to completely dominate the sense of the statement (*la parole*), even to the point of eclipsing the position of the other, that is, interpolating the very moment of understanding that supposedly occurs in the other's mind when s/he performs the sense of the statement. The "I speak" wants only one reply and no other — "yes," "yes," "I agree," "yes," "I understand,' and finally; "yes," "I submit." This is why the subject of language is necessarily mobilized around any point of contradiction, either stated or implicit, which is resolved through repetition and re-phrasing until the opponent is ultimately worn down and concedes, perhaps only to find a little bit of peace, "*to sleep perchance to dream.*" Moreover, in the morality of the dialogical model, this is also why lying is prohibited, in addition to any form of false pretense of agreement (simulation, irony), since these would be precisely the forces that disturbed the peacefulness and the quiet of the *logos* that is founded by a consensus-image. For Lyotard, there is not *a* language, but rather what can be described as a heterogenous field of phrase-particles and genres, all of which are potentially in dispute. Consequently, according to the above observations, language *as a whole* must be reimagined as an arrangement of phrase-particles in a quantum field; consensus (i.e., the moment of understanding or of de-coding the relationship between signifier, signified, and referent) must be eradicated as the representation of *sense*, and replaced by the image of a *differend*, the image of dispute *between* phrase-universes.

I am highlighting Lyotard's theory of language (*logos*) in order to show how far it has divorced itself from classical models and even from modern semiotic theories, which are still based on a notion of language as a structure which still endows language with a unity and homogeneity, albeit a unity that is virtual or "symbolic" in nature, one that must be constructed as the object of a "metalanguage." This is essentially where Lyotard's theory of language would diverge from Saussure, and consequently all subsequent semiotic and structuralist theories, since Saussure, despite his insight into the arbitrary (and thus nonfoundational) basis of language as a social institution, still sought to create a meta-language that would grasp the field of language within a descriptive or scientific framework by creating an homogenous field of pure signifiers from which he could derive a structure.

Perhaps Saussure's first error was at the same time his greatest insight into the *form* of language: his perception of the "arbitrary nature of the sign." By exaggerating this aspect, he effectively neutralized precisely the question of selection, that is, *the emergence of difference* between "signs," the selection of certain signifying relations that belong to a language and the suppression or absence of others. In other words, he neutralized the real question of difference (i.e., the social force that motivates the selection of signs, or of one sign for another) in order to extract from a language pure linguistic values that could be set within a scientific framework. For example, Saussure argues that it is the arbitrary nature of the sign that protects language from any modification, and this makes it immovable and shows the "impossibility of revolution" which distinguishes language from any other social institution.

This distinction is not qualitative but quantitative in the sense that language resists change or innovation to a greater degree than any other social institution. "It blends with the life of society, and the latter, inert by nature, is a prime conservative force."[16] Here, Saussure interpolates an image of "primary matter" (which Husserl called *hyle*) into life and language at once, a matter that to a great degree is dead or inert, where it comes to the closest to being a mere and lifeless thing, an object, or stuff. It is because of the thickness or the density of its material basis that language, of all social institutions, is the least open to "modification." Thus, language at its most fundamental level, which is not yet its ground, is identical to unconscious habit. As we know from Hume, nothing can be rationally grounded in habit; therefore, established by habit, language is revealed as essentially a groundless phenomenon. The "grounding principle" of language is unconscious.

This is the exact meaning of the concept of "arbitrary" at the basis of Saussure's intuition. However, as is evident from the above description, Saussure's argument leads to a vicious circle in which language is grounded in habit (the most inert or dead part of the life of society) and because there is no rational basis for habit, this ground is closed and impermeable to rational justification. The arbitrary nature of the "sign" leads to the discovery of the inability of reason to elucidate the ground of language except by reference to habit, or by extension, to "tradition" or "convention." Thus, it is argument by tautology. As Saussure writes, "because the sign is arbitrary, it follows no law other than that of tradition, and because it is based on tradition, it is arbitrary."[17] Looking more closely at Saussure's argument, we find that the arbitrariness that structures the difference in language, an arbitrariness that closely resembles the invention of rules in a game, is resolved at its base by the fact that there can be no "meta-language" created to discern the arbitrary construction of the rules themselves. It would be like asking, in a game of chess, why there are only black and white pieces, or why the knight can move two spaces forward and one to the left or right, or why the queen can move indiscriminately (left, right, forward, backward, or diagonally), or finally; why a pawn can traverse the board and become a queen? To all these questions there is only one reply possible: because it must, or, because that's the rule. There is no other reason for it other than it makes the game of chess possible.

It is interesting to note in this context that only a two-year old, perhaps *the* subject of language who is *"on trial/in process"* in Kristeva's sense: only a subject who is just in the process of being acclimated to the strange logic of the signifier is capable of posing such foundational questions concerning the arbitrariness of the rules that govern nominative reality. As for adults, on the contrary, we have become so conditioned to these rules that we no longer think to consider them arbitrary, since we are too busy playing the game and, consequently, regard the child's questions why *all dogs are "dogs" and not also "geese"* to be an object of pleasantry and even an opportunity celebrate the child's natural genius and aptitude for language games. The response that it is because dogs are four-legged creatures and geese have two legs and two wings is merely philosophical. However, the real meaning of such an occasion is fatally tragic, an event that most adults have long ago repressed, since it already foreshadows the fact that the child's questions concerning language will never be answered.

Returning to Lyotard's analysis, what we are describing is a situation that is resolved at its base by pure performativity. The condition of all language-events is resolved by being purely prescriptive; there is no basis for translating these prescriptive conditions into denotative or descriptive statements, except that is, by a kind of magical leap. We might see here that the fable of consensus that founds the condition of language and of all speech-acts is just such a leap, since it places every speaker at the origin of language where s/he gives herself the rule that s/he obeys. Thus, the arbitrary nature of the sign is resolved by becoming falsely or pseudo-reflexive — i.e., I speak *as if* I give myself the rule of language while, at the same time, I obey this rule. This reflexive form recounts (or repeats) the origin of social and linguistic contracts alike even though one is always founded upon the other; or more precisely, one is always deduced from the other. The complex patterns of repetition and habit that seem to operate at the foundation of social institutions are deduced from simple instances of linguistic agreement so that, at bottom, they are not heterogeneous but in fact operate according to the same fundamental principle which is then projected backwards to occupy the position of the ground. The problem occurs in the fact that time obscures and alienates this original situation; "tradition" and "habit" are the names given to the two forces of this estrangement from the origin of the social form whatever it may be.

The individual speaker always comes onto the scene too late and discovers himself or herself to be absent from the a prior situation that established the terms of the individual's own speech, even the meaning accorded to the subject. It is essentially a theoretical fiction that social patterns and institutions are basically forms of agreement that operate according to the same principle as the agreement in language. (For example, social institutions like kinship structures and forms of exchange are in fact second-order languages, an arbitrary and differential arrangement of signifiers in a signifying order.) Because of this simple homology, Saussure must struggle with the question of deducing the original situation or terms of the agreement from which a particular social form is derived. We must note that although he first posits the equivalence "language equals a contract between speakers," only to later revise this metaphor, he does not effectively exclude the image of consensus or agreement that the notion of contract implies. He does not say, for example, that the fundamental principle of agreement that is performed by every social institution can in no way be likened to a contract, but rather that "no longer can language be identified with a contract pure and simple."[18] Thus, language is not a contract "pure and simple," but rather it is a peculiar kind of contract, the kind that one tolerates but in no way freely consents to; one tolerates its rule for no other reason than because of habit, convention, collective inertia or indolence, and for the simple fact that it is more convenient to accept its conventions (despite that fact that one cannot ground these conventions in reason) than not to. It is much easier to concede to *a* language and go about one's business as usual.

Why is this rejection of a structure so important for our present study of Lyotard's notion of performativity? How does this relate back to the notion of the critical that is founded upon a consensus-image of reason? On one level, if every social institution finds its true form in language, then we arrive back at the problem posed in the beginning of our discussion: the notion of agreement or consensus that finds its representation in language in the completion of the linguistic enunciation (i.e., the circuit of enunciation and understanding that is performed by a common speech situation) becomes both the internal presupposition and destination of all social phenomena. Agreement is presupposed as the "natural state" of any situation, and becomes the teleology of every event without concern to its social side. If we imagine a universe presented by a phrase is "immediately social in the sense that an addressor, an addressee, a referent, and a sense are situated together within it," and in such a way that none of these terms can be deduced from the others "as if from an origin," then there can be no prior instance of agreement implied in every language situation.[19]

I have been shuttling back and forth between Saussure's argument and that of Lyotard's for two reasons:

1. Because of the importance Saussure's description of *logos* will play in all subsequent theories of society and culture, particularly with the advent of the structural sciences from the 1950s onward. (And in a certain sense, Saussure's description of *logos* is the inauguration of our own understanding of language.)
2. To highlight the difference between Saussure's description and that of Lyotard's in terms of a conflict over the nature of the *logos* itself, of a completely non-

structuralist and even anti-structuralist viewpoint, even an extreme hostility to any consensus-image which I have called *Lyotard's war.*

In one sense, Lyotard accepts the supremacy of the genre of language, which is why he describes the social as a multiplicity of "language-games" each of which operate according to a specialized logic or idiom. However, in place of the genre of language as the totality or structure he inserts the instance of the phrase as the true representative of *logos.* The genre of language is only one manner of linking different phrases, and no phrase can serve as the principle that authorizes another without a kind of magical leap. "No phrase is first."[21] If language is not given priority as the principle for deducing other regimes of signification, or what Lyotard calls "phrase-universes," then there is no reason for giving preference to its image of sense, or agreement. Thus, if the relation between two regions of experience cannot be linked by a principle of homonymy (which the notion of a structure is), then we arrive at a situation of a *differend* or a "conflict between genres of discourse."[22]

Finally, I return to address the problem of consensus that is implied by the phrase *there is a language* from the perspective of Kant, specifically in *The Critique of Judgment*, which is most relevant to the problem at hand. For Kant, the "universal condition of taste" is posed *in principle* (that is to say, as the rule of good taste) precisely at the point where judgments of taste threaten to close around a subjective principle that would remain henceforth impenetrable to reason. Kant's solution was to agree that all judgments of taste were subjective, but in the rigorous understanding that they are not predicated on any attribute of an object but rather on a feeling (*Gemüt*) in the subject. At the same time, inasmuch as all subjects are sensibly structured in a similar manner by nature, and inasmuch as all judgments must be communicable in *a* language which further constrains the positivity of this "feeling," Kant proves that the subjective condition of judgment is "universal" in that it must be grounded on this transcendental agreement between nature and reason (i.e., language) in order even to be possible. First, for this "feeling" to be possible for a subject, the senses must be pre-disposed accordingly; this pre-disposition cannot be said to be singular or unique from one subject to the next since nature only disposes of the general, or the species. Second, for this "feeling" to be communicable for the subject — even to himself or herself, since it must have an aspect of objectivity if only in a psychological sense, that is to say, it must be "real" — feeling is constrained by the relationship between the faculties (the understanding, imagination, and reason) which must in some way have this "object" in common. Thus, the notion of communicability does not pertain to actual communication at first, but rather to the condition of this feeling's objectivity between the three faculties; each of the faculties provide some aspect of this feeling's "object-ity" which gives it depth and reality, but it is language that gives it form. The very fact that I can "have a feeling" already predisposes it to become an object of a linguistic or grammatical structure — that I can think of it as "it," or I can imagine it in comparison with other feelings I have had, even as a new feeling, as something I have never felt before, as in the case of the sublime feeling.

Even though language does not ground the principle of communicability in the judgment of taste, it is the form in which a feeling can become objectively communicable as a signifier for the subject. In the statement, "the rose is beautiful," the term beautiful is a signifier for the subject's feeling and is not to be confused with an attribute of the rose. Kant's final step was to posit, on the basis of the earlier conditions outlined above, that for one subject to declare this rose beautiful, it must also be possible for all other subjects as well. This is where the dispute over judgments of taste begins, since the subject cannot communicate the feeling itself (*ding an sich*), only the form of his or her judgment of beauty. The dispute occurs when we realize that we can only communicate the signifier, having no access to or means of communicating the signified. The feeling itself remains "incommunicable" (or to use Lyotard's term, "un-presentable"), even though it is signaled on a purely formal level of possibility that Kant assesses as "universal."

Even though Kant began by making two assumptions or generalizations concerning the commonness of sense (in a biological and in a psychological or aesthetic determination), he ends by proving the opposite. Both senses of common or universal agreement are not the ground and cannot be referred to in order to establish the identity of a feeling for the subject, and between subjects; rather the ground is the purely formal condition of the universal statement that *there is a feeling*, an "object = x"," which can become only the basis of this purely formal condition, "a signifier for another subject." With Kant, agreement stops being innate, something given beforehand or in "a world of ideas before birth" (in Plato), and becomes the purely formal condition of communicability.

Does this mean that Kant resolves the subjective nature of judgment by *fiat* as I have argued above concerning other such appeals to the notion of an original contract that language performs? That is, does he merely infer agreement (understood as identity) by invoking the fact that *there is a language* as both the condition and final causality? Not at all. This would be tantamount to saying that there is the same "objective feeling" experienced by two different subjects, which would violate Kant's definition of the nature of judgment as purely subjective. To say that two subjects experience the same "feeling" is to attribute some objective quality to this feeling that can be demonstrated effectively by some means other than language or representation. But then, as we know from experience, this is impossible. Rather, this "thing" (*Das Ding, la chose*) can only be inferred by mere convention to be the same referent, which is why there can be normative standards of taste in a culture. Although we can dissect and measure two experiences of the statement "this is beautiful," we will never establish the objective conditions of the feeling that occasions this statement. We are then effectively barred from the thing itself (*Das Ding*), which is the "signified" of the statement "this is beautiful," or "I find this beautiful," or even, "we agree that this thing (this moment, this object of art, this sunrise) is beautiful." It turns out then that the only "thing" we truly have in common is that we are both placed before this unspeakable *feeling of a feeling* and this, in principle, becomes the form of our being in common, which in Kant, is the form of our subject-hood that is mediated by the institution of language.

*Language disposes of the thing-in-itself,* in every sense that this phrase implies. The fact that *there is a language,* in Kant's hand's, is precisely what bars us from establishing the object we have in common as an identity; but at the same time, it allows this object (as "object = x") to be communicated as the *a priori* condition of having something in common, as well as the *a posteriori* condition of any subsequent agreement concerning its possible significations. This means that the condition of our agreement cannot be grounded in the thing itself, but only grounded in its presentation as a signifier. This is why all judgments concerning taste will ultimately fail to establish the same feeling for all other subjects *in actuality*; what we have rather is an agreement to postpone the question of the identity of taste indefinitely, to defer the question to convention (which is itself a kind of provisional agreement), or to what Adam Smith defined as the "third man" (the little judge who resides within us) as a kind of stop-gap measure or compromise.

Recalling our discussion of Saussure, what is language but the historical "tradition" of all conventions, the sum total of the conventions of "signs"? Thus, it is here that language enters into Kant's analysis of the subject, and where a metaphysical expression of "agreement" is determined to be un-grounded, unable to be founded upon the identity of the thing in itself. Because of this insight the metaphysical notion of agreement becomes in Kant the purely formal, which is to say "universal," condition of the subject. More importantly, this is why for Kant the condition of universal agreement is not placed in the past as some ground or origin, but rather in the future as the "goal" or the "end" of the subject. Finally, perhaps most importantly for our purposes, this is why the notion of "critique" in Kant attaches itself to the destruction of the metaphysical conventions that determine the subject's experience; not in order to discover an original meaning or essence that has been distorted by accumulated tradition of History — Kant is not Heidegger — but rather to release this experience itself, this thing in itself ("the Subject") to its future signification — all the way to the "universal" which can never be demonstrated in the present and always remains, in a certain sense, *the future of every presentation*.

In a very roundabout way, *via* Saussure and Kant, we have finally arrived at the place where we might understand *Lyotard's war* against Habermas' ideal of *consensus* ("communicative action"), or more importantly, against all forms of nostalgia concerning the "Universal" and "Humanity" (or transcendental forms of consensus). Both amount to mythic forms of authorization by which language offers the transcendental principle to settle all *differends*; Lyotard's argument is that the appeal to a universal-Man or to a common sense is an attempt to totalize all language-situations past, present, and future. The image of a final consensus, in whatever form it takes, may in fact be a manner of avoiding the conflict caused by the clash of heterogeneous social elements; in short, the real nature of interest that is posed in the form of politics is replaced by the myth that *a language* provides — that of a "common sense" (*sensus communis*). This is why I stated above that the image of consensus, which is given prior to or even at the same moment as a concrete language situation, can be likened to the serene calm of a landscape following a night of battle. If Levinas' great protest against "the language of Being" was "ethics before ontology," then here we might argue that Lyotard's war-cry against "the Being of language" is *politics before language*. "It is, if you will a state of language, but it is not *a* language. Politics consists in the fact that language is not *a* language, but phrases, of that Being is not Being, but *there is's*."[23] Therefore, politics is not a genre of discourse but the eruption or the constant threat of *a real differend*.

## III(c) *Dueling meta-narratives*

After this long digression on language (*logos*), we might concludethat the conditions of "critical" knowledge will, at the same time, be the conditions of a truly critical subject of politics. However, both must be derived from the presence of a *real differend* and cannot be ascribed to a genre of discourse, a "narrative" tradition, or even to a "critical theory." The moment we take the "critical" as a purely formal procedure (which can be emulated, mastered, and reproduced in the manner of a style or a program), then we lose sight of both conditions, and most importantly, of the real relationship between knowledge and society that the specific conflict of the critical purportedly enacts.

Perhaps Lyotard's most pressing observation concerning the fate of critical knowledge in contemporary society, therefore, is that today all criticism is "on the defensive" and, in general, this defensive position underscores a period of "slackening" (as he defined it in the postscript to *The Postmodern Condition*, "Answering the Question: What is Postmodernism?")[24] This comment comes to the fore very late in his work and appears most explicitly formulated in *Postmodern Fables (Moralités postmodernes)*, but can be detected even earlier in the critiques of Marxism from the 1980s onward.[25] Thus, the notion of the defensive or reactive attitude of criticism, if accurate (and I think it is, at least, in the context of first world societies) could signal for us the most visible sign of the passing from the phase of modernism to postmodernism. There is enough evidence to entertain such a hypothesis and I need only to list a few indications. First, in most cases (if not all) the debates and struggles in which critics and intellectuals of the Left are embroiled today are not of their own making; rather, they are often reacting to the attacks of the Right or of some other social power. In most cases, they are attempting, through a period of intense self-reflection, to salvage something of their earlier programs and language from what many have perceived as the fatalism of late-capitalism. It is significant that the primary location of social critique is found in universities, a fact which has produced some strange contradictions, and that binds the fate of the critical today even more closely to the fate of this social institution.

We should recall that in the foundational essays and manifestoes which inaugurated what Octavio Paz has called "the Age of Criticism," the spirit of modernism was essentially a critical spirit, at least in a sense that was dramatized in the character of its leading personages, from Baudelaire to Nietzsche and Rimbaud.[26] Foucault later defined modernism not as a period of cultural history, but as a fundamental *ethos* that he derives from the portrait of the modern critic first drawn by Baudelaire.[27] The critical spirit was portrayed as active, creative. The modernist critic could be described as someone who was always on the cultural offensive, not only in the sense of offending common tastes and mores of the class in power, but who in most cases would be the one *to initiate the conflict with culture*. In the early campaign against the bourgeoisie, for example, the modernist impulse was to attack the false notion of consensus on several different cultural fronts: in art, the consensus of "taste"; in morality, the consensus of bourgeois sexual prohibitions; in language, through "experimentation" and "poetry," the consensus of linguistic and cultural agreement upon which social institutions are based (politics, economics, and architecture, for instance). At this point, I will not enter into a long thesis on modernism, since what I am referring to above has been described in much more detail by others and is generally well known. What I wish to highlight is the character of *conflict* that belongs to the nascent period of modernism, which seems to follow Kant's earlier intuitions concerning the change in the speculative mood (that is, the inclusion of the psychological state of "terror" as a fundamental relation to "the Whole"), even though modernist art would employ this mood more strategically than Kant may have intended or even thought possible. In a manner that recalls Freud's earlier description of the first encounter between consciousness and the *real*, the organization of the understanding, whether in perception or in language, is thrown over against another totality causing, according to the famous thesis by philosopher Gilles Deleuze, "a general de-regulation of the faculties of understanding and the imagination."[28] The finite organization of the concepts of understanding and the even more narrow and limited power of the imagination that defines the subject of bourgeois institutions is "blown open."

Lyotard's observation that the condition of postmodern critical knowledge is one of *ressentiment* (Nietzsche) is, in my view, an insight into a problem — perhaps even *the problem* — that bears great importance for the contemporary situation of what is called critical knowledge, and may help us to diagnose a shift from the critique of "totality" to the partial and invested subjects that constitute the scene of critical in the academy today. For Lyotard to observe the essentially "defensive attitude" of current critical subjects (such as Marxism, first and foremost, but we might also detect this attitude today in the discourses of feminism, minority and race criticism, eco-criticism, and so on) signals something much more striking than a simple extension of an essentially modernist impulse, as Habermas has argued many times concerning the notion of the postmodern. On the contrary, it may even signal something more akin to a reversal or becoming "reactive" (to refer again to the Nietzschean term) of an earlier critical spirit.

Lyotard's observations can be further supported by referring again to Derrida's remarks in the conclusion of "*Mochlos*, or the Conflict of the Faculties," where Derrida points to this "disorientation" (between left and right, between critical and conservative) as a problem that determines the current conflict of faculties as well. In fact, the guiding pun that is given in the term *mochlos* refers to "a lever," or more specifically, to the "leverage" attained by pushing from the right foot in walking or running. At the conclusion of the article, Derrida quotes a very interesting note from Kant's *The Conflict of the Faculties*:

> Experience teaches us that if we have our shoe measurements taken from our left foot, and if the left shoe fits perfectly, then the right will be too tight; and we certainly cannot lay blame for this on our parents, for not having taught us better when we were children. The advantage of the right foot over the left can also be seen from the fact that, *if we want to cross a deep ditch,* we put our weight on our left foot and step over with the right; we otherwise risk falling into the ditch. The fact that Prussian infantrymen are trained to start out with their left foot confirms, rather than refutes this assertion...(*my emphasis*).[29]

In the above passage, we can see that the orientation between left and right is based to a large degree on myth and folklore concerning the natural "weakness of the left side of the body" (which also bears an echo of sexual difference). However, it is interesting to note that in these anecdotes, particularly the last, it is the left foot that is put forward first, a strategic or martial metaphor that is also found in the notion of an avant-garde. This only highlights the sense of disorientation that both Lyotard and Derrida seem to detect at the basis of the current conflict, in which it appears that today it is the right that is out in front and the weaker left that seems to bear the full weight of the assault (even at the risk, as Kant says, of falling into a ditch). In short, this has caused a general disorientation over the sense of the "critical" today.

In order to illustrate this last statement, I will take up what could arguably be called the two dominant "meta-narratives" of the critical that, as the sub-title of this section suggests, are "dueling" over the representation of critical knowledge in the academy today: the meta-narrative of Marxism and the meta-narrative postmodernism (that is, post-structuralist theories generally premised upon the critical performativity of some privileged semiotic region of culture, whether of "the text," the media-image, or "the body" for example). I refer to these two meta-narratives as dominant, not in order to exclude other possible representations of the critical today, but rather to acknowledge that these other representations have already incorporated, perhaps fundamentally, elements from either one or both of these earlier meta-narratives within their specific discourse or critical program, or many of the principle concepts these other theories might employ. Feminism, to take the most obvious example, has early on incorporated a principle of dualism or opposition that was borrowed from Marxist critical theory, but more recently, has also been greatly influenced by semiotic (or structuralist) and psychoanalytic theories in its critical constructions of gender and sexual identity. Another example is post-colonial theories, which we could not even imagine without the notion of "core and periphery" that has been derived from the early Marxist analysis of the relation between town and country in early industrial societies. At the same time, beginning with the work of Homi Bhabba, there has also been a great deal of attention to the formations of subjective resistance in post-colonial societies that are based on semiotic performativity of some privileged region of cultural expression. There are many other examples I could refer to. In each case we would find a thread of either narrative (or, in many cases, both) underlying each critical theory and providing, so to speak, the principle rationale concerning the two following questions: *how knowledge can become effectively critical,* and *how a subject is revealed to be in a relationship of conflict with a particular society, past or present, in which he/she/they are located.*

Most importantly, we might notice that the notion of the "critical" itself functions as a mode of self-legitimation and, in a certain sense, already gives the principle of reason concerning the nature of the conflict that critical representation enacts between knowledge and society. The subject does not need to ask *why* or even *how* the relationship between knowledge and society is mediated by a critical consciousness. A narrative is already provided which responds to these questions and sets the critical subject in a tradition of other like subjects who are already in agreement or who supposedly share in this consciousness. What I am suggesting by this is that there already exists a certain unspoken *consensus* concerning the *how* and *why* of the conflict that the critical subject performs, which is why critical theories do not need to do the work of justifying their knowledge of society in the first place. (In short, I am suggesting that the mode of self-legitimation of critical knowledges has assumed the form of a modern *dogma*.)

Returning to Lyotard's argument, we might have also noticed that the appeals one often hears to an older image of the "critical" strategy of dualism (or opposition) are becoming more and more ineffective, since this earlier principle no longer functions as a "narrative that binds the subject to an ongoing social or political project." Therefore, the justifications of a critical knowledge one often hears in the university today (more recently, in the new genre of department mission statements) as either producing, for example, the conditions of "critical citizenship" (an argument that piggy-backs itself on the idea of the university as a social institution of the bourgeois public sphere, or as an instrument of the nation-building project), or as creating the conditions of a more radical constituency in public life now appear as strangely archaic and even nostalgic. Again, this development echoes Lyotard's primary thesis concerning the inability of the contemporary critical subject to bind itself to an effective master-narrative in order to legitimate the social reproduction of its own knowledge. Fundamental to this thesis is the argument that the principle of dualism that underlies the historical modes of critical knowledge is itself in default, and no longer pertains to the form of knowledge in late-capitalistic societies. There may be no legitimation for critical knowledge according to this earlier principle, at least not in the dualistic sense of "the critical" that was first established by Marx.[30]

Turning first to an assessment of the Marxist notion of critical knowledge in light of the above observations, Lyotard's own narrative of *The Postmodern Condition* perhaps represents a final rejection of the genre of political idealism, or "utopianism," associated with the name of Marx, as Jameson correctly perceives in his Foreword to *The Postmodern Condition*. Consequently, the outline of a critical methodology which Lyotard calls "narrative analysis" must be understood as the procedure of critical thought that has finally discarded — as patently "archaic, and fatally outmoded" — an earlier procedure of the dialectic which is based upon a dualistic model of knowledge. The motivation behind Lyotard's critique of Marxism is both personal and historical: personal in that it stems from his own idealism in the early years corresponding to his participation in the *Socialisme ou barbarie* group, and with the writings around the period of *Libidinal Economy* (1971); and "historical," but only in the sense of "the historical moment," what Lyotard calls the "balance sheet" that shows how the critical model of Marxism has become incorporated, absorbed, or "recuperated" into the programming language of capitalism itself as one of its internal perspectives or poles of attraction. As Lyotard writes: "Everywhere, the critique of political economy (the subtitle of Marx's *Das Capital*) and its correlate, the critique of alienated society, are used in one way or another as aids in programming the system."[31] Recalling Lyotard's metaphor of a chess-game, the failure of Marxist critique can be assessed from the perspective of strategy. Its mode of conflict or "agonistics" is so well known to the adversary that it can no longer be determined as a "good move," that is, one that is likely to win the contest over the social bond. What Lyotard is calling into question here is the principle of dualism upon which all Marxian thought is founded: first, the dualistic principle of *conflict* itself (understood as opposition, struggle, or war); second, the assumption that it is only from a true place of "opposition" to the social whole one is placing in question that knowledge can become effectively "critical," that is, which can enter into conflict with the dominant institutions of culture that have been shaped by the "performative" regimes of late-capitalist societies.

On a practical level, this last assumption concerns the existence of a subject who occupies a position that is external to the interests of capital in order to launch an effective critique against these interests. (This subject is an expression of the classical dualistic structure of Marxist critical knowledge, which is why its existence can be posited without referring, as of yet, to any actual historical subject-group.) For example, the position of the proletariat is "external" to the interests in capitalism in the sense that this subject would gain nothing from the current society's maintenance, or even the improvement of its social and economic institutions, under the criteria of "justice." This criteria informs Marx's rejection of liberal humanist political emancipation, which Marx called the final form of emancipation *within* the existing social order, but accused of not achieving total or human emancipation, since it leaves all class-bound contradictions intact, and simply denies them or pushes them to an unconscious level of society.[32]

> The state abolishes, after its own fashion, the distinctions established by *birth, rank, education, occupation,* when it decrees that birth, social rank, education, occupation are *non-political* distinctions; when it proclaims, without regard to these distinction, that every member of society is an *equal* partner in popular sovereignty. However, far from abolishing these *effective* differences, it [the State] only exists in so far as they are presupposed.[33]

Here Marx is implicitly ascribing the presence of unequal differences within the civil society to the ideology of the state-form, which depends upon their continuation for its own form of sovereignty. The presence of discrimination and prejudice gives the state "something to do" as well as a principle for expressing its sovereignty over other competing institutions such as the family or religion. If this appears as a contradiction — on the one hand, the state encourages inequalities and, on the other hand, goes about its business of declaring them "non-political" or unlawful — it is because Marx discovered it to be the principle of contradiction upon which the liberal state is founded. After all, a society in which there were no competing private interests would be a society that no longer required a state "to rule" over these interests; therefore, it is always in the best interest of the state itself that there be conflict between the various groups and identities that compose its sphere of influence (or *dominion*) and, in those cases where there is none, to stimulate the creation of new conflicts as the principle of its own sovereignty over competing institutions.

Marx remained "anti-Hegelian" in that he refused the possibility of mediation, since two ideas of the "Good" cannot be become regulative of the same social totality. As Hegel had shown earlier in his commentary on Sophocles' *Antigone* in *The Phenomenology of Mind*, two notions of the Good cannot exist within the same social totality without entering into contradiction, a contradiction that concludes by the further act of self-cancellation, or sublimation. Thus, spirit cannot suffer contradiction without suiciding itself, just as Antigone and Creon come to mutual self-destruction at the conclusion of the play. However, Marx adds, this notion of "contradiction" is still too abstract when it is conceived philosophically, since it subscribes to a form of illusion which is the inner consistency of reason itself (as *spirit*) and the extrinsic or "contingent" nature of contradiction. Hegel asserts that the essential nature of reason (spirit, mind) is the removal of all contingent accidents, that is, all forms of contradiction. What if, Marx replies, the essential nature of Reason is not spirit unified within itself, but rather the extraneous and multiple forms of "contradiction"? In other words, what if "logical contradiction" was simply the most abstract expression of the *real* division that determines the nature of the social bond? Thus, Marx reverses the Hegelian image of reason, or rather, wagers that the essence of reason is contradiction itself; the strategic point is to make contradiction real and thus to found a new form of rationality which erases the "false image" (or ideological distortion) that is latent within the abstraction of logical or philosophical reason.

In Marx's later critique of the liberal construction of political emancipation, *On the Jewish Question,* he further argues that the emancipation of particularities (or social identities) does not achieve a point of human emancipation (that is, man as a "species-being"), because it remains abstract, and leaves intact the fundamental contradictions that determined the inequality in the first place. For Marx, of course, the fundamental contradiction is situated in the division of labor, and the inequalities of race, ethnicity, and gender are secondary effects of this primal form of inequality; only by rectifying this primary injustice can all the secondary inequalities be adequately addressed. Otherwise, by declaring certain particularities and social identities to be equal with others, but then leaving all the barriers and prejudices that effectively determine real inequality intact, one ends with an "abstract" and essentially lifeless notion of equality that will continue to haunt the political sphere, *which even today remains a valid observation concerning the problem of equality in late-democratic societies.* In a certain sense, this "disavowal" or contradiction is responsible for creating the critical conditions for early theories associated with the "hermeneutics of suspicion," and more recently, the dialectical form of ideology-critique that takes as its object "the political unconscious" (Jameson), that is, the critical revelation of those real contradictions that undergo repression and can be found in the unconscious processes of cultural and social life.

Phrasing this in a more psychoanalytic manner, that of Lacan, the form of liberal or political emancipation merely *forecloses the real contradictions from the social symbolic order.* Yet, as Lacan cautioned, what is often foreclosed from the symbolic *always returns in the real.* This is one possible explanation why, for example, the relative success of gay rights in certain modern institutions (such as in the university or in the courts) is often accompanied by the shock and horror of atrocities committed against homosexuals in the larger society, usually taking place at the "periphery" of society such as the desolate stretch of a rural highway, that is, in places that are far from any institutional "enclosures" (what Foucault called *les enfermements*). Thus, liberal emancipation either blinds itself to its own inherent contradictions, or limits the sphere of equality and the representation of *access* to a highly rarified social space (such as the modern university); and finally, to the certain privileged subjects who serve as symbolic representatives of a class (or "species" to use Marx's original designation) often at the price of disavowing the quantitative reality of those who live in a place where equality is definitely not the case. These symbolic representatives are defined by anthropologist Jean-Loup Amselle as the "social actors" who can mostly be found *inside* late-democratic institutions and thus the form of cultural identification they enact is predicated on the rise of the modern media. As a result, Amselle writes, henceforth "for a culture to *become a culture*, it must now have the capacity to interest certain social actors and only if the latter are successful in projecting it before the political and social scene of *recognition*."[34] However, this performative or symbolic form of "recognition" itself sometimes represents a contradiction that recalls Marx's original criticism in the sense that these "social actors" do not *necessarily* have any real ties to the group they supposedly represent, and it is the performativity of "cultural identification" itself that often supplants the real social or political basis of a collective tie. "Yet without such ties," Amselle argues, "there is no culture, no society."[35]

For Marx, of course, the true principle of identification rested on the division of classes, or more precisely, on the conscious experience of a political subject *who knows* that society is not a unified totality, but rather fundamentally divided, and that the "state of all knowledge" (including culture, history, morality) is only representative of one part of society in such a way that this subject's own knowledge is effectively non-existent as a perspective that is maintained and reproduced by dominant social and cultural institutions. The classical proletarian subject witnesses on a daily basis the *absence* of his or her own experience in the representations of culture and history; or rather, discovers this experience to be represented in a distorted form that is filtered through the imaginary of another dominant class. In Marx, therefore, "theory" or "theoretical knowledge" (that is, the "theory of political economy") must always have a character of certainty, that is, *of something that happens to a subject,* even though this knowledge cannot find its representation in a dominant discourse (for example, the sanctioned official or representative discourses of culture and history). Marx defined his knowledge as a "science" (*Wissenschaft*), and not as "ideology," — which is to say that it was not a "philosophy"— because a specifically Marxist reason appeals to a "subject of certainty" as the ultimate guarantor of its truth. An original Marxist perspective, therefore, is founded upon the absolute "heterogeneity" that lies within the principle of knowledge itself, and upon a "subject of certainty" who henceforth bears witness to a repressed knowledge that refers to a completely "other" experience of the same social totality. (As an aside, one can see here the original Marxist inspired critical subject of historical feminism, and one can even trace the tradition of feminist discourse to its early Marxist influences.)

However, the above experience is not simply one "perspective" that is buried or hidden in the first and could be accommodated through some type of mediation (hermeneutic or consciousness-raising, representative or democratic), but rather the critical consciousness of the subject who rises up and enters into conflict with the total organization of knowledge (and, indeed, with the principle of "Life" itself). Thus, the principle of dualism one finds at the basis of Marx's political economy can be formulated as follows: *only "real" oppositions are critical and properly theoretical; all "false" oppositions are inevitably recuperated, since they in fact were expressions that already belonged to the system itself as one of its opposing poles.* In the latter case, the appearance of the opposition to social totality was unfounded and thus only appeared as such, but was actually a "blind-alley" or an ideological expression of the system's attempt to pose its contrary in the form of its own internal presupposition (its "Other").

As we have already noted, it is precisely this unresolved or archaic image of dualism that Lyotard defines today as fatally "out-moded." As he writes concerning the opposition between a purely functional or positivistic knowledge vs. a purely critical or "reflexive" knowledge:

> I find this partition solution unacceptable. I suggest that the alternative it attempts to resolve, but only reproduces, is no longer relevant for the societies with which we are concerned and that the solution itself is still caught within a type of oppositional thinking that is out of step with the most vital modes of postmodern knowledge.[36]

Consequently, as Lyotard writes:

> the social foundation of the principle of division, or class struggle, was blurred to the point of losing all its radicality; we cannot conceal the fact that the critical model in the end lost its theoretical standing and was reduced to the status of a 'utopia' or 'hope,' a token protest raised in the name of man or reason or creativity, or again of some social category — such as the Third World or the students — on which is conferred *in extremis* the improbable function of critical subject.[37]

What Lyotard is referring to in both of the above statements, or rather condemnations, is the critical subjects that are associated with the post-1960s in first world industrialized countries. In many cases, the changes in class identification have led to an "abstract" or "academic" Marxism that we often see in the university today, in which considerations of class and origin, social solidarity, and actual interests are effectively split from a discursive position (narrative) or representation, what Lyotard calls a "language game." Habermas himself makes a similar observation in the conclusion of *Legitimation Crisis*, when he writes that the "partiality of reason [i.e., ideology] just as little justifies the retreat to a Marxistically embellished orthodoxy, which today can lead at best to the establishment without argument of sheltered and politically ineffective subcultures."[38] What is implied in both judgments is that the dominant critical subject who emerges in this period (and afterwards) does not attain a true image of conflict, since its knowledge is not rooted (which is one of the meanings of the term "radical") in the division of labor and class struggle; therefore, the critical model it employs is not theoretically extrapolated from a completely different experience of the same social totality. As a result, the "knowledge" that this critical subject extrapolates from its own experience, as Lyotard says, loses its authentic "theoretical standing."

By saying that "when the critical model lost its theoretical standing and was reduced to the status of 'utopia' and 'hope,'" Lyotard is addressing the situation whereby the critique of Political Economy becomes "mythic" in procedure, and in this it has much more in common with religious narratives, or "utopian" narratives of an organic society (both of which have frequented Marxist discourse throughout the twentieth century). That is to say, its means of narrative legitimation flows upstream to a source (or origin), rather than downstream as part of an ongoing "project"; or which amounts to the same procedure, the notion of a Marxist project has itself become speculative in its method of authorizing truth, even to the point of becoming metaphysical in form. We might notice, for example, that today many Marxist critiques legitimate their knowledge by means of a procedure of "close reading," that is, by referring up-stream to Marx's "text" in order to authorize its representation of "critical knowledge." It is precisely this procedure that Lyotard identifies by the term "narrative," which again does not refer to a *genre* but rather to a *mode* of authorization (following Gerard Genette's earlier division of these two terms) as well as to a chain of addressees that can be identified by a common "language game."[39]

When I suggested above that the contemporary Marxist form of knowledge is "metaphysical" in procedure, I am employing this term in its original Aristotelian sense, which designates the "first *book* of the physics," the book of first principles which provide the "frame," so to speak. Is this not the position of authority that defines "the text of Marx" today? Consequently, all subsequent statements must refer back to in order to be authorized as consistent with the first principles outlined in Marx's own writings. This procedure would even allow for some of these principles to be rectified, perhaps others subsequently abandoned (such as the subject of the proletariat, or even the primacy of the concept of class itself as in the case of Weber); however, the requirement for either argument would inevitably have to refer back to "the text of Marx," even though this text no longer designates Marx and Engel's writings alone, but rather the tradition of Marxist discourse. In both cases, the form of critical knowledge has taken on a narrative mode of legitimation, one that assumes the form of a meta-language. Critical concepts must be "rectified" in the terms of their original source — they must continue to reproduce the "text of Marx" — only then are they authorized to interpret empirical reality. As a result, one observation we might make is that many Marxist analyses today spend a great deal of time and effort dealing with what could be called the "states of exception" that now belong to the original Political Economy, that is, precisely those empirical realities that appear aberrant or which exceed the original "frame" that Marx provided.

By the above statements I am not necessarily rejecting the concepts found in Marx's materialist critique, nor implying that they have no pertinence for de-scribing the current social and economic reality. That would be absurd, and would even contradict my own citations of Marx's earlier analysis in many passages of this report. I am simply suggesting that the form of the critical within much of contemporary Marxist discourse is itself narrative or even epic in form, following Lyotard's original definition, and thus the very conflict that this discourse performs today may no longer be *grounded* on the reality of a *differend* between knowledge and society. Concluding my brief (and no doubt inadequate) commentary on the Marxist form of the critical, perhaps the time is coming for a revolution in this knowledge which is comparable to the revolution enacted by seventeenth century science, when scientific knowledge was no longer legitimated by "the text of Ar-istotle," but rather by a new procedure which found its referent in the real. But then, wouldn't this simply be to follow the very gesture of the later Marx himself — to purify "critique" of any residue or language of philosophical narrative (hence, the overcompensation represented by the turn to a scientific framework in *Das Kapital*)? In our own contemporary situation, such a procedure would enact "A Return to Marx" (*sans* "Marx"); however, such a return would not necessarily be effected by the faculty located in English departments today, since the critical capacity and expert knowledge in "reading and interpreting the text of Marx" may no longer be a primary requirement for the new *Political Economy*.

At this point let us turn to our second example of a meta-narrative of the "the critical," the postmodern. Rightly or wrongly, this strategy has been associated in the United States with the writings of Derrida, particularly the writings from the period of the early 1970s such as the essay "Structure, Sign, and Play within the Human Sciences" where a certain strategy of structure and play is clearly proposed in what could be called "the manifesto of deconstruction."[40] However, it would be much more accurate to identify the writings of Julia Kristeva, specifically, *The Revolution in Poetic Language* (1984), as the primary influence in this regard even if contemporary theories do not in fact explicitly avow this influence any longer.[41] Her book was read widely in classrooms from the early 1980s onward and the argument offers a blueprint of sorts concerning how to make revolution with *a language*. There we find the concrete prescriptions concerning how to "link" poetic transgression to symbolic institutions of society and culture through the intermediary of a certain revolutionary practice of writing. At the same time, Kristeva's argument already prepares the way for the de-legitimation of the "text" (and of the narrative form in particular) and even language per se as privileged sites of transgressive or semiotic performativity, since language and textuality are clearly bound to the symbolic, or to what Kristeva redefines as the *thetic*. Consequently, in order to be truly effective, critical practice must re-open the symbolic determination of language (the "order of the Signifier") to the semiotic or pre-symbolic organization of the body; not, however, the body as it is already determined by the symbolic institutions of society (as already castrated or subjugated to a position within the family, or within the political economy of gender identifications), but rather the vocalized and poetically charged body of desire which appears as the *dis-organized organization of the drives* (the semiotic *khora*) — that is, the body such as it is prior to the moment of "interpellation" by the symbolic order of castration.

The importance of Kristeva's argument lies in having offered a manner of linking a generalized notion of play (transgression) and a practical or political subject: the subject of sexual identity, which has emerged lately in first world societies, particularly the United States, as the new representative of the critical subject. Thus, an alternative image to the postmodern or the "deconstructionist" has emerged more recently around the body as a site of symbolic contestation and "performance" (particularly the critical subject of "queer theory" which has become associated with the work of Judith Butler).[42] But here again, this image of the critical agency of the de-regulation of gender and "sexed identity" that binds the body to its symbolic designation is based on the same principle: that this "performativity of gender" (its de-regulation from the symbolic) will produce lasting and profound effects in the dominant institutions that fundamentally determine sexuality and gender (marriage, heterosexual ideology) although, in actuality, there is no evidence that this will in fact ever occur. The subject this strategy is bound to is *the subject of the unconscious*; hence, the final term of this process is inevitably suspended, left to chance, if not foreclosed altogether (or, more accurately, "disavowed").

This has been one of the more dominant criticisms of the "transgressive" character of postmodern theories that privilege the "playful" constructions of textuality and form, the hybrid constructions of *image* and *text* as, in fact, enacting highly critical interventions into the symbolic institutions of society. But again, the coherence of this "critical strategy" must invest itself in the principle of a structure, first of all, and the primacy of language or discourse as containing the grounding principle of all other structures). Postmodern theories must base their idea of critical agency on the belief that the principle of "play," that is, the de-regulation and creative transformation of signs and of signifying practices on one level of structure (that of the text, of culture, or of the body for example) will register important effects on a much deeper level of the "social symbolic." This, in some ways, is analogous to a mythical procedure of consensus that performs this critical function by a kind of magical leap of faith in its symbolic efficacy.

The problem with this strategy, as Fredric Jameson and Slavoj Žižek have each pointed out on different occasions, is that the critical subject can have absolutely no knowledge of exactly what kind of "effects" his or her semiotic peregrinations will have in "the Symbolic," and consequently, this gesture cannot in any way be defined as "political" *as such*, since the term demands a clear relationship between the "act" and a "subject of representation" (traditionally, a collective subject). The "postmodern theorist," on the other hand, seeks only to liberate *a language* in the blind hope that this will engender effects in other semiotic regions that are linked together in the form of a signifying chain (politics, economy, sexuality, ethnicity). *Yet, to liberate the Signifier is not an act that can be defined within the genre of politics, but rather belongs to the genre of poetry.*

To refer briefly to Jameson's argument from *Postmodernism, or The Cultural Logic of Late-Capitalism* (1991), the strategy predicated on the play of representations is in effect a symptomatic solution at best, which is why he demotes the strong meaning attached to "play" (parody) as merely "pastiche," turning the transformative potential of inter-textuality into a simple patchwork of signs.[43] Jameson often employs Althusser's notion that such a strategy represents, on the level of the real subject, the form of an "imaginary resolution of the real contradictions" that structure the social bond through the position of the subject, which is that elementary point of symbolic contact, what Lacan had earlier defined as the *point de caption* (or "quilting point") where the living being is sutured to a symbolic order through the medium of a signifier (for example, a name).[44] The subject is "interpellated" (hailed) by the symbolic order, or in Althusser's phrasing, by the ideological institutions of society (the family, the school, the state, and so on).[45] Metaphorically speaking, the subject is pinned down like the butterflies under glass in the famous passage from Conrad's *In the Heart of Darkness.*

However, Althusser also argued (rather strenuously, in fact) that *there is no such thing as a subject outside an order of interpellation* (i.e., ideology). The existence of a "subject" is facilitated by the order of interpellation in which a subject appears like a rabbit through the looking glass, and which effectively gives *a subject (that is, a signifier or a name) to a subject*, which is the condition of symbolic identity — or as Lacan had earlier formulated this, it is the condition whereby *the subject can become a signifier for another subject* (that is, where the name can acquire meaning, consistency, recognition, and symbolic value). Interpellation refers to that process which makes it possible for the subject to be "for others," on the basis of which there is also the possibility of being "for oneself." Where there is no interpellation, there is no subject either. Consequently, the fantasy of non-interpellated subject which is frequently proposed as the political desire of the postmodern critic, that is, of a subject that is purely "in-itelf" (*an sich*), or a language without or beyond the order of interpellation, can be likened to the brilliant stripes on the butterfly's wings in the Borgesian fable of Choang-tsu's dream. As for the real butterfly (that is, Choang-tsu when he is awake and appears as a subject for "others"), he remains pinned under the glass.[46]

This is a good illustration of the "imaginary resolution of real contradictions," according to Jameson's critique of the postmodern critical subject. Sooner or later this subject must inevitably wake up. Usually this occurs when he or she stops "writing," even for a moment, and glances up from the page. More frequently, however, this rude awakening occurs as the result of some encounter with the *real* order of interpellation (at work, school, when applying for a credit card or a car loan, receiving a rejection notice, upon being snubbed by a more famous colleague, etc. — the possibilities for such encounters are endless). This awakening *to the Symbolic* refers to an event that Lacan once humorously recounted under the notion of *tuché*, of being "knocked up," that is, of finding oneself, even at the deepest point of interiority, always already impregnated with the "Other."[47] The result of repeated or frequent "awakenings" usually leads to what could be called the *disenchantment of the postmodern subject*, which is often remarked by a growing feeling of malaise or depression, a turn to cynicism and irony — in general, all the traits that belong to a certain fatigue or "slackening," as Lyotard diagnosed. The final outcome of this tendency is to divorce completely the idea of emancipation one carries forward on the level of the text from any hope of ever achieving the desired effects of social and political transformation, which seems so remote as to not be worth considering any longer. Accordingly, perhaps it would be necessary to return to Sartre's concept of "bad faith" in order to understand the process whereby two contradictory ideas can be entertained at the same time, although under the sign of "negation." The revolution in poetry, I would argue therefore, has produced two subjective tendencies in the postmodern critical genre: cynicism and *glossolalia* ("speaking in tongues").

The notion of the ideal form of the social bond that is often represented by these postmodern strategies is founded on the most acute contradiction, since in fact it refers to a place that is purportedly *beyond* or *before* the social symbolic order," a place that is relatively free from "an order of interpellation" (i.e., ideology) that can be likened to the position of the dream in the psychoanalytic topography. Moreover, this ideal place is already dependent on position of another, which bears the characteristic of being relatively autonomous, that is to say, which can already be found at a certain distance from normative social space. The position of "the text" (of writing) was the first representative of this "other place" where identity could be constructed (or transgressed) according to the creative rules of what Lyotard called a different phrase regimen ("poetic," "literary," or "para-textual"). More recently, as I suggested above, the subject's body itself has become a "text" which can therefore be more plastic to different manners of phrasing, as in the case of "queer theory" where linguistic or semiotic performativity has become the creative principle of critical social constructivism.[48] However, in the final analysis both strategies are fundamentally speculative. Why speculative and not political? Using again Lyotard's definition of narrative procedures, we can say that both the critical narratives of post-structuralism and queer theory are not exactly mythic in procedure in the sense we have argued above concerning many contemporary Marxist narratives, since they do not often refer upstream to a source for the narrative form of their authorization. On the contrary, they seem to resemble political narrative in the sense that they ultimately refer downstream and bind the "subject to an ongoing project." However, as in the case of contemporary academic Marxism, we must ask whether this direction is merely formal, which is to say, is based on the appearance (or simulacrum) of an "ongoing project," which has become merely discursive.

I am echoing Lyotard's claim that in this case the critical has been reduced, in procedure and in form, to a "language game," and the nature of the *differend* — understood as the unspeakable conflict, or underlying issue (*pragma*) of a critical subject of knowledge — is subsumed under a language of pure gesture, *whereby the differend appears in the performative "act" of a subject who invokes it or claims to represent it in discourse.* As a result, its critical sense is effectively transformed into a formula that can be invoked by any subject who repeats it, and which might help to explain the multiplicity of such subjects today, all of which lay claim to the representation of a *differend* with the given social bond, whether this refers to the underlying issue of race, ethnicity, gender (or sex), colonial or post-colonial order. The success or failure of this formula's "performativity" in representing the position of an actual *differend* for society, however, will often be dependent on other factors that cannot be known beforehand, and here I recall Amselle's observation that this success or failure for the registering of this conflict is very much contingent upon the success or failure of various "social actors" in creating a symbolic form that is identifiable and open to repetition. Amselle writes, "one could hold that identity is the agreement on the very subject of disagreement....

The ability to name, to give a first name [to this subject of disagreement] is of course essential; it reveals the rifts and the relations of forces at work within a given social field."[49] (In this text, I have employed Lyotard's term in order to underline the generic quality of this act of naming.) Theorists Slavoj Žižek and Ernesto Laclau have both addressed this situation from a Lacanian framework as essential to a notion of political conflict that falls outside the limits of signification (i.e., the symbolic order); for both, this "outside" takes the form of an "empty signifier," whether that of the empty category of the "universal" (Žižek) or of the possibility of politics itself which very much depends on "the production of empty signifiers."[50] However, one would be wrong to see in this situation the conditions for a kind of free-for-all in which the chance of the political can be compared to winning a game of charades.

In all the above arguments, the existence or reality of the *differend* seems to be very much dependent on its production via signification and seems to be nothing without it, owing its very existence, on the one hand, to the success of certain "social actors," and on the other, to the production and citation of "empty signifiers." But then, this all seems quite arbitrary and leaves the question "who decides" to some unknown power — perhaps the inscrutable agency of power itself — that selects certain identities and certain conflicts as candidates for signification, opening us to the possibility that there are an equal number left in the shadows in a state of dumbness and inarticulation, in suspense like the picture of the damned in Virgil's *Aeneid* "extending their arms for the other shore." The virtue of an earlier understanding of Marxist theory was in the certainty that there was only one *differend* that deserved the dignity of the name, the real *differend* produced by the inequality of the classes. Or as Althusser once wrote, "For us, the 'real' is not a theoretical slogan; the real is the real object that exists independently of its knowledge — but which can only be defined by its knowledge."[51] Today things are very much changed and *differend* now has many names. However, this exposes us to the most dizzying problem, which I will address in the next section around the formulation of the ethical: the problem of discerning whether the *differend* itself precedes its signification, or whether it is simply the effect that is produced in the manner of a slogan, that is, by the almost ritualistic citation of one of its many names.

I will conclude my observations on this old debate (or "dueling meta-narratives") concerning which subject (or "strategy") is one that best represents the critical condition by which knowledge becomes transformative (i.e., producing real, not abstract, opposition). We might discern in Jameson's earlier commentary on Lyotard the makings of a fundamental opposition in the critical models that are dominant today and which are struggling for "hegemony" over the proper form of critical knowledge, or rather, over the question of which "meta-narrative" will in the final instance represent the real *differend* between knowledge and society. This opposition can be illustrated by pointing to a basic alternative that will locate a critical model on one side of this divide or the other. The first model would accept the fact that capitalism is here to stay and, therefore, would seek out manners of developing new forms of resistance and new critical subjects. For example, despite the Marxist leanings of many of its leading representatives, "Cultural Studies" can be located on the former side in the sense that it promotes an aesthetic and cultural knowledge that might allow us finally, as Jameson himself suggests with regard to Postmodern architecture, to "learn from Las Vegas" (Robert Venturi).[52] The second critical model, primarily associated with Marxist thought, would never cede or capitulate to the glories of Capital, but would continue to believe in a version of an end of Capitalism first prophesied by Marx in *The Grundrisse*. Accordingly, Jameson's argument is that many French thinkers of the post-1968 generation, such as Lyotard, Deleuze and Guattari, and even Foucault, can be placed on the first side of this divide; while Jameson's own position is clearly "utopian" and can be placed on the other.

Jameson's preference is fairly transparent and his image of critical knowledge can be illustrated most strikingly in the following passage:

> On a political and social level, indeed, narrative in some sense has always meant the negation of capitalism: on the one hand, for instance, narrative knowledge is here opposed to scientific or "abstract" as precapitalism to capitalism proper. Yet — as became clear when the narrative legitimations of science itself were evoked at their moment of crisis and dissolution — narrative also means something like *teleology. The great master-narratives here are those that suggest that something beyond capitalism is possible, something radically different*; and they also 'legitimate' the praxis whereby political militants seek to bring that radically different future social order into being.[53]

In this response to Lyotard, however, Jameson could be accused of nostalgia for the "great master-narratives," and his argument could be seriously challenged on many different levels. What does he mean [when he writes] that, "narrative has always meant the negation of capitalism"? Is "negation" meant here in a creative or Hegelian sense of the progression toward Absolute Knowledge, or in terms of a communitarian sense of narrative as restoring a previous social bond that was dissolved by capitalist relationships of exchange? Can the comparison offered between narrative knowledge and scientific knowledge and pre-capitalist and capitalist societies be supported or even rigorously applied to the actual history of pre-industrial and post-industrial societies, or to the emergence of scientific knowledge from the seventeenth century onward?

Finally, in saying that some form of teleology is necessary to "legitimate" the praxis of militants and revolutionaries — *but is this not also the mode of legitimation for the praxis of terror as well?* — does this not simply reproduce a tendency on the part of first world intellectuals, which is the confusion of a certain narrative of "universal history" with the actual political struggles that were taking place in the third world during this period of the 1980s, in Central America and Africa in particular. Is this not the tendency of Protestant intellectuals of the *center* who continue to create heroic narratives about *the periphery*, narratives whose symbolic meaning was always directed back to the core as an "imaginary resolution of real contradictions"? According to Lyotard's criticism cited above, Jameson's own prescriptions could be described as representing a spirit of "utopianism" and "hope." In the end, it is Jameson's unwillingness to consider giving up the idea of master-narrative that pits him in an irreparable opposition to Lyotard's major argument. More precisely, this concerns an unwillingness to sacrifice the dialectic in its modern form, the methodology of which is now hermeneutic, and whose primary object continues to be the "great master-narrative" of *Universal History.*

If in the previous part we discovered a certain "nihilism" that was present in the Kantian pretension of the "autonomy of reason" (embodied in the philosophy faculty), then we might find the complimentary, albeit postmodern, expression of nihilism is present in the "purity" of the critical faculty today. As we have just shown in the case of the earlier critical narrative of postmodernism we discovered a desire that is called political, but is founded on a belief in the possibility of a "non-interpellated subject," that is, a subject who is political in the sense of being purely "for itself" and thus is given the power to resist any social designation (or name) originating from the perspective of the "Other" (or in psychoanalytic terms, the "symbolic order"). However, because this movement is founded on an abolition of "who the subject is for the Other as well as for others" (whether we are speaking here of the subject of gender, race, ethnicity, or sexual identity), this critical strategy can be associated with the conflicts that surround what has been called "identity politics."

Here again I recall what Lacan once said concerning Choang-tsu, who dreamed he was a butterfly: "In fact, it is when he was a butterfly that he apprehended one of the roots of his identity — that he was, and is, in his essence, that butterfly who paints himself with his own colors — and it is because of this that, in the final instance, he is Choang-tsu."[54] As in this passage, what keeps Choang-tsu from going mad is that he can only apprehend himself as a butterfly "who paints himself with his own colors" while he is Choang-tsu, that is, "when he is awake and Choang-tsu for others, and is caught in their butterfly net."[55] If he should try to become the butterfly by annihilating Choang-tsu, then he loses the possibility of both identities. Likewise, if the critical strategy underlying the politics of identity is in fact a desire to withdraw to a "safe space" where one can paint oneself with one's own colors (in short, to create one's own identity), then this strategy is in danger of losing both the possibility of identity itself and of being a subject "for others" (which is fundamental to any collective politics), and by this I do not simply mean one's own kind (or *semblable*). It is for this reason that we might wonder if the final term of this strategy is nothing less than the *annihilation of the subject of the political itself,* what Deleuze calls "a line of abolition" which draws in its path the future possibility of collective or social desire as well.[56] It is because of this that earlier on I identified this critical strategy as perhaps a new form of cynicism.

On the other hand, in the case of Marxist inspired models of the critical we have shown the demand for the critical subject who is purified of any interest (assuming that power is not a form of private interest). However, since the Marxist representation of "critical knowledge" has become paradigmatic in the academy since the 1960s, the early schism between partial or political emancipation and total or human emancipation has returned many times in the constant impeachments of this or that critical subject (for example, "the first world feminist," or the "post-colonial cosmopolitan critic"). We might conclude from the long history of the "impeachments" of the critical that it may be the severity of the demand for what Wallerstein calls "*an ideal type*" that structures the conflict that is internal to the Marxist critical model itself.[57] (In the United States, for example, given the appropriation of this critical model by feminist and minority critics, this trial and inevitable impeachment of this or that representative "social actor," to again use the term coined by anthropologist Jean-Lupe Amselle, has reached a nearly hyperbolic intensity.) The problem we must inevitably encounter at some point is that *this ideal can belong to no living subject,* delimited by interest and by enjoyment (bound up with the problem of life, not as a general problem, but as a living particular) and, thus, it is this *demand for the ideal* (or, "the universal"). This leads us to the return of the contradiction that structures the subject of political desire itself, and which gradually brings with it the depression, malaise and cynicism that inevitably results from the repeated betrayals of this subject's desire for *a pure political reason.*

*Gregg Lambert*

### III(d) *Who bears witness for the witness? On the ethical turn*

After the advent of structuralism and semiotics in the early 1970s transformed the discourse and basic methodologies in many Humanities' disciplines, many people began to speak of a "linguistic turn" in critical knowledge. Partly, this notion of a "turn" recalls the influential description of a "paradigm shift" in Kuhn's *The Structure of Scientific Revolutions*.[58] Today the signs are everywhere of a second turn, an "ethical turn" of knowledge. We might see indications of this, for example, in Lyotard's own discourse, and his call for "small narratives" (*les petites recits*), or in the turn to overt religious subjects and to ethical discourse in the fields of philosophy and theory. The early influence of Jewish philosopher Emmanuel Levinas is exemplary of this shift, and his categories have become more pronounced in the writing of other philosophers. Among other signs of this, one could list the recent series of works by Derrida on the subject of religion, followed by the publication of John D. Caputo's *The Prayers and Tears of Jacques Derrida*; finally, the recent emergence of British "radical orthodoxy" in the fields of American continental philosophy and religion.[59]

Outside these fields, I could also refer to developments in literary criticism and historiography, such as recent post-colonial theories that are less concerned with forging a new image of the deliberative potential of cultural forms, in the sense of binding the subject of culture to an ongoing political project (Lyotard), than with recounting the episodes and events of past wrongs under the world shadows of European colonialism or American imperialism, or of the current impact of the globalized market in the third and fourth worlds. By "the ethical turn," therefore, what I am suggesting here is the possibility of a certain modulation of the critical genre itself, where today the concern for "doing justice" has in many ways supplanted earlier objectives of the critical, and which might indicate a new procedure for determining the language game of what had earlier been understood as the task of the modern critic.

In the closing pages of *The Postmodern Condition*, Lyotard himself recommends that because "consensus has become an out-moded and suspect value…we must arrive at an idea and practice of justice that is not linked to that of consensus."[60] According to this prescription, the theoretical genre still takes the form of narrative analysis; however, there is also attached to this procedure a practical subject of knowledge as Lyotard outlines, which would be the subject of "justice." Moreover, consistent with the description that this subject would not occupy the point of "the Universal," the number of language games themselves would be finite and there will be several forms of justice that will emerge as a result of the somewhat "monadic" arrangement of knowledge and power in postmodern societies.

We might imagine that this arrangement has been caused by two dominant factors: first, the rise of global marketplaces and the effect this has had on new distributions of information and knowledge by cyber-technologies and; second, the disorientation of the classical political sphere that has resulted from the fragmentation of a model of "civil society" that was premised on the power of the nation-state to *unify* the conflicting forms of private interest within its own territorial boundaries. We see in both developments the conditions for the decline of an idea of consensus that is predicated on the rational organization of society as a "whole" — since *each society is being organized, it seems, always from the periphery* (that is, from transformations that are taking place elsewhere in globalized markets), and the classical political sphere is always found to be two or three steps behind each transformation in the flow of capital, but more importantly, the flow of information and knowledge required for decision-making (including the decision of the political). This was a principle factor in Lyotard's analysis of the form of knowledge in "computerized societies," which could be redefined at this point to address the flow of knowledge and information in societies tied together through computerized markets or exchanges, as illustrated in the following passage from Thomas L. Friedman's recent study of globalization, *The Lexus and the Olive Tree*:

> There is no question that in the globalization system, where power is more evenly shared between states and Supermarkets, a certain degree of decision-making is moved out of each country's political sphere into the global market sphere, where no one person, country or institution can exert exclusive political control — at least not yet. Think how many times you've heard the expression "The markets say…," "The markets are demanding that…."[61]

This change, as we might have noticed already, will certainly have an effect on what both Jameson and Lyotard (and Habermas) have observed, with a certain foreboding, concerning *"the political question of knowledge."* It will not only have effects on the form of knowledge (that is to say, on its "institutional objectifications" [Jameson] as I have argued concerning the university), but equally important for our current discussion, on the political subject of knowledge (the critical subject, or what Kant had earlier defined as the "pure practical subject of reason"). Consequently, we might rephrase Kant's earlier admonition to this subject in the current situation. Today perhaps the question that defines this subject is no longer "What should I hope for (or desire)?" but rather *Where?"* That is to say, where should I address my desire in the hope that it will become critical or transformative of my current relation to other social desires? How does the whole question of desire become a political concern which presupposes that my desire is not solipsistic, but rather whose origin is in some way collective and bears within it a latent accord or harmony, or what Kant called a "voice" (*Stimmung*)?

The question *Where?* presupposes a disorientation, as I have argued in the preceding section, concerning a distinct place or location in society where the political question of desire takes on a definite voice and even harmony with regard to a particular group. In this moment, the idiosyncratic and solipsistic nature of many desires begins to *harmonize*, using Kant's analogy, and is transformed into a desire-in-common which functions much like a scale that unifies the many voices of desire into one chord. It is only on the basis of this harmony, moreover, that what was formerly regarded as merely private or solipsistic in the expression of desire can suddenly acquire a new collective or political resonance — in short, that the *personal becomes the political*

Each in its own way, modern critical theories have located the place of the political question of knowledge in the position of a displaced or repressed representative of culture, or in the critique of the socially repressive forces that shape personal and social identity such as race, gender, and sexual identity. That is, each has in some way responded to the absence of this question in the political public sphere and, instead, has shown that the place where the relationship between knowledge and society becomes most critical and transformative is effectively "repressed" and is now "unconscious." (Simply put, its location — *Where?* — is unknown.) As a result, what is revealed is that it is in those places where the subject's desires were considered "non-political" (such as preferences in sexuality, matters of cultural taste or pleasure, or considerations of origin or race) — that it is precisely these places where the whole political question of desire is now being organized.

A further development occurs when the modern subject is made responsible, even guilty, for the political question of desire. This constitutes one partial explanation for "the ethical turn," given that this development has occurred more often in first world societies and particularly among a new generation of middle-class intelligentsia who feel most acutely the responsibility for a certain practical subject of ideology (whether this subject is registered in terms of class or racial membership, gender identification, or national sovereignty). The social privilege that this new class enjoys generally, although through no labor of its own but is rather owed to inheritance, has created the conditions for the ethical character that dominates the scene of "the critical" in society today and the demand for "justice" that has gradually replaced the earlier demand for "the political."

We might conclude that any earlier notion of the political, defined as the "narrative that binds a subject to ongoing project of emancipation," has changed sense and direction. It no longer refers to the future, but rather to the past, and the concern for emancipation has become instead an occasion for the expiation of guilt and the acknowledgement of collective responsibility — a discourse of ethics and, properly speaking, not politics.

The situation I am describing is accompanied by no judgment on my part. On the contrary, I am merely reporting of one the possible factors of a "turn to ethics" in the area of critical knowledge. According to a Marxist perspective, however, this turn to an ethical mode must be underscored by the fact that it has taken place most of all in first world institutions, that is, in precisely those places of the world economy where there is the highest concentration of accumulated capital; therefore, the turn of the critical itself into an occasion for collective responsibility rather than deliberative action is, in itself, a telling sign of the nature of the class consciousness behind recent developments in the critical genre. Thus, the most acute critical subjectivity in these societies does not belong to the working classes, which is obvious, but rather to a younger generation of the middle class itself. Here we might be witnessing a certain historical irony if we recall the often-cited prophetic statement from *The Communist Manifesto* that in the creation of a property-less class, the proletariat, the historical bourgeoisie were in fact "producing their own grave-diggers."[62] The irony is that, at least from the perspective of current first world societies, this role (of "grave-digging") has been assumed by the children of the middle-classes themselves, that is, by those who were *biologically and culturally produced* by the bourgeoisie.[63]

One possible explanation for this development, as well as for the frequent identification with a proletariat consciousness that is often performed by the middle class intelligentsia today (and is especially pronounced in first world universities such as in the United States), can be discerned in Wallerstein's observation that a large portion of the modern bourgeoisie have become "property-less" in the sense that they can no longer live off their own profit, but must live off their "rent" (i.e., future income). In short, this class has become a class "indebted" (and debt in a credit society is the new form of enslavement). As Wallerstein writes,

> they cannot translate present income (profit) into future income (rent). That is to say, they cannot one day represent the past off with which their children will live. Not only do they live in the present, but so must their children and their children's children.[64]

This phenomenon is made more even more acute among the children themselves, especially when they find themselves located in economic sectors that are being *de-capitalized* (i.e., "down-sized"), such as in certain departments of the contemporary university, where the former promise of living on one's "rent" is becoming more remote, if not impossible. This creates the conditions for a class consciousness under the traditional term of "proletarianization," which has been applied to the recent political formation of graduate students in universities today, particularly in institutions that continue to draw a higher proportion of their student populations from the upper middle classes. According to Wallerstein, the term "proletariat" actually refers to any economic subject who "only has his labor to offer on the market, and no resources (that is, no past) to fall back upon."[65] This definition does seem to apply to the current situation of graduate students and faculty who can be found in former Humanities departments in the institution, which has become the fundamental basis for the "politicization" of these groups, even unionization of labor as in the case of the teaching assistants at Yale and the University of California. Yet, we must recognize that, for the most part, this new "class struggle" which is being enacted today, mostly by graduate students in contemporary first world universities, is actually a conflict between two different segments of the modern bourgeoisie itself — the struggle between those who can-not live off either their profit or their rent ("the have nots") against those who can ("the haves") and who, in fact, *are performing quite well in the current market.*

Returning to our earlier assessment of the different "moves" (i.e., strategies) that can be said to define the form of the critical today, we might ask whether this last development is consistent with Lyotard's argument for what he describes as "a politics that would respect both the desire for justice and the desire for the unknown."[66] In attempting to construct a practical subject of critical knowledge from Lyotard's prescription, we might ask what would be the practical subject of politics? What would be "the theoretical standing" (in Marx's sense) for the subject of justice? Surreptitiously, with such certainty that we might not have noticed, Lyotard's own explanation of a "loss of consensus" and the submission of all knowledge to "the goals envisioned by a practical subject" itself takes the form of a certain meta-narrative.[67] This is what Jameson critiques in his forward and elsewhere under the name of "postmodernism." It refers to the critical narrative that posits the question concerning the current relation between knowledge and society and, based on the observation concerning how this relationship works today, or how knowledge performs a social bond, comes to several conclusions:

1. the impossibility of consensus;
2. the failure of older meta-narratives;
3. the failure of an older critical model based upon dualism to "resist" this state of affairs;
4. the social "illegitimacy" of the critical function of knowledge according to the new social bond to which knowledge belongs;
5. the submission of every social bond, which are multiple and bear a greater degree of complexity in modern social systems, to the "perfor-mativity" of language games;
6. finally, the fact that there is no possibility that language games and be unified or totalized in a meta-discourse.

This set of observations certainly appears to describe the current state of affairs, or the underlying axioms of the current social bond, as Lyotard claims. And yet, there is also a narrative procedure as well; as Jameson has argued, this occurs when Lyotard's narrative itself attempts to legitimate a new practical subject consistent with the state of knowledge that belongs to *The Postmodern Condition*. Contrary to the terms of Lyotard's own critique of the impossibility of meta-narrative, the problem occurs when Lyotard's denotative statement becomes a prescription for a new practical subject that is the postmodern subject: act in such a way that one's actions take place outside the possibility of any consensus. Even though it reverses the Kantian categorical imperative (i.e., the condition by which a rule becomes a principle of conduct is its universality), Lyotard's ethical prescription becomes categorical nonetheless precisely in its rejection of any possibility for "the Universal." Of course, this subject has no pretension, as it did under the older regime, to assume the role of "the Universal," but rather only legitimates a finite number of "language games" that currently occupy the place of the Humanities in the University, under the general or umbrella term of "critical knowledge."

In many ways, Jameson's criticism of Lyotard is identical to Habermas' earlier critique of Luhmann, and one wonders whether this was in fact the same debate translated by a different set of terms, by a different "language game" that belongs to the United States. As Jameson comments, "the moment when aesthetics gives way to ethics, in which the problem of the postmodern becomes that of one's more fundamental attitude toward a new social formation — the moment, finally, in which what I have called the deeper repressed or buried symbolic narrative of *The Postmodern Condition* comes at length into view."[68] What Jameson is suggesting is that by offering a set of prescriptions which can bind a new practical subject to "a fundamental attitude toward a new social formation," creating an attitude or even *ethos* named "postmodernism," Lyotard's own speculative narrative may have a deeper symbolic function of which he himself is unaware. Of course, this amounts to a charge of a deeper "positivistic" function that serves the practical goals of Capitalism, even though this practical subject is mediated through what Jameson has called the "political unconscious." Althusser put this even more succinctly, although not in response to Lyotard but rather to a tradition of humanism: "Simply put, the recourse to ethics so deeply inscribed in every humanist ideology may play the part of an imaginary treatment of real problems."[69] Therefore, we might ask the following in attempting to discern the critical relationship that this narrative performs: Who benefits from the loss of all consensus? What is the social bond performed by a situation of knowledge which is described as a "heterogeneous" field of "language games" without any possibility of unification or meta-discourse?

Lyotard's description would also become a "meta-narrative" under the condition that it would bind a practical subject to an attitude, a set of behaviors, even to a common *ethos* this subject could be said to share with others. As Jameson has argued, this has been true for a certain postmodern practical subject one finds in the academy today. In rejecting all forms of consensus, this subject seeks out "instabilities" through the procedure of paralogism, and ultimately seeks "to undermine the very framework in which the previous 'normal science' was conducted."[70] Thus, Jameson is in a certain sense correct in saying that Lyotard's solution returns to the earlier solutions to a positivistic function of knowledge offered by Stoicism, Cynicism, Sophism, by the Skeptics and Pyrronists. As Jameson writes:

> The rhetoric in which all this is conveyed is to be sure one of struggle, conflict, the agonic in a quasi-heroic sense; nor must we forget Lyotard's related vision of non-hegemonic Greek philosophy…, as the guerilla war of the marginals, the foreigners, the non-Greek, against the massive repressive order of Aristotle and his successors.[71]

For this reason, however, we might conclude that the alternative critical model that Lyotard offers for *The Postmodern Condition* is possibly the most archaic and philosophical, and *perhaps the least modern of the alternatives we have reviewed in this part.*

On the other hand, Lyotard's use of the term "justice" as a replacement for the term "critical" is important enough here to examine further. Jameson and the Lacanian critic Slavoj Žižek have diagnosed this shift as typical (that is, paradigmatic) of the postmodern "move" from the political to an ethical register of emancipation, or from the horizon of a "real act" as the only true form of justice, to the imaginary horizon of a purely symbolic action, which Jameson calls "proto-political" (or mythic) and Žižek names "virtual" (in association with the transformation in the nature of the Symbolic itself, which has been effected by the new virtual reality technologies of a modern computerized society). Concerning this "postmodern move" and its implications for producing social and political effects (that is, its possibility for intervening or transforming the current social bond), Žižek has written extensively and most critically concerning the above shift that appears to encompass Lyotard's solution. "The political as the domain of appearance," Žižek writes,

> has nothing in common with the postmodern notion that we are entering the era of universalized simulacra in which reality itself becomes indistinguishable from its simulated double.[… ] The key to today's universe of simulacra, in which the Real is less and less distinguishable from its imaginary simulation, lies in the retreat of 'symbolic efficiency.'[72]

In response to both general criticisms, we have to ask if this move to the ethical register is all that Lyotard means here. That is, does this do justice to the concept of *justice* that Lyotard announces as the primary concern of a post-critical knowledge? In order to do this it would first be necessary to recover a sense of this concept and to do some of the work that, for some reason, Lyotard himself did not feel it necessary to perform on this occasion. I will show in what sense the concept of "justice" that Lyotard refers to is, in fact, at the heart of his theory of performativity. In order to demonstrate this, however, we must refer to the work of Emile Benveniste who, it could be argued, is one of the foremost historians of Western institutions. The importance of Benveniste's work is to have added a critical and political, properly genealogical dimension to Saussure's theory of language as a dominant social institution. In fact, through his comparative etymology, Benveniste creates a vivid profile of the ascendancy of Language as a dominant institution in the shaping of political, social, and economic reality. He does this by showing the evolution of forms of speech to nominative realities that determine political institutions. As he writes concerning the frequency of the historical relationship between terms that designate institutions and verbs used in order to denote in one way or another *to say,*

> There is often a close connection between the act of speech and law or rule in so far as they organize certain social functions. In particular, political institutions are sometimes called by terms which involve some specialization of the notion of 'speech' in the direction of authoritative pronouncement. [...] The work of the comparatist can be instructive in determining the point of departure for the terms which denote 'to say' that have become words and names for authority.[73]

The above is true, as we will see, particularly in the case of the notion of "justice" which was originally associated with the act of "swearing an oath."

As Benveniste shows, the concept of justice (*ius*) has evolved alongside two other terms (*thémis* and *díke*) that belong to the Indo-European institution of law, all of which originally designate types of speech, ritually bound forms of utterance, or a specific class of utterances that have a definitive location and social or technical meaning (for example, a marriage vow or the sentence of execution pronounced by a judge). Moreover, the concept of *ius* covered an area of human law (i.e., the laws that govern the relationships internal to the family or between families) and develops in opposition to another type of speech (*fas*) which covers the enunciation of divine law. In his analysis of this concept, however, Benveniste raises the question of the derivation of this notion of law from the act of swearing. "How did this verb come to diverge semantically from the basic noun in such a strange way?"[74]

In seeking to discover the cause of this divergence, Benveniste discovers the basic root of justice in the Iranian formula *yaoš*, which designated the act of purification and thus referred both to a "place" and to the action of "making a place conformable to prescriptions" (i.e., the act of purification according to prescribed actions performed by the participants in a ceremony or other ritual occasion). The etymological meaning of this term reveals the religious sense of justice (the act of purifying or removing pollutants from a particular place or region of society, of cleansing, preparing or sanctifying the social relationships that belong to a place or raising it to a state of the sacred), a sense which still can be found in the uses of justice today (such as "social justice," "environmental justice," or "economic justice"). Yet, is this original religious meaning of the term enough to solve the dilemma announced above, or to cover the secular order of justice relating to human law?

Benveniste shows that the secular meaning of law emerges in the Roman period when the formula for religious purification came to be regularized to extend beyond particular occasions and places (i.e., those associated with religious ritual and with sacred places) and became "formulas for normality." However, this normative and civic function of justice would in no way remove the religious significance associated with "purification," but rather provides civil prescriptions and ordinances with a mythic justification for demanding the observance of rules in prescriptions. For example, why does everyone obey traffic signals and parking signs (at least, most of the time)? One explanation easily comes to mind: chaos, that is, the destruction of the regularity and orderliness that governs the space of the *polis*, even though the experience of this chaos is always speculative in nature, (i.e the "rationalization" of the subject who always obeys traffic signals.

As Benveniste argues, the notion of "justice" (*ius*) originally designates a formula (which could sometimes take the linguistic form of a prescription, or a maxim), since "what is constitutive of 'law' is not doing it but always pronouncing it."[75] It is a formula that, inasmuch as it takes an institutional form, only certain individuals or corporations can enunciate in the sense of giving a formula a performative value, or "force of law." This is where Benveniste locates the derivation of an abstract concept of law from the original meaning of "swearing an oath." It is in the Roman period in which this connection is established, Benveniste argues, that "a new chapter in the notion of law is opened."[76] As Marx later discovered, there is a properly ideological dimension to the institution of certain corporate notions of "purity," "cleanliness," "order," and "equity" just to name a few subjacent notions that belong to the ritual space of justice. This dimension appears, on the one hand, when these notions are bound to formulas that take on a normative or universal prescriptive function and; on the other hand, when these formulas are located in institutions and certain subjects who are endowed, structurally, with the privileged site of locution, that is, of the "subject who says the rule" (*iu-dex*).

Here I will skip to the conclusion of Benveniste's rich analysis of this concept. His analysis separates the content or the text of the law itself to the purely formal or procedural event of the law's enunciation, its performative character. It seems that there is an abyss that separates these two dimensions of the law, an abyss which is echoed later in Kant's separation between pure reason and practical reason, or finally in Lyotard's strict division of prescriptive and denotative phrasing. It is this separation that gives the notion of law its performative and secondary character, inasmuch as the subject invested with its enunciation is always in some way "citing" a previous instance of discourse. It is here that the connection between law and oath is clearly underlined:

> The taking of an oath requires two persons: the one who *praeit verbis*, who 'precedes with words,' who pronounces the *ius*, and the one who really *iurat*, who repeats the formula, which is called the *ius iurandum* or 'the formula to be formulated,' that which must be repeated after the person '*qui praeit*'' has pronounced it, the formula fixing in stereotyped and time-honored terms the text of the engagement.[77]

The fundamental problem, which Benveniste outlines for us, and which Lyotard locates as the problem of knowledge, is that the notion of law, as it has historically evolved in Western institutions, has no foundation other than the power of the one who *praieit verbis* (who "*pronounces the ius*"). Within the very concept of justice, there is the presence of the "witness" (*the arbiter*) whose judgment cannot be verified or founded, the presence of which would create the possibility of what Lyotard would later call *le differend*. According to Benveniste, there is no way to establish the law since its meaning primarily refers to the manner in which the notion of law itself is established by only two criteria: one, its citability, and; two, its location in the subject who gives the formula of *ius* a performative, obligatory, or binding character, which has the power to bind other subjects to its reproduction. The example I referred to above may have seemed trivial — the obedience of traffic laws — but perhaps it is in its most quotidian and habitual force that best exemplifies the non-foundational and non-consensual character of the notion of justice we are examining.

Who, then, has the power to "say the rule"? In many ways this question echoes the earlier one posed by Lyotard concerning knowledge: "Who decides?" In the conclusion of Benveniste's analysis of the concept of "justice," this power and privilege is to be located in position of the "judge-arbiter."[78] What is most striking about this subject is its character of secrecy, of being a clandestine or unseen observer of events and things, or might also characterize the "unforeseen" nature of certain events that falls under the judge-arbiter's power to discern the rule. At this point, allow me to repeat the examples that give the historical uses of these terms and the best sense of the arbiter and arbitri.

> '*Come over here, please, a way off, so that the arbitri cannot arbitrari [witness] our words*';
> '*Let us go into the house; this is not a suitable place for us to talk about your conduct, the passers may be arbitri*';
> '*The neighbors are arbitri of everything that goes on in my house; they look through the windows.*
> '*Follow me and at the same time look around to make sure that there is no arbiter present.*'[79]

In each of these terms, we might witness the original sense of justice (i.e., of being bound to an oath) is inextricably linked with the presence or absence of another subject (the arbiter) who bears the force of this binding through critical scrutiny.

As Benveniste notes, what characterizes the arbiter is the extent of his power; "he judges by coming between the two parties from outside like someone who has been present at the affair without being seen."[80] It is precisely this invisibility that gives the arbiter an omni-present and binding force; because the subject may not know at any time if there are *arbitri* present to witness his or her actions, and so more often than not the subject's actions will conform to the rule. Today, in American society, the police enact this ancient function of the *arbitri*. Recalling my earlier example of running a traffic signal, one never knows if they are present in the event that you break a rule; in other cases of crime, the police-arbiter (or model detective) reproduces the facts of an event between two parties (theft, or murder) until he or she assumes the position of a "witness" to the event itself without being seen by either party — without, in fact, having been present. The detective solves the case and represents the event as if he or she had been there to witness what had transpired. In addition, most critical social transformations are always accompanied by the creation of a new class of *arbitri*, from cases of domestic violence where the neighbor will become *arbitri* (as in the above example that Benveniste cites from Plautius), to new laws and social policies that are enforced by the constant possibility of every subject to become an arbiter. Thus, social gossip and rumor must be included as expressions of the power of the *arbitri*, as narratives and testimonies that effect a certain pressure on the subject to insure his or her behavior conforms to the normative rule.

I think we can see the relevance of this archaic social and legal institution to understanding the modern concept of justice. What distinguishes the modern form of this institution pertains to the Freudian discovery of a figure of the arbiter within the subject's own interiority, and here of course I am referring to the "super-ego" (*Über-Ich*) in the Freudian topography. This archaic institution has evolved through seventeen centuries of Christianity until the position of arbiter is no longer tied to a particular social personage, but in some ways becomes absolute or universally present in the subject's own psyche, illustrating the sense of ferocity and violence of intrusion that accompanies its modern avatar. It is perhaps Lacan more than Freud who shows the true face of this new arbiter as something truly horrible and monstrous. Why? Because we live at the end of the period of the decline of religion and socialized rituals that bind this *arbiter* to the circumscribed space of a community in the sense of binding the character of the *arbiter* to a definite social and cultural context. What has emerged at the end of this long period is a new *arbiter* who both is *ab-solute* and seemingly contextless and, at the same time, a permanent fixture in the topography of the Ego; it can be occupied by any social norm that emerges in the unconscious and assumes the position of "the norm."

This is why Lacan suggested many times that "the death of God" (the absolute witness of witnesses) was not necessarily something to celebrate, since this event forecasts the emission of the law from a point in the unconscious. Consequently, Lacan suggested that "the death of God" only means that God now belongs to the field of the unconscious. This underlines a situation in which one is not conscious of the origin of law, its essential arbitrariness or its own interest, but also its absolute imperative to conform or to adapt oneself to the normative rule even if this rule might violate ethical consciousness. Of course, Lacan was addressing the possibility of fascism among other modern developments, and particularly the unfolding of anti-Semitism in Europe to its terrible conclusion. At the same time, we need to remind ourselves that anti-Semitism in National Socialist Germany enacted the archaic sense of "justice" for the German people who became its *arbitri* — both in the religious sense of a ritual purification of place, and in the Roman sense of *ius* as normative rule. Thus, "Auschwitz" is perhaps the most vivid and terrifying example of what can happen as a result of the fact that ultimately, to paraphrase the words of the German poet Paul Celan, there is *no witness for the witness.*

In addition to the works by the German poet Paul Celan, this shift is perhaps nowhere better illustrated than in Kafka's *The Trial,* which begins when K. wakes to the intruding stare of the concierge of his apartments looking in from the window, and ends when K. is executed, "like a dog." The last thing K. sees from a distance is the figure of a woman outlined in the light of a window. Can we not see in both these figures which frame the narrative of K.'s brief and unhappy engagement with the law the central concern of the novel — the problem of justice? Everything that happens to K. occurs in the full presence of witnesses, before the gaze of the *arbitri,* and in such a way that K. must conclude that what is happening to him is, in fact, a form of justice in the sense that it conforms to a norm, regardless of whether the law is in fact an archaic representative of justice, the blood-oath of racism and prejudice. Kafka's novel provides a vivid illustration of the unfounded nature of the "arbiter" ("the witness") that has been demonstrated many times during this century.

It is perhaps in response to the non-foundational character of the "normative rule" (including the rule of *consensus*), that the modern reaction can account for the meaning of the term "arbitrary" today, meaning the "arbitrariness of the rule," or the factor of power that determines the subject who says (represents) the rule (the norm). It is this sense of the "arbitrary" or non-foundational character of "the one who says the rule" that is the basic tenet of ideological critique: that the social subject who establishes the rule is prejudiced, partial, and whose entire justification is founded by a principle that cannot be deduced (i.e., the power of performativity). As Lyotard argued, "the law cannot be deduced," since there is no phrase of cognition properly speaking, without reducing or canceling out the aspect of force or the obligatory character of law, in which case it is no longer law but rather its theoretical representation, or as Kant said, its "maxim." Thus, "*You ought to* implies an addressor who is undoubtedly a mystery, who is 'incomprehensible' and 'inscrutable.'"[81]

Kant had also seen the danger of this situation, since "the arbitrariness of the rule" implies the absolute character of law and of the "one who says the rule" (*ius*). Kant's brilliant and often misunderstood solution to this problem takes the form of the categorical imperative: act in such a manner *as if* (*als ob*) the maxim of your action is also a universal obligation. Simply put, Kant's solution to the arbitrariness of the rule was to affirm it by universalizing it. Here, action conforms to "the saying of a rule" that must be given a universal character. Hence, every subject is the position of the *ius*, of the "one who says the rule," and who thus demands obedience from every other subject. But here is the difference. It only appears *as if* Kant is establishing the essential arbitrariness of any rule in the fact that any subject whatsoever can assume the position of establishing the normative rule; however, the second part of the categorical imperative is the true test of this rule's universality. It demands that the maxim (or descriptive representation of the principle of an action) must be able to be communicated; and for this it must be able to assume a universal form of a *sensus communis*. In order to be "communicable," the representation of every action must be translatable into language or discourse; therefore, it is constrained to the historical conditions of sense and meaning, since no action or command can assume the form of "law" outside language. Law is essentially and supremely a linguistic phenomenon. Rather than being "arbitrary," the universal is precisely the form of the rule's auto-legitimation. It requires agreement. Here, the absolute and arbitrary character of justice (*ius*) is constrained by this universal requirement. The law requires universal agreement in order to be absolutely obligatory; however, since no law can ever attain universal agreement, then the very nature of law is something finite and historical and reserves for the subject the space of freedom to resist or to disobey.

At first glance, Kant appears to be saying contradictory things concerning law. First, all laws must [be] universally communicable. Second, there is no law that so far has assumed such a test to prove its categorical validity. Third, there is no universal law and every law is contingent and historical in character, that is to say, unfounded in a categorical sense. Here Kant is playing out the distinction between human law and physical or natural law in order to underline their essential difference. It would be absurd to say to the apple that it must make a maxim of its action before it falls from the tree to land on the head of Newton. Likewise, Kant suggests, it would be absurd to say to a human being that he or she should simply obey the law the way an apple "obeys" the law of gravity. Between natural and human (or artificial) law, there is the intervention of language or discourse, or more precisely, "the universal," which is created by the possibility of language. For the human, there is no law without language; whereas, for things there is no language and thus no "universal."

Perhaps we can locate the most original and authentic sense of the "critical" in this figure of the arbiter (the social or critical force) who binds the subject to an oath or a promise. The critic must perform this function of the arbiter in order to re-enact the social meaning of this obligation, which would also include the two meanings of *ius*, that is, both the religious sense of "purity" and the civil sense of "regularity." One can witness this sense in most applications of the concept of justice today, which involves both an "illumination" of transgression as well as a recalling to an earlier obligation. Consequently, it is this sense of "justice" in the sense of recalling one to the terms of an original oath, to responsibility, that may underlie what I have called "the ethical turn." In addition, the basis of the Marxist critique of bourgeois values enacts both these senses as well; that is, both the religious sense of "justice" as purification, and the civil or secular sense of justice as conforming to a state of regularity, which can be represented by "the Universal." Yet, we find here in the "critical" nature of justice that there is also a contradiction between these classical notions of justice, something that was prepared for, as Benveniste suggests, by an inherent flaw in the concept itself in western institutions and which highlights the very problematic character in Western notions of justice. *It is a flaw or structural lapse, I would suggest, that may in fact be fatally irresolvable and perhaps the founding condition of a permanent conflict of the critical social faculties, or between a pure subject of justice and the various historical or social representatives who assume the power "to say the rule" concerning the social bond (including, I might add, those who assume the power to "say the rule" of performativity).*

As we might recall, the first divergence occurs when the religious and ritual sense of *ius*, that of "swearing an oath" or "conforming to the rule of the ceremony," becomes associated (according to Benveniste) in the Roman institution of law with a "normative rule" or "state of regularity" (*civilitas*). In this stage, as Benveniste recounts, the *ius* is still associated with a formula of conduct or of law, that is, with a prescription that must be obeyed or conformed to by the subject in order to remain in the space of civil society. To transgress this rule of normativity would cause the subject to fall outside or beneath this space, to become a barbarian at the gates of the city, or the criminal in its most dark and hidden sectors. Already at this stage, however, we might see the ground laid for the constitutive ideological or imperial dimension of law (something that Marx already outlined in his critique of "Roman Law"), since there is no way to guarantee that the formulas of justice (*iu-dex*) are themselves properly founded and correct. In fact, there is only the power of a certain *arbiter* or class of *arbitri* whose "saying" assumes the position of the Universal. The notion of justice historically will always be publicly articulated by the corporate interests that assume the instruments of the *iu-dex*, and these instruments are primarily the social institutions where the formulas are maintained and the "legitimate" class of *arbitri* are reproduced (including, historically, the institution of the modern university). Therefore, the power of the subject who "says the rule" must be jealously guarded, that is, authorized and regulated, since this power to establish one's own rule as normative as the rule for everyone, is Universal. This leads to the second divergence, which Benveniste emphasizes, which is the shift in the meaning of the formula of justice from a highly delimited ritual or ceremonial occasion to the formula that determines the state of normality or regularity in the *polis*. From this point onward, the notion of justice cannot be easily separated from the "police," and from the institutionalization of normative rules that determine the space of *civilitas*.

After the above development in the concept of "justice," it is only the briefest of steps to get to Marx's critique of liberal and idealist notions of civil society as, in truth, composed from the powerful interests of the dominant class who, following the Roman transformation of justice, can establish their own rule as also the rule of the entire *polis*. The primary struggle of Marxism, for example, is the struggle to assume the position and the instruments of the *iu-dex*. These "instruments" are primarily the social institutions where the arbiter-judge is to be located, such as the instruments of the state, commerce, law and culture. In point of fact, the Marxist project is founded by an appeal to most primitive form of justice: the appeal to the position of the arbiter-judge who comes from outside the domain of conflict of particular interests, who is hidden from the conflicting parties, and "who makes his decision not according to formulae and laws, but by a personal assessment and in the name of equity."[82] This is the archaic mechanism of justice that was practiced first in Sicily: the appointment of a stranger to arbitrate local disputes over land-claims between colonial occupations.[83] In Marx, this social stranger and arbiter appears as the subject of the proletariat who, we recall, has no vested interest in the current social organization of private interests and, therefore, is in the best place to judge, or to "say the rule."

As we know, however, Marx still subscribed to a metaphysics of history in that he assumed that this history takes on a teleological form: that the emergence of the proletariat, as the final flower of the primordial logic of this original division, will cancel out all previous contradictions and usher in the "End of Capitalism." Marx's fundamental error was to believe that in the encounter with the bourgeois subject and the working class, the political subjectivity that emerged from this conflict would assume the position of the "next one" in the order of an historical succession. He did not consider, at least in his early speculations, that the bourgeois subject would have much staying power, or was not "the last" in an historical series of economic subjects that have been engendered by this division, or that the proletariat subject would in fact never appear *in the present*. Marx wagered on the tide of a contemporaneous conflict and based his theory on the premise that the current conflict was in a certain sense also final. He wagered and he lost, as history rolled the dice again, repeatedly transforming the nature of this division into new configurations just as class conflict has been re-configured by the creation of new political and economic subjectivities that belong to "our capitalist era" (which, although it is growing "late" has not yet shown any signs of setting).

Concluding our observations on "the ethical turn," we can clearly see from Benveniste's historical analysis that there is a split or opposition within the concept of justice itself. According to our argument, the selection of "the stranger" to embody the position of judge-arbiter has left permanent and lasting effects within the concept of justice itself, as well as on the very character of judgment in Western philosophies. Why is this divergence in the notion of justice, at the same time archaic and distinctly modern, so significant for our analysis of the social institution of the university or to the nature of "critical knowledge"? First, it shows a divergence within the saying of *ius* itself, which does not belong to a formula or to a table of already established laws, but concerns something that is not written, covered by statute or rule, something hidden, or unforeseen. (To these adjectives, we might also add those events and disputes that are "unconscious," that is, conforming to an as yet unknown rule.) Second, this notion of justice is coupled with a certain kind of arbiter, the stranger, whose privilege and power to decide stems precisely from the subject's invisibility or impartiality. In Plato's description of the Court of Tartaros in *Meno,* for example, the most perfect judges are described as dead, a metaphor for having no interest in the affairs of the living that could create the possibility of bias, and as having no eyes or ears, that is, no senses that occlude or make their viewpoint partial to their own subjective interest.

Concluding our observations on "the ethical turn," we can clearly see from Benveniste's historical analysis that there is a split or opposition within the concept of justice itself. According to our argument, the selection of "the stranger" to embody the position of judge-arbiter has left permanent and lasting effects within the concept of justice itself, as well as on the very character of judgment in Western philosophies.

How did the stranger assume such a powerful role? In answer to this question, there is no explanation except to say that this practice must have received the agreement of the conflicting parties, as a kind of stop-gap measure invented to forestall the undecidability of the issues involved, to have their conflict settled by someone who has no interest in the affair and could gain nothing by taking sides. There was a consensus that first gave the stranger-arbiter the power to decide the whole affair. This was seen as the best solution to the problem of justice, one that continues to determine metaphorically the figure of the judge-arbiter in our courts today. The philosophical principle of justice (*ius*) upon which the concept of law is founded has not changed that dramatically since the time of Plato. And it is the return of this schism between a pure subject of justice (the stranger arbiter) and the partial or practical subject of politics that underlies the conditions of the conflict of the faculties in Kant's time, as well as in our own.

### *Summary & transition*

Although the preceding discussion may have seemed to digress from the primary topic of parts one and two (the university), I have argued throughout this report that there is a necessary and historical relationship between an earlier philosophical representation of the critical position of the university with regard to society, on the one hand, and the nature of critical subject of knowledge that is located within the university, on the other. As I expand upon this relationship in part one, the understanding of this critical function is founded upon a notion of "autonomy" enjoyed by the institution as well as by the critical subject, an autonomy which is necessarily and even constitutionally heterogeneous to the dominant forms of social interest and power that belong to the surrounding society. And yet, major statements concerning the university by leftist and conservative critics alike share one common assumption: that the current institution is no longer founded upon a principle of autonomy, but rather is open and permeable to the dominant, primarily economic, interests of late-capitalist societies in which it is located. Today the university is a "business," and for this reason the relationships between its various social segments, classes of labor, and intellectual or academic sub-units can be organized accordingly, just as administrators have been doing now for the past several years. However, if the institution in which the contemporary critic is located is no longer organized around the principle of autonomy, I ask whether this would also imply a change in the sense of the "critical" itself? That is, can the claim for critical autonomy or distance from dominant social interests be made from within a social institution that itself is in the process of dismantling any such "position"?

This is perhaps the most *critical* observation in my report, which in the conclusion will take the form of a question concerning the *critical* itself. With the emergence of the critical theorist in the late seventies in the United States, and the growing array of "critical subjects" in the institution today, there is a tacit assumption of the critical formation of knowledge and its direct or, more often than not, indirect connection to the field of politics. This is something that could even be called an *Ur-doxa*, that is, a grounding dogma or an unreflective aspect that belongs to contemporary representations of critical knowledge. In my view, Lyotard is one of the few philosophers associated with the left to have broached these questions and to have risked misunderstanding and even enmity for calling into question the continued pertinence of critical narratives that may in fact be based on an earlier relationship between knowledge and society. It is for this reason that Lyotard's writings assume a more prominent place in the last two parts of my report.

More recently, however, there have been signs of disillusionment and growing confusion over the weakening of this critical function, which seem to be confirmed by the loss of social investment for procuring this type of knowledge, or in Kantian terms, in the "reproduction of the critical faculties" (i.e., the downsizing of the Humanities and the under-employment of recent doctorates in various fields, particularly literature and languages). Here, Lyotard's earlier diagnosis of the decline of certain grand narratives, which first appeared too abstract to some, takes on a strikingly concrete expression when viewed from the perspective of the current moment, since the relatively recent social dis-investment of certain faculties (in terms of size, but also in terms of worth or "purchase value") is the clearest marker of the devaluation of the corresponding knowledges, which have been slated for extinction, and the non-maintenance of certain narratives in which the knowledge of these critical faculties is situated. (Again, I am referring to text-based knowledge specifically and to the techniques of reading and critical analysis.)

At the center of these debates, I have argued, is the loss of faith in the consensual function of social institutions which earlier philosophical models of "criticism" and "critical theory" depend upon in order to operate — something that has been implicit in the modern critiques of Enlightenment reason and in the critiques of representation in general that critics and theorists have been engaged in for several decades. As with any social contract, these are provisional agreements that are valid only as long as the different parties adhere to them. In the modern period, it is precisely the representation of this consensus that has been placed in question in the most acute manner, under a general critique of Enlightenment reason. However, as Lyotard announces, these are precisely the narratives that in modern post-industrial societies have lost much of their credibility, and this loss of credibility (or faith) can be evidenced by the frequency of "anti-Enlightenment" and "anti-essentialist" rhetoric of the critical faculties themselves.

The loss of consensus, which was addressed in III(a) and III(d), leads to a failure of the narrative as a sufficient explanation of "how things really work," and of one narrative in particular, the Enlightenment narrative of reason, as the sufficient ground for determining the nature of the contemporary social bond. At the same time, I have suggested that Lyotard's argument represents perhaps the most extreme case of the rejection of consensus, which he sees only as the result of a repressed or annihilated *differend* within his general notion of communicative "agonistics."[84] However, the rejection of the idea of consensus as either an ideological notion or as a social and political myth has unexpectedly turned against the historical models of the critical itself that still depend on a certain idea of consensus — even in the "negative form" of *dissensus* — in order to justify their social function. This situation, I argue, has often engendered a turn to the remaining alternatives expressed by the critical subject today: a turn to *cynicism, poetry*, or *ethics*.

# Part IV  *Conclusion*

*Anent: The question, "What is* critical *in critical knowledge today?"*

Throughout this report, my primary subject has been the nature of the conflict that determines the epistemological conditions of critical knowledge. I have argued that this conflict must be better understood in its contemporary setting so that the critical representation of knowledge can be better adapted to it. In the preceding part, we followed Lyotard's hypothesis that earlier notions of the "critical" in the social formation and reproduction of knowledge may no longer be pertinent to the contemporary social bond. In the conclusion, I will address this same question in the following manner: "What is *critical* in critical knowledge today?" The notion of critical I am evoking here does not refer to a certain historical discourse or genre of narrative, as it so often does, based in part on tradition, and in part on a series of presuppositions which are internal to the form that the critical relationship between knowledge and society takes at a given historical moment (that is to say, on a particular tradition or institution of "meta-narrative"). As I have discussed, both with regard to the modern philosopher and the postmodern critic or theorist of the social bond, one of these presuppositions concerns the existence of a purely theoretical subject (a subject of reason), in the case of the former, and for the latter a purely practical subject (a subject of politics). Therefore, to ask *what is critical?* is to repeat the question that guided the preceding sections, although this time from the perspective of the critical subject who occupies the university today — who knows? Who decides? What, in fact, is *critical* today concerning the question of knowledge?

I have argued that, inasmuch as this "critical" activity takes place in a social institution that is either sanctioned by the state, or is created to serve the dominant forms of social interest (and, of course, prejudice is a form of interest as well), there has never been a form of the critical that has not in some measure served these interests by virtue of the very place where the critical faculty is housed, and by this faculty's dependence for reproduction on a certain consensus with a form of government. It is because of this fact that any notion of absolute autonomy that belongs to the critical subject in the academy has been led into contradiction precisely around the problem of "recuperation." What is broadly defined as "critical" (although not necessarily in a Marxist sense as we have outlined above in section III[c]) would, as anyone might assume, ideally resist any such "recuperation" or positivistic function. However, the irony is that we can observe the constant tendency on the part of critics themselves to discover a hidden positivistic function operating at some level in every instance of critical knowledge itself, whether this might take the form of "partiality of reason" or "self-interest" on the part of the critical subject, or an a priori "recuperation" having to do with the nature of *form* itself as an ultimate ideological value. This, for example, has been a dominant critique of modernist experimentation for many years.

Lyotard questioned the very nature of dualism in knowledge that is linked to this problem and whether or not "critical" knowledge should be founded upon a division that has repeatedly been shown to be either essentially false, or which has undermined the very objectives that critical knowledge sets out to accomplish. The idea of "multiple language games" might be seen as a temporary solution, one that avoids the potential of "terror" at the basis of a dualistic model — *that there be only one language which would henceforth totalize all the possible moves (or strategies) concerning the social bond.* Lyotard's solution, however, is also somewhat unsatisfactory and I agree with Jameson that the notion of "multiple language games" and the strategy of a "general agonistics" in the absence of any possible consensus is almost a pre-modern return to the strategies of stoicism and cynicism. We might recall that the hallmarks of these schools of philosophical resistance were withdrawal from the city and the creation of an opposing and antagonistic image of knowledge and reason based on a virulent principle of *anti-logos*. Although the stoics and cynics would form "schools of thought" like mobile bands that wage guerilla-like attacks against the Aristotelian principles of a royal "state-form" of knowledge, one would always find them outside the city, living in some cave, or in the city square dressed as beggars — never in the *paidea* itself.[1]

As I argued in section I(c) concerning the figure of the "subject at large," identified with Derrida's position in the American academy, one reason for Lyotard seeing this as a possible form of resistance was, to a great degree, owed to his "post" in the American university: that of a stranger, a mobile intellectual and theorist, moving freely from one institution to the next (Columbia, Irvine, Emory), free for the most part from the obligations, constraints, and social rituals that bind most domestic or native academics. Thus, as in the case of Derrida's "position," Lyotard's image of resistance to performativity is not purely a philosophical strategy, but is materially conditioned by the relative autonomy his subject enjoyed in the American institution, "a position" that cannot be generalized as a general "strategy" without engendering contradiction. (This is because such a strategy is already contingent upon one's "position" in the university.) The difference between Derrida and Lyotard on this issue, as I have shown above, is that Derrida was acutely aware of this privilege and admonished his American audience to take his point of view with their "eyes wide open" to its drastically schematic and somewhat exceptional perspective. I think that one of the factors behind the contemporary backlash against the subject of theory in the United States is precisely a latent suspicion, and even rejection, of the stranger's point of view as a guarantee of objectivity.[2]

However, as I have argued in the preceding section III(d), the guarantee and the privilege accorded to the stranger can be understood as nothing more than a stop-gap measure or compromise formation that was historically invented to resolve the problem of the arbitrariness of "the one who says the rule." In short, it is an archaic convention that underlies several institutions in the West (most notably law, science, and philosophy) and, therefore, is dependent upon the consensus of society itself to maintain the credulity of a stranger's perspective as one that guarantees the highest measure of objectivity.

What remains valid in Lyotard's rejection of dualism is his recognition of a positivist spirit that has always haunted every model of "critical theory" and operates, in short, as an inner pole of attraction stemming from this unresolved model of dualism that continues to determine the critical or transcendental employment of knowledge. Lyotard's thesis that Marxism and radical critical theories post-1960s have only become "aids in programming the system" is merely an extreme and even exaggerated assessment of this problem. *However, it is the tension between these two kinds of knowledge, and ultimately the failure of critical knowledge to remain "critical" to society, on the one hand, and to resist the inevitable moment of "recuperation," on the other, that defines perhaps the question of the state of current knowledge, including the critical social knowledges that are found in the university today.* Not only in most commentaries on the question of the university, but in the daily experience of those who are located in this institution, there is an explicit conflict between these two kinds of knowledge which has reoriented the new conflict of the faculties in the most striking manner. For example, what has often been defined by critics as "the corporatization of the university" can be ascribed to this conflict, or what Bill Readings in *The University in Ruins* constantly alludes to as "the idea of excellence" that has become the principle behind many of the recent initiatives to improve the university's performance and efficiency in all areas. It is precisely the success of this new positivism that has been the concern of many critics and philosophers, beginning with Derrida's own 1983 address at Cornell. What has been most devastating and apparently insurmountable is the perceived role played by late-capitalism in this state of affairs, which has left some critics questioning the possibility of any effective form of resistance before its own solutions to the problems of organizing the social bond.

In part one, I argued that this relationship addresses the eighteenth century image of reason that institutes the idea of the university's speculative mission (the study of knowledge for its own sake). This image is also dependant on a notion of "autonomy," which has been discussed throughout the report: the belief, although today one might say "myth," that the form of interest that defines this speculative mission is relatively *free from* the dominant interests that comprise any given historical society, which charges the university with a transcendental mission in relation to the particular society in which it is situated. As I have shown, this is a narrative of the university that was created to serve the interest of only one branch of knowledge, that of the philosophers. Of course, these narratives are for all practical purposes not based in fact, as has been demonstrated many times by critics over the past one-hundred years. However, given its philosophical and speculative origin, the modern notion of critical knowledge, or more recently, "critical theory" are both equally founded on these internal presuppositions of a speculative mission with regard to the future of the social bond and the presupposition of autonomy, the freedom from dominant social and economic interest (in short, tradition, culture, and history).

If Lyotard earlier had rejected a dualistic distinction between "information" and "knowledge," it is because this divide rests upon a very metaphysical pretension for a form of thought devoid of social interest, and of a subject of knowledge that responds to no *a priori* social demand or obligation. This subject would be "a stranger" in the sense of occupying the role of the *arbiter* (judge and witness) in the appeal to "ethics" addressed in the previous section. But then, Lyotard asks, what language would this subject be speaking? Language, as Saussure has shown, is the primal contract that the individual or the community cannot sever since one was never *free* to elect it in the first place. Thus, Lyotard's critique of the principle of the autonomy of reason — that is, the principle upon which the distinction of knowledge and information ultimately rests — participates in a long tradition of critique from Hamman to Gadamer concerning whether reason is ultimately a social phenomenon which is bound to the conditions of *a language*. For example, Kant's maxim of reason's individual autonomy, "think for yourself," was criticized by Hamman as the source of reason's "misunderstanding with itself," and later by Gadamer as an "abstract antithesis" between individual and tradition (or language, culture, and society).[3]

In some ways the entrance of a more radical notion of autonomy that one finds in the subject of Marxist discourse, a radical subject of knowledge that is completely divorced from dominant social interests, is already occasioned by the earlier idealist and philosophical narrative. This may explain why Marxism was able to establish itself within the liberal institution of the university in many late-democratic societies, since it could apply its narrative to the transcendental pretension at the basis of the institution itself, particularly the teleological aspect of the interest of reason that concerns the "future of society" for which Marxism provides an epic denouement in the "end of Capitalism" and the future of a "classless society." However, it is this notion of autonomy that has itself led to the repeated disenchantments of the critical subject that have occurred precisely around the contradiction between a notion of reason at odds with the social institution of the university founded (and *funded*) by dominant interests in a given historical society.

In his later writings on the subject of pure reason or upon the philosophical mission of the university, mostly in response to the acts of censorship against his critique of the subject of religion, Kant himself was forced to retreat from the earlier arguments for the transcendental status of reason. This withdrawal occurs in the section of *The Conflict of Faculties* concerning the conflict between the faculty of philosophy and the faculty of theology, as well as in the famous text in response to the question, "What is Enlightenment?" On both occasions, Kant divides the nature of reason itself into two opposing aspects: public and private. The first (the public aspect) concerns the exercise of reason in the public domain, primarily in the form of discourse or debate and in printed matters. The second (the private aspect) concerns the exercise of reason that belongs to the "performance" of some duty, position, or role in society or one of its institutions. Many of Kant's critics, beginning with Hamman, accuse Kant of being self-serving in this matter by seeking to preserve his own interests, as well as the right of the "educated class" to which he belongs: the *right of access* to the public media (to printing presses, pamphlets, journals, and newspapers), and the instruments of public persuasion and privilege that might influence the decision-making process. As an aside, it is somewhat striking to notice that recent debates concerning "public access" (Bérubé) today so closely parallel Kant's original concerns that sometimes it seems that we are only repeating history. In Kant's time, however, the famous *freedom to think* which is represented as a universal right of the human being, is in reality the self-interested right of a particular class of men, and does not address in the least the rights of other subjects, particularly women, social and ethnic minorities, and the uneducated classes as Hamman pointed out as early as the eighteenth century.

Even more pertinent for us today, however, is Kant's argument concerning "private reason," which also extends to the duties of university professors, in their non-public capacity as a "teacher of the youth." In this case, Kant's definition of the private use of reason applies as well, inasmuch as the role of university teacher is sanctioned by the authority of the state, and that the university teacher occupies this position of authority in the service of state-sponsored goals, the professor's duty is *"to obey!"* just as much as it is the duty of a soldier. Above all, it would be an illegitimate use of reason for either subject to use the vested authority of his or her office, or "position," for an overtly public purpose — to persuade, influence, or otherwise, criticize openly the principles that underline his or her "official post." Such a "public use of reason" in a private capacity, Kant argues, would lead to a contradiction, and worse, to an anarchy of principles.

On the basis of the above observations we might risk the following speculation: the image of "autonomy" (of a reason purified of social interest and obligation) was, at best, a compromise formation. Kant's formula for it was *Think, argue, debate in a public capacity as much as you want and about whatever you want.*

*But obey!*¹ By extension, we might argue that this condition of autonomy or the freedom of reason also covers the modern determinations of the critical subject. What if there was an original arrangement (or contract) by which the critical use of knowledge could be pursued within the province of a certain social institution, the university, only under the condition that, and as long as, this knowledge is not attached to a prescriptive or social obligation. This would constitute something like the original social contract between the modern state and the critical faculties that are housed in the university. The original interest of the state would be that criticism is a social good, that conflict is productive and stimulates both the production of new knowledges (which can be adapted to its own ends) or the refinement of older knowledges (in part, deciding which knowledge is *critical* for the contemporary society and should be maintained, and which is obsolete and should be slated for dis-investment). The conflict of the faculties is a social good as long as it does not lead to outright war or to a situation in which the faculties attempt to use their offices to undermine the state's own ends. On the other hand, the philosopher's interest would be served in that this would allow "him" a public office and a means of livelihood to serve the interests of reason itself which, as I have said above, cannot be divorced from the particular interests and desires of a class of the intelligentsia. To summarize: it was Kant who first brokered a deal with the state, in which the state acceded to the philosopher's right to think in exchange for the philosopher's sacrifice of self interest in "power."

Of course, the idea of an original contract is a fiction, but it is useful for clarifying the current conflict of the faculties. It is important to notice, moreover, that the terms of this original deal have, for several centuries, now been set into the meta-narrative of reason itself, which is described as an autonomous form of self-interest, and has been divorced from practical interest in prescriptive powers. The question that concerns us today is the possibility of the abandonment of this early contract between the university and the state (or, at least, its latest modern representative). On the one hand, we can say that the first party (the state) has reneged on the earlier agreement to guarantee the freedom of thought, including critical thought (the public use of reason); on the other, the philosopher (or at least his modern representative, the critical theorist and social activist in the academy) has reneged on his or her agreement to not overtly seek influence or power over the social bond. It is difficult to discern which party breached the terms of the original contract first, even though it is clear that both parties have left the table and are busy in their own corners shouting *foul!* at the other side. This is the current state of what I have called the new conflict of the faculties.

If I am casting this conflict in terms of a legal conflict, in some ways following Kant's earlier rhetorical framework, it is because I see this debate very much as a kind of long and tempestuous divorce-proceeding between the higher and lower faculties, and between the modern philosopher and the state. On one side, we have what is commonly referred to as "the right" accusing university professors in their capacity as "teachers of the youth" of using their authority to distort time-honored cultural values and institutions of value (such as the canon or family morality), and converting the very same youth to more radical and potential anarchic belief-systems. In most cases, the arguments of "the right" can be seen as citing the earlier Kantian division between a public and private use of reason, almost in the sense of holding this new class of professors, academic activists, and "public intellectuals" to the terms of the original contract. On the other side, "the left" accuse "the right" of being secret agents of the state or of a dominant class morality that they accuse of bad faith in not honoring the absolute right accorded to the exercise of the critical function of judgment, or the right of new political subjects to have access to the centers of decision-making and authority in a contemporary democratic society. In other words, "the right" often reduces the function of the university professor completely to "private reason," while the left often characterizes its own function (in all of its aspects including teaching and service) as completely consistent with a "public use of reason." What is clear from this most recent conflict of the faculties — although conservative pundits and politicians such as Pat Buchanan, William Bennett, and the indefatigable George Will are not faculty, they can be seen to occupy a similar role as the censors or the clergy in Kant's own time — is that the original terms of the understanding have been violated, which is why they are today often cast in the form of an extreme antithesis.

If there is any criticism which can be brought to bear on this debate, it is that both sides assert that their position in this affair and the values that each side espouses — that of "Culture" on one side, and "Criticism" on the other — are eternal, rather than being very contingent to a certain historical arrangement of knowledge in society, an arrangement which is subject to "assessment" and renegotiation from time to time. Another way of putting this is that as these same values undergo conflict, the identities that are dependent upon them would suffer a period of intense disorientation — sometimes registered in terms of a loss of value or "function," and at other times, in terms of outright hostility and war. Moreover, this conflict has been inflamed by the rise of the administrative class as a party to the conflict itself, a class that in some way acts to dispose of the interests between these earlier parties according to a new set of principles that are responsible for transforming the social institution today. Thus, as I highlighted early on in Part I, this subject not only has been endowed with a philosophical authority over the *idea* of the university (thus supplanting the earlier position of the philosopher), but also has been granted executive or practical authority over the social institution (thus supplanting the authority of the faculty) and, therefore, has been invested with the power of making its idea of the university prescriptive. I have highlighted both these aspects only to underline the discrepancy between this arrangement and the earlier one, which bestowed upon the philosopher certain ideational powers, but certainly not executive privilege to transform the institution as he saw fit since this would violate one of the primary conditions of the original contract.

Today it is the administrator, and not the philosopher (or any representative of the faculty), who demands that all knowledge be submitted for examination, under the contemporary term of "assessment." That is to say, in response to Lyotard's earlier question, it is this subject who decides what knowledge is *critical* to the contemporary social bond, and who has been invested with the power of deciding what knowledge is maintained and which is left to fall into extinction or be erased and over-written (i.e., revised, adapted, up-dated) from the contemporary data-bank of society. The effects of such decisions are tangible and can be registered very concretely in terms of what faculties are retained and reproduced (through the creation of new faculties), which programs and departments are invested with new capital and which are left to a process of gradual attrition and eventual extinction (such as the department of classics, or the study of languages), or are adapted to a new set of initiatives and institutional priorities (such as the separation of writing from the English curriculum). Finally, this "decision" can be indicated by the general investment and real worth to the institution, measured in terms of annual budgets and average salaries, which sharply distinguishes the value of different programs, departments, and even individual faculty in the university today.

It is interesting to note that this transferal of administrative power, concretely impacting the nature of autonomy enjoyed by faculty, is something that constantly returns in the form of a "symptom" at the department level, the last refuge (or "reservation") of an earlier notion of autonomy. I invite my readers to survey their own departments to identify administrative functions from those I identified strictly by "research". These are in most cases easy to discern since they are most often located in identifiable individuals. For example, on one side one finds the department administrator or officer who has little or no active engagement with a research project to justify his or her role in the "creation of new knowledge," and who takes on administrative or service duties to compensate. On the other side, one finds the active researcher who busies himself or herself with publication and the cultivation of national networks, whose value in the role of knowledge production appears self-evident, and therefore, is free to elect only such service duties that might fit his or her own professional interests. The animosity and even historical resentment that exists between these two classes of faculty is the constant staple of day-to-day academic life, and constitutes the underlying conflict of all "academic politics." From this example alone, it appears that Marx was correct is saying that the first and foremost social division is the division of intellectual labor, the abstract division from which all other divisions of work and value in society are derived.

Perhaps we are just at the beginning of this process of transforming the social institution into a form the best fits the contemporary social bond. It may take a generation before the decisions that have already been set in motion concerning the above matters will finally take effect, primarily as the result of the death or retirement of tenured faculty in existing departments. It is for this reason, more-over, that the question of tenure has been such a volatile issue nationally since it poses the greatest obstacle to the "pace of anticipated future change" (from the language of the Report cited in part one). Perhaps this is why the recent conflicts over the tenure system between administrations and regents, on one side, and faculty unions and departments, on the other, have been closely monitored in the pages of *The Wall Street Journal*, often appearing in the column on page one, for the last ten years (along with regular reports concerning the current growth of university endowments).

Today the figure of the modern day administrator is one who is concerned with the ranking index of institutions in the yearbook of *U.S. News & World Report*, reports in the latest issue of a trade journal covering the latest endowment and grant revenue figures, proposed legislative reforms that affect higher education institutions, creative trends in distance learning, the re-packaging of academic delivery programs, recent lawsuits involving colleges and universities, all the while attempting to stay abreast of what students are saying about the process of education itself, about faculty, programs, politics, and student life. All of these represent sources of feedback to the decision-making process itself. Although, as I argued above concerning the fable of Kant's second-coming, Kant would have identified this class of administrators as "agents of the government" precisely by the executive power they hold and by their intermediary position between the university and its various "publics." Although, as Lyotard later revised the role of what he calls "technical managers," they cannot any longer be defined as state-agents since the state itself is only one "public" (or user) among others. One only has to track the change in state and federal funding allotments from the late-1970s through the current moment to see that what is commonly referred to as "the state" (meaning in the United States a combination of federal and state legislative interests) has less of a controlling influence over the university than it did during the height of the cold-war, or even earlier, in the immediate post-war years when the federal government was bullish on higher education. Thus, when Lyotard writes that the control of information is more than ever before a question of government, we must separate this determination from the form of government represented by the state-form. "Government" probably means in this context something closer to its original meaning, that of "economy." The control of information (or knowledge) is, thus, more than ever before the question of *economy*, which, in its modern definition, refers to the statistical organization of social interests (or goods). For the last century, this notion of government has gone by the name of "capitalism," or "market capitalism," and today by "global market capitalism," which is the "invisible hand" (Adam Smith) that rules both the state and the modern university.

These days it has become a platitude to say that the university is modeled after a "big business," although many of the social critics and humanities scholars who most often make this charge have very little experience of how "big business" actually works and often, as a result, fall back on clichés and popular cultural sentiments drawn from contemporary films, such as Oliver Stone's *Wall Street*, that create narratives to represent the greed and impudence that define this new race of masters. This is certainly the case of Bill Readings' argument in *The University in Ruins* (1996), where the complex principles of "corporatization" or "privatization" that have been installed as the organizing principles of many contemporary universities in the United States are reduced to one simplistic and over-arching myth, "excellence." Another way of understanding the principle of "corporatization," however, can be related to the changing conditions of Capital and the "global market." For example, in the United States we could highlight the growing internationalization of student populations and the relationship this might have both to the concentration of a highly skilled work-force in one national center and, at the same time, "the Americanization" of global markets and skilled workers as part of an overall trade strategy.

As I have argued we can perceive all of the above developments, and more, as signs of a new model of "government" that has replaced the somewhat republican model first outlined by Kant. Yet, we again recall the fact that Kant himself imagined the form of the university in his time to be essentially adapted to the emerging industrial model, noting that one of the university's primary functions was to *"create doctors"* by a division of labor that was for all intensive purposes, *"mass production."*[5] Taking our cue from this early industrial term, which is hardly metaphorical, we can see the lasting traits of this earlier mode of production on the division of labor and the nature of higher education today. A student who matriculates into a contemporary university or college still enters what could be seen as a long conveyer belt ("a course or program of study"). The student passes through various departments, classrooms, offices, and comes out at the commencement ceremony in order to be placed on display with all the other finished products of that particular year's line. More recently, of course, what is basically an eighteenth and nineteenth century analogy has been turned into today's "cafeteria model" of education, in which the student is now placed somewhat *to the side* of this process of production and is no longer identified completely with the object that is being constructed or assembled. Rather, the student moves through a vast lunch line, choosing an entrée (a major) and various side dishes and deserts (options and electives). This is a model that Readings vociferously criticizes, since it places the student in the position of "the subject who is supposed to know" (employing the Lacanian phrasing), not only what to choose, but also the criteria that make a good choice, and how these choices will make up a balanced diet of education and experience.

The question that Readings poses in his criticism of this *ad hoc* or cafeteria model of education is justified. As opposed to the earlier model in which the student is definitely a "fabricated subject" (that is, manufactured according to the specifications of particular class assumptions concerning what it means to be "educated," "cultured," or "a citizen"), the question is whether these *ad hoc criteria* are intentional in design. The authority that is seemingly invested in the student as the subject *of* and no longer subject *to* the "process" of higher education seems to fit best many of the ideologies that have been vigorously promoted in the contemporary university in the last few decades, not only by administrative reforms that place the student at the center of the process, as either "patron" or "consumer," but also by the history of pedagogical reforms that have placed the student at the center of the classroom and even of his or her entire program of study, and have invested the student's own judgment or assessment of the process itself with a new and unprecedented authority.

In point of fact, students *are* at the center of the process today — this is something that we, meaning anyone who works in higher education, can no longer deny — and in many ways faculty (those earlier points of authority) are very much subject to a new regime of assessment, by students first of all, but also by administrators who are in the process of assembling a new system for the delivery of knowledge that will define the twenty-first century university. Of course, this last series of statements must be qualified, and cannot be taken at face value. When I say that the student today is placed in a position to "judge" (to assess, to evaluate) the very process of education that he or she is engaged in, I mean this as much symbolically as literally, which is to say that the student is placed today in the position of *censor*. This does not presuppose that the student knows what criteria to use in order make the best judgment — in fact, most of the time they do not — but only that they are categorically placed in a position and have the responsibility to "judge." This obligation is part of what it is to be a student of the university today. Students are not only given the "right to evaluate" (their experience, their professor, their program or major, even their discipline or area of specialized knowledge); they are in fact placed in a situation where this right becomes a "duty," almost in the Kantian sense of "moral duty." As for faculty, those who resist this new form of censorship and cling to the idea that they are the only subjects invested with legitimate authority over the process are penalized either by being viewed by students and other faculty as being "conservative" and backwards, or by gradually losing student numbers in their courses and thereby coming under scrutiny at the department and administrative level for "bad teaching." (Of course, I am speaking here more to what is taking place in the Humanities, than in the sciences and professional programs where there is a clearer definition of knowledge that still belongs to a traditional model of top down authorization.) What makes the Humanities especially prone to this newer model of assessment is the fact that the concept of authority in many humanistic disciplines has come under suspicion as subjectively and ideologically motivated. Today, students and faculty are very much defined as "co-learners" in a process that is still under construction. This in itself may not be such a bad thing, although one of the effects this will have in a stage of transition is that it will be a site of great confusion and disorientation, since it will require that the historical structures that define *what knowledge is*, partly defined by dominant social interests and partly housed in the traditions and the disciplines that make up a disciplinary form of knowledge, be re-defined to better facilitate this new process that is based less on the acquisition and reproduction of distinct content and more centered on the nature of judgment itself.

Returning again to Readings' argument, it is the loss of an earlier criteria or tradition of judgment (Culture), which he sometimes decries and at other times affirms, that might signal a change of reference concerning what is to be known and who knows — that is, the subject of judgment. *We might hypothesize, therefore, that the shift in authority and position of censorship over the process to the modern administrator, on the one hand, and the modern student, on the other, might reveal the fact that today society itself doesn't know the criteria by which to judge.* As I said above, the student is symbolically placed in the position of "the subject who is supposed to know," which in a Lacanian understanding would also imply that this subject is itself an imaginary construction, a fantasy that is projected onto a certain subject but which in fact defines the point of the unconscious as the position of "knowledge" (*savoir*). What I am suggesting, therefore, is that this position is structural in essence, and that we must begin to ask the following questions: what is the state of an institution that invests the point of "judgment" in a subject who doesn't in fact *know*. To what end? And why? In response to these questions, some might define this phenomenon as a final expression of nihilism that has taken hold of the institution itself under the guidance of consumerist ideology, and see this as the "end of knowledge" (or at least, as an illegitimate or aberrant episode in the progress of knowledge). Others like myself might see it as an opening move in a new game of knowledge legitimation which directly corresponds to Lyotard's guiding questions in *The Postmodern Condition*: "Who decides what knowledge is?" and "Who knows what is to be decided?"

Many have argued recently, including Lyotard, that there has been a general de-structuring, or at least, a change of the modern relationship between the university and an earlier form of the nation-state; although this must be distinguished from a relationship to any "state-form" has been argued by Etienne Balibar.[6] Most would agree, however, that there is some connection between the so-called decline of the modern nation-state and the decline of the centrality of the university as a site where the question of who has the right of access to instruments of power that determine the social bond is asked. My concern however has more to do with the following observation: at the same time that the question of *access* (of historical groups and underrepresented classes of individuals) has become increasingly situated as the central concern of the university as a social institution, the relationship of the university to the institutions of the state (or nation), and more importantly these days to the instruments of Capital, has become more and more uncertain. This uncertainty has been most acutely expressed by leftist critiques that reveal this relationship as repressive, or based on some underlying ideological expression of class or racial hegemony. However, programs for diversification of student populations and affirmative action measures must still presuppose the centrality of the university as a social institution that is directly linked to the political sphere in order to justify the efficacy of these programs, in short, *to effect a change in the composition and distribution of power and advantage that currently defines the social bond.*

This is not to say that students who attend universities today are in line for a greater probability of economic advancement, or that the contemporary university reflects a greater degree of access to historically underrepresented groups because of these programs. Both of these things are certainly true. *However, economic advancement, or the increased access of formerly under-represented groups to one social institution, does not necessarily translate into the improvement of surrounding political institutions, or even lead to the social and political conditions of these groups themselves, the majority of which remain outside the still relatively privileged sphere of the university.* A more draconian reading of the contemporaneousness of these two developments might posit the shift of the question of *political access* to the university precisely at a time when this institution is being disinvested from — or, at least, is more remote to — the *political question of knowledge* (according to both Jameson and Lyotard), as part of a strategy of "isolation" or "containment." The new critical social faculties would be effectively "distanced" (recalling that this is one of the senses that Marx originally accorded to the concept of alienation), and from the distance they occupy in the academy and would find it increasingly difficult to register their *differend* with the larger society. What is more troubling, however, is the possibility that leftist critics themselves are lending a certain force to this process of alienation. Therefore, we must note the presence of a certain contradiction in the arguments made by critics who seek to dismantle the institutions and values of the "old bourgeois public sphere," on the one hand, and to promote the political cause of underrepresented groups on the other, precisely by appealing to the power of institutions like the university *and* the state as critical instruments of a new social agenda. In effect, this would be like cutting the ground out from under one's own feet.

In section III(d) I argued that the presence of this contradiction can be traced to a certain "split" in the ends of the critical itself, one that is owed to the genealogy of the Marxist doctrine. It is a split that has symptomatically been acted out in many episodes of "critical" theory: the split between total human emancipation that is premised upon the demolition of the institutions of civil society (including the university and the state), and political (or liberal) emancipation, which is premised upon the maintenance and adaptation of these very same institutions to certain "particular purposes," including the political objectives of social minorities who seek access to the institutions of the public political sphere. Perhaps like the "Death of God," the refrain that marked an earlier critical period, the decline of the nation-state, our current refrain, is not necessarily a cause for celebration, at least as I have argued throughout this report, with regard to *the political question of access.*

Bill Readings' *The University in Ruins* is a case where the argument concerning the so-called end of the nation-state is advanced most starkly, albeit simplistically, although his central object of contention is less the "public sphere" than it is the notion of "Culture" in an approaching era of what he defines as "post-nationalism." Consequently, Readings repeatedly declares not only the end of the "Nation-Form," but also a consonant notion of "Culture" that is determined by "national characteristics." In the age of "Cultural Studies," Readings announces at several points, the concept of culture is now an "empty signifier"; therefore, he offers a vision of what he calls the "post-historical university" (and by this I understand him to mean "post-national") which can be defined as a space to think "being-in-common without any unifying idea."[7] In response to this declaration, we must ask the following: In whose interest is such out-right hostility to the relationship between the university and the nation, or to any idea of "community" based on identity or unity? What is the political status of the desire to promote a concept of culture as essentially "empty," that is, as having no intrinsic relation to collective or communal experience and expression? What is the status of the "knowledge" of the faculty of such a university, defined as "thinkers," who are described as thinking nothing but "Thought itself" (in Readings argument Thought is always capitalized) that is, thought "beside itself," as inhabiting a shared space where there is an attempt to think *nothing* together?"[8]

Today the only force that can be said to be responsible for placing individuals "in common" without any recourse to an experience of community (defined in terms of unity and identity) is the force of globalization. Thus, on one level, Readings' description of the "post-historical university" can be read as a blatant attempt to cast these values into an ideological form that can best define the social role of the institution in late-capitalist societies. He directly responds — even provides an answer! — to the question of what knowledge is and who decides. In fact, almost all of Readings' proposals can be read negatively, as promoting the conflict between the older understanding of the university's affiliation with a particular community (whether this is a "nation-state" or a particular class), even championing many of the new values which are inherently in conflict with these earlier ones. Thus, in place of "community" we have an assemblage of faculty and students who are attempting to think through their being together in terms of non-identity, and non-unity. At the same time, in many ways Readings counts on the current animosity of the critical faculties themselves against "the old nation-form" as well as to democratic institutions founded by the ideology of consensus, both of which have evolved into a clear set of prejudices or *doxa*. That is, he is appealing to the consensus that already belongs to a certain critical narrative (or "language-game"), which can be defined very much along the following lines: the impossibility of consensus (or what amounts to the same thing, the idea of *dissensus* as enacting a permanent condition of conflict with "society"), hostility to the nation-state (or to any "state-form" for that matter), heterogeneity vs. homogeneity of collective desires and, finally, the *prime facie* value of "thinking" (which needs no further legitimation than it be "interesting"). In effect, what Readings is arguing for is something similar to the Kantian argument for a "critique of taste," only in this case, the critique would take as its object the judgment of thinking itself and would therefore replace the half-thought or un-thought administrative criteria of "excellence."

The relationship between Readings' argument and the earlier one by Kant in *The Conflict of the Faculties* is almost too uncanny. At many points, the parallel is clear and the attempt that Readings makes to broker a "new deal" for "thinkers" (the new philosophers) is patently visible. He seeks to position the "thinker" once again in the role of the classical philosopher, as the *censor*, the subject who decides what is critical to society and what is not. For example, at one point he recommends the dismantling of earlier disciplinary structures under the rubric of "Cultural Studies" (which is empty, "de-referentialized" from any inherent signification or value), but under the condition that "university administrators *plough back* these savings into funding pedagogical initiatives (such as short-term concentrations for teaching and research, mini-humanities centers) that allow *interesting work to be done*."[9] Readings even suggests the abolition of tenure for temporary contracts, but only under the condition that there is a deal worked out beforehand that would guarantee a set ratio of faculty and students. "Thought," the principle of any evaluation, assessment, or censorship, should be divested from the administrators and vested in "thinkers" under the terms of the conditions he sets forth, among which are abolishment of disciplines and of tenure. A bargain, it seems, is being struck with the forces of inevitable change, and Readings defines his own position as being one of "institutional pragmatism" (although some might consider it flagrant opportunism).[10]

Yet, we have to ask, who is the "addressee?" Although it would seem to be the administrators and technical managers of the "university of excellence," in fact, Readings is appealing to the despotic personality of power that is behind this class and not to them directly. Like Kant, Readings is appealing to, or attempting to persuade, a power to intervene on the behalf of the weaker party in this new conflict of faculties, where, as I have suggested above, the modern day administrator occupies the equivalent role of the higher faculty in Kant's day. Readings is appealing to a sovereign power — that is, quite amazingly, he is appealing to the power of "performativity" itself — in order to divest the administrative class of the authority of assessment, and to invest this authority within a new class of faculty, "thinkers,"under the criterion of "judgment." In contrast to Kant's argument, however, we must keep one thing in mind: Kant was addressing his argument to an identifiable form of sovereignty, a real despot, Kaiser Wilhelm. Readings, on the other hand, is addressing a mere shadow, the phantasm of "the invisible hand" behind the emerging global marketplace.

The argument of *The University in Ruins* is in many ways a "translation" (although I use this term loosely) of many of Lyotard's major arguments put forward in *The Postmodern Condition*. Not only does Readings expand on the question of the university in the wake of the decline of the nation-state, which is the central concern of Lyotard's earlier argument, but also recasts many of Lyotard's most important terms into the language of the contemporary administrative reforms in the United States. Thus, for the notion of "performativity," Readings substitutes the administrative shibboleth of "excellence," and for a form of cultural knowledge that is emptied of any specific content (i.e., the form of knowledge under the rule of de-legitimation in Lyotard's original account), Readings substitutes the current debates around the "de-referentialization" of the notion of "Culture" that are taking place around the emergence of "Cultural Studies."[11] What is most interesting, and I would argue most symptomatic, in Readings' argument, is his application of Lyotard's prescriptions for a form of knowledge that has rejected the idea of consensus as a goal, and opted for the creation of multiple language games governed by the principles of "small narratives" and "temporary moves." In Readings' account, however, when he tries to adapt this "strategy" to the

contemporary university, we end up with the idea of historical disciplines being dissolved into temporary clusters of research projects, which are periodically
constrained "to reinvent themselves…in order to be attentive *to the terms* of their
production and reproduction"(my emphasis).[12] But then, isn't this also a strategy
that many administrations are already beginning to employ in order to "assess"
the value and productivity and "vision" of academic departments: constant, even
perpetual, self-assessment?

If I have spent a great deal of time refuting many of Readings' arguments, it
is because I see in this last position, concerning thought as inherently "empty"
the ultimate flowering of the spirit of nihilism, or "other-worldliness," which has
been latent in the concepts of philosophical autonomy and pure reason as well.
Readings' account is influenced not as much by Lyotard in this regard, as by two
works that appeared in France in the late-1980s: Jean-Luc Nancy's *Community at
Loose Ends* (*La Communauté Désoeuvrée*, 1986) and Maurice Blanchot's *The Un-
avowable Community* (*La Communauté Inavouable*, 1983). In these philosophical
works we can find many of the principles that Readings espouses concerning
"negative community," or a "community for those who have no community."
Yet, to my mind, these works represent perhaps the fullest expression of the trait
of postmodernism that Lyotard has defined by the term "slackening," and the
philosopher Gilles Deleuze defines more explicitly in terms of the expressions of
"fatigue" or "exhaustion" that marked the end of this period in particular, sound-
ing like a death knell of the jubilant forces that were first released in the streets of
Paris during May '68. Thus, if Readings indicates that "the time of study" for his
*The University in Ruins* is May '68, then it is significant that the time that marks
my report falls at the end of this period, in the Y2K.

*Summary (of the five theses)*

By taking up and reading different historical perspectives on the crisis of philosophy in the University (resulting today in the crisis of humanistic knowledges and the reproduction of the critical faculties), my argument was to show that this crisis arises with the very inception of the idea of a University. It is a crisis as old as the University itself, implying perhaps that it is constitutive of the relationship between knowledge and society in the form of this institution.

There are five underlying theses to this argument, which I will now summarize:

1.  Throughout this report I have investigated the concept of university — that is, the university in its purest, most philosophical determination — which I show was invented to solve two critical social needs: storage and reproduction of knowledge or information (systems of writing, or *mneumotechnics*). Although in many ways the historical institution corresponds to an eighteenth century conception of absolute knowledge, I demonstrated that it embodies a speculative trait endemic to the form of information itself (a tendency toward totalization, institutionalization or centralization). The university fulfills these social needs by gathering all knowledge together into one site under a principle of the autonomy of reason ("knowledge for its own sake"), and by operating a mechanism of selection (or *censorship*) that directly responds to the problem of discerning what kinds of information should be stored and reproduced and what information should not be stored and thereby slated for the possibility of extinction or forgetting. It is in the nature of these two activities that we might locate the underlying terms of the current conflict in the most striking manner. As regards the first aspect (*mneumotechnics*), in part two I have argued that with the advent of new technologies for storage and reproduction, the university may no longer operate the most critical data-bank for the current society and thus appears more remote to fulfilling a critical social need today. The objective form of the centralization that belongs to information under the first aspect (such as the earlier form of the encyclopedia in the age of the book) is being located more and more in virtual data-banks, and this is having an impact on the modes of archiving and, most importantly, on the *political question of access* to knowledge. Under the second aspect, discrimination or censorship, we may be witnessing a change in the principle criteria of how knowledge is assessed. This may explain why certain historical knowledges are undergoing a gradual process of dis-investment or, at least from the perspective

of the current moment,"de-legitimation" (Lyotard). At the very center of this conflict is the question concerning the validity of the criteria of censorship and the powers of the subject who emerges today as the one "who decides" what knowledge is critical for the current society and should receive capital investment or growth, and what knowledge is obsolete and should be slated for eventual extinction (i.e., forgetting). The question concerns the criteria for deciding which knowledge should be part of the most critical databases maintained by society and which should not.

2.  Second, I have discussed why the historical position and function of the university in society is bound up with the character of the *autonomy* of the university as a social institution that is, in some ways, positioned both inside (at the very heart) and outside (at the very borders) of the society it inhabits. We have seen this position of autonomy framed in several different ways throughout our discussion, from Kant's early discourse where it is understood as the principle of reason and as the "freedom" of thought (which must be protected from any finite determination, pathological interest, or utilitarian end), to Derrida's understanding of this character of autonomy precisely as a certain "lifting of repression," that is to say, freedom from the normative commands and obligations that bind representation to a determinate social function. On a very simple level I have approached this question by using the analogy of *territory*, but then I have tried also to show that the metaphorical determination of this institution is often the most important aspect of its function. It is this very determination that allows us to picture the university as a place where the question of the "end" or "goal" of society is posed and, at the same time, as the border (or "outpost") where cutting edge and new knowledge enters into society. Like all borders, it is highly regulated and policed and the questions of legitimate entry and visa are always highly sensitive and subject to ongoing assessment. It is in this sense that the university is always at the border or boundary of the current society, since its function is often to bind new knowledge to an apparatus of social legitimation, and at the same time, to introduce it into the relationships that comprise the current social bond. Such a function often does not occur without a great deal of conflict, misunderstanding, and even a certain repression of new knowledge itself. This, in my view, is the essentially conservative function of the university as a social institution: *its mission is to adapt new knowledge to conform to the current form of legitimation while, at the same time, preparing the social bond to receive new information.* This function has an aspect of "programming" to it, which by a more antique and philosophical term could be called "progress." The university, as a place where cutting-edge and critical knowledge enters into society, also implies another sense of "bordering": it is also a place where seemingly

frivolous and "fringe" knowledge enters. Thus, both senses of new knowledge must be allowed to co-mingle in the same space: the most innovative and new knowledge often associated with some discovery or the invention of a new process that will "move" the social bond, as well as the most obtuse and obscure and seemingly inconsequential knowledge whose importance for society is not easily demonstrated. In both instances, credibility is not guaranteed to either kind of new knowledge and its repression will often be the dialectic that determines its initial place, under the requirements of censorship that we discussed above.

3.  My third thesis was that along with this character of autonomy there is also a form of *conflict* and it is precisely the nature of this conflict that assumes a historical form of the dialectic of knowledge. Like the character of autonomy above, this conflict has assumed many different forms since the inception of the university as the social institution where this kind of conflict is ritualized and takes place routinely, if not permanently. Kant, perhaps, first saw this conflict as constitutive of knowledge and sought to establish a form of government in the university in order to regulate it. Thus, the Kantian conflict of faculties is in many ways not that different from a modern wrestling match in which there are certain rules that determine the nature of the conflict as well as proscribe certain legal and illegal "moves" for how this conflict can be developed to the advantage of the different players. Later, in the position taken by Lyotard, we saw the most extreme and perhaps fatalistic expression of this conflict, which takes the form of a complete incredulity toward any of the prescriptive rules that would safeguard or regulate the conflict of reason. In a strange way, Lyotard's position is that with the rise of the performativity principle there has been a promotion and even triumph of what Kant had earlier defined as "the illegal forms of conflict" (for example, the resort to a means of bribery, overt threat, and force in settling the dispute over reasons). *Thus, "performativity" can be understood as the supreme principle of an illegal conflict of the faculties*, by which all conflicts are settled beforehand and all dissenting voices are silenced by a new form of consensus in which they become *de facto* and *de jure* extinguished or absorbed *differends*. (I have also suggested that this perception represents, perhaps even *contra the Marxists*, a return to an earlier position of Marx himself concerning the failure of liberal political reform to address the situation of real conflicts with society.) As a result, Lyotard concludes, we should play the game of knowledge under the principle that *all bets are off*; that is to say, we should either adopt the tactic of "paralogy" (seeking our opponent's weakness and making a move that will annihilate him), or "strategy" by which we might discover the means of changing the rules of the game — *our only ways out!* It is because of the extremity

of Lyotard's formulation of the modern character of conflict that I choose to privilege his perspective in my report, not necessarily because I agree with his solutions or even his recommendations for that matter.

4.  My fourth thesis is that bound up with the previous characteristics of autonomy (which determines the position of the university in society and the principle of reason upon which this place is founded or rationalized) and conflict (which is the form of the social dialectic of knowledge by which knowledge as such is historicized, or at least institutionally located), there has been a certain *subject of reason* that has historically embodied both principles within the university and toward society at large. Of course, the earliest representative is the philosopher, whose discourse is supposed to safeguard the principle of reason and, at the same time, whose autonomy is assured by the fact that the philosopher has no "interest of his own" in the present conflict. This is the basis of the idealist narrative of the subject of philosophy, whose modern representative would be the Marxian "pure" subject that provides the foundation for a critical image of autonomy that has been the principle of many contemporary critical knowledges. We discovered in the subject of the modern day administrator a new subject of reason who belongs to the contemporary university, and perhaps a new higher faculty that must be contended with. The problem with this new form of autonomy is twofold. First, adapting the arguments first developed by Niklas Luhmann, it is a "symptom" of the founding principle of late-democratic institutions, the principle of freedom, which is redefined to mean "contingent selectivity." I have used the psychoanalytic term "symptom" because it best expresses the unconscious causality of this subject in late-democratic social institutions, and the modern university in particular. The social power and "confidence," a term often used by sociologist Georg Simmel, which is bestowed upon this class of individuals to "manage" or "steer" the university, is in part the unconscious symptom of the arbitrary principle that haunts the democratic form. This is because a democratic form of organization is based on the spontaneous creation of a new social bond which did not exist previously to the performative moment of its linguistic creation, "We, the people—," which henceforth only exists from that point onward. If this is true then the social form of organization that an historical people might choose has no other basis than this purely performative character of foundation, there is no basis for determining whether a particular form of organization has any more validity than any number of others that could have been chosen. There is no basis to ground a democratic organization of society other than the contingent and arbitrary nature of the democratic form itself, which henceforth must be validated by force. (This is what Slavoj Žižek calls a "forced choice," since my free election is actually a forced choice.)[13] As the history of the twentieth cen-

tury has demonstrated, one way in which this aspect of force appears is war and another is competition, which we have witnessed in two world wars, the cold-war competition with another form of government, and, in the last decade, the various "moral wars" that the United States has been involved in from Desert Storm to the war against Serbian aggression in Kosovo. It is interesting to note that the most successful of these wars are those that provide the archaic image of a despot (or *pater familias*) from Adolph Hitler to Saddam Hussein, as if democratic institutions that are founded on the exclusion of this older and despotic image of authority are constantly haunted by its return, and thus at war with the other face of their own ideological choice. My analysis of this history is not very original in many respects and follows the work of many others who have already underscored these aspects of our "political unconscious" to employ again the term that was first coined by Fredric Jameson. In the current geo-political moment, however, I wonder if it is no longer the case of the internal struggle of democratic ideology with its archaic representatives (real or imagined), but something radically new that defines "our political consciousness." *Perhaps what is new is the almost hyperbolic increase in self-organization that is accompanied by the burgeoning creation of new ideologies of self-management, efficiency, and re-organization.* Most of these ideologies — I call them that only for the sake of convenience, since the concept of "ideology" must today be revised to account for these new strategies of organizing the social bond — are not overtly political in appearance, even though one could say that any program or institutional initiative that seeks to transform or adapt the social bond to some end (real or imagined) is *immanently* political and it is precisely this "new language" of the political whose relation to the classical language of democratic institutions must be analytically constructed.[14] Explicitly, I am suggesting that the very "arbitrariness" of this subject's power to re-organize the social bond of a particular institution is a potential place to launch a critique of this subject's authority. Thus, the emergence of all the different alternatives, of new methods of organizing the social institution that are occurring around an administrative function, threatens the identity of the social institution itself with contingency, and there is an irony here in that most of the criticisms of the right that are directed against the left for being nihilistic and for tearing down the structures and traditions of the modern university are, in fact, misplaced. In actuality, it is the contemporary administrator who is perhaps the most nihilistic of all the faculties in the university, since this subject has *no reason of its own with which to protect or safeguard this particular social institution from becoming organized just like any other.* As a result of the lack of a "principle of reason," the university can be organized like a factory, or a business; it can take the form of a bureaucracy or a church; it can be organized according to any other institution, whichever one in the present seems to provide the model of "the best one." Relationships between faculty and students can be redefined along the lines of "service-personnel" and "customers," "counselors" and "patients," "clerks" and "clients." But then, this proliferation of organizational schemes, borrowed from other social institutions, begs the question: "What exactly is a university?" "What are the distinctive social relationships that distinguish it from other social institutions?" A utilitarian or positivistic solution to this problem is by far the most visible and can be expressed by the following maxim. *The institution should be organized in whatever manner that works in the present.* This is the performativity principle that is the most plausible criteria for selecting a method of organization since the effects of this organization can be measured in practical terms (i.e., desired outcomes, goals, quantifiable values). However, one problem, like the proverbial wrench in the machine, is that no method of organization actually works that well *in the present.* This is because the nature of the institution is partly "historical," meaning that it is not completely *in the present* (defined by consciousness), but also *in the past* and is defined by tradition or habit, that is, by socially ritualized practices and conventions. In part, this is why most organizational initiatives fail — because they do not recognize the historical nature of the social bond they attempt to adapt or conform to new principles. Because the past is the condition of repetition itself, it often proves to be the greatest point of resistance to any new definition that attempts to install itself or institute itself from the perspective of the contemporaneous moment, under the criterion of what seems to be the best manner of organizing the social bond. To answer the above questions concerning the university today, therefore, we would need to return to clarify its two primary functions: storage and reproduction of knowledge, which is deemed *critical* to the perpetuation of the contemporary social bond. In turn, these questions presuppose a certain judgment concerning the social nature of knowledge itself, and the problem of legitimation of judgment which cannot be resolved by mere "decisionism," that is to say, by a subject who is authorized to decide this question simply by the fact, according to some unfathomable principle of social evolution, he or she happens to occupy the position of a subject "who decides." This is a tautological form of legitimation (or as Lyotard says elsewhere, "*tautegorical*"), one that might very well correspond to the current principle of reason (i.e., functionalism or performativity); however, in a strictly Kantian sense, it is a position that does not produce sufficient grounds upon which to base a claim of authority.[15]

5. My final and fifth thesis is already implicit in the question concerning what today is *critical* in critical knowledge. I have argued that the passage from

modern to postmodern also might signal a consequent passage from critical to *post-critical.* By the term "post-critical" I do not mean the end of the critical as such. Rather, it could mean something closer to what Derrida intended by the term "closure" in the phrase "the closure of metaphysics," which is not an end of metaphysical forms of knowledge and experience by any means, but rather the point where the question of their repetition and habituation is taken up and situated from the perspective of a second text, from the perspective of their reading and analytical (de)construction. The procedure of "deconstruction," which as Derrida has reminded us many times is not a "theory" since it doesn't presuppose the over-all view, a new ontology, or even a cosmology, is nothing more than the privileging of this double perspective that any critical reading constructs. However, rather than taking up Derrida's procedure, which answers the question of the "critical," and even provides a definite example of a "post-critical" solution to the problem at hand, I have chosen to follow Lyotard's lead in asking what form the critical will take when it can no longer be legitimated by its earlier meta-narratives. This im-plies that I agree with Lyotard's thesis that earlier narratives that perform the critical function of knowledge must again be placed in question as to their pertinence to the form of the contemporary social bond. To continue to re-peat or rehearse these narratives without regard to the empirical conditions of the conflict over knowledge that the critical function supposedly enacts in the relationship between knowledge and society would constitute a return to dogmatism. What is *critical* in critical knowledge today? In response to this question, we can only rehearse all the old narratives. To provide "critical citizenship." To promote "a democratic ethos and a spirit of free expression." To "recognize new social and political identities." To "perform justice." Yet, all these explanations ultimately fail to become persuasive because they already assume a certain consensus with the surrounding society, which may, in fact, be a "thing of the past." Is the "age of criticism" now past, in the same way that Hegel announced that the age of the artwork is past? Perhaps. Yet, like the meaning of Hegel's statement, which does not mean the "end of art" as such since the growth of the modern art world has not effectively proved him wrong, but only that the social function of the artwork has been surpassed by the emergence of other forms of communal expression, including the power of modern popular culture and mass media. One explanation concerning the fate of the critical that this report has investigated concerns the changes of the university itself as a social institution that no longer defines itself *apart* from society, but rather *a part* like any other institution or corporate body. As a result, as I have argued throughout, *where the university goes today, there goes the critical as well.* The only question that remains concerns which subject will emerge today, the contemporary administrator or the contemporary philosopher (or "theorist"), as the one who will offer a solution to the most critical question of society: the question of judgment and evaluation that is already implied by the term *critical* itself. Such an evaluation (or assessment) is already being performed in first world universities, particularly the United States, and this assessment, as well as the decisions that flow from it, is not being conducted by the faculty themselves, but rather by those who are being charged with the authority to decide which knowledge is critical to the future of the contemporary social bond, and which is not. In my view, it is precisely around the tangible and real effects of these decisions that *a new conflict of faculties* should ensue concerning their principle of "legitimation" and the authority of the subject who effectively decides. My own recommendations, therefore, are more Kantian in spirit. What I recommend is that faculty begin to engage in a newly invigorated conflict of faculties within their respective institutions and departments, that executive power not be confused with philosophical authority, and, finally; that the very moment that administrators claim to "know" what a university is today, or is becoming, they should also be required to submit their knowledge to an examination just as faculty and students must in their own respective claims to knowledge. This, in my view, is the only method of "legitimation" that remains tied to the specific institution and traditions of a university; consequently, it should be employed again as the only means of investing the claim of knowledge with a real position of authority over the future of this institution.

Respectfully submitted,

Gregg Lambert
*Syracuse University*
September 5, 2001

## *Acknowledgements*

This report grew from many conversations with friends and colleagues concerning the changes that are occurring in the contemporary university. Some of these conversations took place as early as 1995, which is also the year I began to think and write on this subject. Because they are too many to recount in this space, I cannot begin to acknowledge everyone who contributed materially to this report, so its publication is my way of saying thanks. However, I particularly want to acknowledge Joel Reed and Charles E. Winquist who, as close friends and colleagues, gave their time and attention graciously and often suffered through long dissertations over dinner when they probably would have wanted to talk about something else; and, my friend Gregory Flaxman who read and commented on drafts of the manuscript.

Although the title is taken from a short story by Franz Kafka — an allusion I have decided to leave unexplained so not to spoil the laughter for those readers who might discern a little humor in it — it was also the title of a document I co-authored in the spring of 1994 as part of a concerted effort by several graduate students and faculty of the University of California to call attention to the changing working conditions for recent doctorates in the humanities, both at U.C. and in other research institutions across the United States. This document is still available on-line at http://www.ags.uci.edu/~clcwgsa/academy.html and I include a reference to it here in order to acknowledge the very practical concerns that originated what follows. An earlier version of part one, "The University in the Ears of its Publics," appeared in *Crossings* (special issue on "Universities as Spaces of Resistance," winter 1997) and I wish to thank the editors of this journal for first giving my argument a little bit of space. I would also like to thank Professor David Miller (William P. Tolley Professor of the Humanities, Syracuse University, 1996-1999) who invited me to present a talk from this earlier article to the faculty of Syracuse University as part of the Tolley Lecture Forum in the fall of 1997, and who has always encouraged my work on the current "assessment" of the faculties.

I want to extend my gratitude and appreciation to Victor E. Taylor, editor of the Critical Studies in the Humanities Series, for his creativity and his astute vision concerning the shape of the "critical" to come; and to Keith Davies of The Davies Group Publishers for his personal and professional dedication to the survival of the academic monograph, his commitment to the rights of the academic author and his studied concern regarding the changing nature of intellectual property. I am indebted to Grayson Snyder who proofread the final manuscript version, and to Fredric Filice for his aptitude in "computerized knowledge."

Finally, I want to express my gratitude to two philosophers and former teachers who figure prominently in this report. First, to Jacques Derrida, not only for his unwavering sense of responsibility regarding the "question of the University," but also for his sense of obligation to those like myself who have followed this question both with and without his guidance. Second, to Jean-François Lyotard, who throughout the course of my reflection and study of this question over the past five years I have come to regard as a thinker who has struggled — perhaps to a degree more than any other modern philosopher — with the issues I will address in what follows, concerning the university and the current state of knowledge, to be sure, but more importantly perhaps, concerning the question of what, today, is effectively *critical* in the contemporary discursive formations of knowledge. I would like to conclude these acknowledgements, therefore, by dedicating my report to the memory of perhaps *the last philosopher* of the West.

About the artist:

Jorge Sicre is a Cuban-American artist living in Long Beach, California. He received a BA in art history from the University of California, Santa Barbara in 1980. His oils and watercolors have been exhibited in New York, Philadelphia, southern California, Florida, Mexico and South America. He has collaborated with the author for some time and his paintings have been used as the basis for illustration of several other academic books. The original painting from which the cover art is drawn is titled "Living like rats." More information concerning the artist, as well as reproductions many of his other works, can be obtained through the following web site:

http://justart.com/home/sicre/default.html

# *Notes*

## *Notes for (Preliminaries)*

1. Immanuel Kant, *The Conflict of the Faculties*, trans. Mary J. Gregor (Lincoln: University of Nebraska Press, 1979). For two different perspectives on this "power," see Jacques Derrida, "*Mochlos*, or the Conflict of the Faculties," *Logomachia: The Conflict of the Faculties*, ed. Richard Rand (Lincoln: University of Nebraska Press, 1992), pp. 1-34; also Bruce Robbins, "Less Disciplinary than Thou: Criticism and the Conflict of the Faculties," *the minnesota review* (nos. 45 & 46: 1996), pp. 95-116. Many other recent studies have utilized Kant's earlier document although, for the most part, I do not refer to them in this report. For other readings of Kant's argument, in addition to the other essays collected in Rand's volume cited above, see especially Peggy Kamuf, *The Division of Literature: Or the University in Deconstruction* (Chicago: University of Chicago Press, 1997), and Stephen Melville's "Art History, Visual Culture and the University," *October* 77 (1996): pp. 52-54.
2. Martin Heidegger, "Introduction," *Being and Time*, trans. Joan Stambaugh (Albany: SUNY Press, 1997), p.72
3. Jean-François Lyotard, *The Postmodern Condition: A Report on Knowledge*, trans. Geoff Bennington and Brian Massumi (Minneapolis: University of Minnesota Press, 1984), pp. 41-52.
4. Kant, *The Conflict of the Faculties*, p. 53.
5. Jameson, "Forward," *The Postmodern Condition*, p. xii
6. Bill Readings, *The University in Ruins* (Cambridge: Harvard, 1996). For Habermas' discussion of the concept of the "bourgeois public sphere," see Jürgen Habermas, *The Structural Transformation of the Public Sphere: An Inquiry into a Category of Bourgeois Society*, trans. Thomas Burger (Cambridge: MIT, 1989).
7. For an example of several arguments along this line, see the special issue on "The Crisis of Education," *Telos* (no. 111, spring 1998).

## *Notes to Part I*

1. Louis Althusser, *Pour Marx* (Paris: Maspero, 1975), 172n.
2. Epigraph to Report, p. 1.
3. The report I refer to was issued to "members of The University of California community" by vice-chancellor and provost Walter E. Massey, dated November 22, 1993, and titled, "University of California Long-Term Planning Retreat, Sept., 1993." Hereafter, all references to this public document will be cited as "Report."
4. Jacques Derrida, "The Principle of Reason: The University in the Eyes of its Pupils," *diacritics* (13:3, fall 1983), pp. 3-20. Also see "Les pupilles de l'Université: Le principe de raison et l'idée de l'Université, *Du droit à la philosophie* (Paris: Galilée, 1990), pp. 461-498.
5. Report, p. 1.
6. Report, p. 1.
7. For information concerning the source of this public document, see above: "Introduction," n. 8.
8. Report, pp. 11-12.

9. See Jean-Loup Amselle, *Mestizo Logics*, trans. Claudia Royal (Stanford: Stanford UP, 1998).

10. Report, p. 14.

11. Kant, *The Conflict of the Faculties*, p. 27.

12. Kant, *The Conflict of the Faculties*, p. 25.

13. Kant, *The Conflict of the Faculties*, p. 25.

14. Kant, *The Conflict of the Faculties*, p. 41.

15. Kant, *The Conflict of the Faculties*, p. 25.

16. Kant, *The Conflict of the Faculties*, p. 25.

17. Kant, *The Conflict of the Faculties*, p. 25 (my emphasis).

18. Kant, *The Conflict of the Faculties*, p. 47ff.

19. Kant, *The Conflict of the Faculties*, p. 31.

20. See Benedict Spinoza, *Theological-Political Treatise* (New York: Dover Publishers, 1951), particulary chapter 16.

21. Kant, *The Conflict of the Faculties*, p. 25.

22. Karl Marx, *The Communist Manifesto*, ed. Fredric L. Bender (New York: W.W. Norton, 1988), p. 57.

23. Derrida, "*Mochlos, or The Conflict of the Faculties*," p. 29 (emphasis mine ).

24. See Readings, *The University in Ruins*, pp. 21-43.

25. Jürgen Habermas, *Legitimation Crisis,* trans. Thomas McCarthy (Boston: Beacon Press, 1973), pp. 133ff.

26. Jürgen Habermas, *Legitimation Crisis*, p.135.

27. Report, p. 15.

28. Immanuel Kant, *The Critique of Pure Judgment*, trans. J. C. Meredith (Cambridge: Oxford University Press, 1997), especially §49.

29. Kant, *The Conflict of the Faculties*, p. 29.

30. Ferdinand de Saussure, *Course in General Linguistics*, trans. Wade Baskin (New York: Philosophical Library, 1959), pp. 1-16.

31. Martin Heidegger, "Introduction," *Being and Time*

32. Jacques Derrida, *Of Grammatology,* trans. Gayatri Spivak (Baltimore, Johns Hopkins, 1974).

33. See William Bennett, "The Shattered Humanities," W*all Street Journal*, Dec. 31, 1982.

34. Derrida, "The Principle of Reason," p. 19.

35. See Alexander Kojève, *Introduction à la lecture de Hegel* (Paris: Gallimard, 1959.)

36. Derrida, "The Principle of Reason," p. 19.

37. Derrida, "The Principle of Reason," p. 19.

38. See Evan Watkins, *Work Time* (Stanford: Stanford UP, 1989).

39. Quoted from Derrida, "The Principle of Reason," p. 18.

40. Derrida, "The Principle of Reason," pp. 6-7.

41. Kant, *The Critique of Pure Reason*, trans. J.M.D. Mieklejohn (London: J.M. Dent, 1934), p. 83.

42. Derrida, "Roundtable discussion at Villanova University" (on-line: October, 1996).

43. Qtd. from Derrida, "*Mochlos or The Conflict of the Faculties,* p. 31.

44. Paul de Man, *Blindness and Insight: Essays in the Rhetoric of Contemporary Criticism* (Minneapolis: U Minnesota P, 1971), p. 165.

45. One can interpret De Man's dominant allegory of blindness and insight as a great trope, one that has clear European origins, which had powerful and authorizing effects on the

concept of "reading" as a heterogeneous social space capable of producing new distinctions in social and institutional space as well. Of course, it found an easy fit in the space opened by formalist methods of interpretation, as well as in the tradition of criticism itself, where one person's blindness is always another person's insight — that is, it is an avatar of the classical subject of the ironist. Yet it also placed a great deal of privilege on "slow and careful reading" as well. As an anecdote of this, I recount the following story. In a telephone conversation I once had with a De Manian critic, I mentioned that I just spent the morning reading James' "Figure in the Carpet." After a long pause, my interlocutor replied: "Really? Why it took me two months to read that text and you read it all the way through in one morning?" Of course, I knew right away that I had been insulted. The underlying accusation was that while I read James, in fact I did not really "read" him according to the rigors of the De Manian criteria of textual scrutiny; thus, whatever insight I felt I had gained was without authority, since it was ultimately blinded by my own "allegory of reading."

46. Kant, *The Conflict of the Faculties*, p. 45.

47. Lyotard, *The Postmodern Condition*, p. 9.

48. The above conclusions, more speculative and predictive than factual, are made on the basis of several second-hand reports from other academics concerning publication projects that were suddenly cancelled after news of the Sokal affair hit the national presses, or accepted articles that were placed on the waiting lists indefinitely, or at least until the authors finally withdrew them I experienced the effects of this event myself when an edited collection on Literature and Science in which I had a chapter was placed on the back-burner by a noted academic series in science and postmodern theory and, even after additional reports were solicited by scientists concerning the validity of the scientific knowledge in some of the chapters, was finally passed on by the editorial board of the press for the stated reason that they didn't want to take the risk of being "*sokalized*" and thus threaten the credibility of the entire series which had already been made vulnerable by the event.

49. Kant, *The Conflict of the Faculties*, p. 45.

50. Sandra Gilbert, "Presidential Column," *MLA Newsletter* (Spring 1996), p. 3.

51. Michael Bérubé, *Public Access* (London : Verso Press, 1994).

52. This incident took place soon after De Man's death in 1983 around the revelation of the critic's earlier anti-Semitic views expressed in several articles published in a Flemish national journal during the war. Several academic antagonists of deconstruction saw this as an opportunity to use the revelation of a leading deconstructive critic's earlier complicity with National Socialist ideology as a platform to censure deconstruction generally, including the writings of Jacques Derrida. An intense debate ensued both inside and outside the academy and was widely publicized in newspapers and various national journals such as *Time, Harpers,* and *The Atlantic Monthly.* As I mention below, this debate was preceded by a similar debate concerning Martin Heidegger's affiliation with National Socialism while rector of the University.

53. See Bruce Robbins, "The Insistence of the Public in Postmodern Criticism," *Secular Vocations Intellectuals, Professionalism, Culture* (London: Verso, 1993), pp. 84-117.

54. Derrida, *The Other Heading: Reflections on Today's Europe*, trans. Pascale-Anne Brault and Michael B. Naas (Bloomington: Indiana U P, 1992), pp. 54-55.

55. Yury Lotman, "The Text with the Text," *PMLA* (Volume 109, n. 3, May 1994): pp. 377-384.

56. See Fredric Jameson, *The Geopolitical Aesthetic: Cinema and Space in the World System* (Bloomington: Indiana UP, 1994).

57. Gilles Deleuze, *Negotiations* (New York: Columbia UP, 1994), p. 146.

58. Kant, *The Conflict of the Faculties*, p. 45.

59. Kant, *The Conflict of the Faculties*, p. 47.

60. See especially part two of *The Conflict of the Faculties*, "The Conflict of the Philosophy Faculty with the Faculty of Law," pp. 140-171.


*Notes to Part II*

1. Lyotard, *The Postmodern Condition*, 1.

2. Lyotard, *The Postmodern Condition*, 4-5.

3. See Etienne Balibar "The Nation Form: History and Ideology," in Etienne Balibar and Immanuel Wallerstein, *Race, Nation, Class: Ambiguous Identities*, London (Verson, 1991): pp. 86-106.

4. Lyotard, *The Postmodern Condition*, p. 5.

5. Lyotard, *The Postmodern Condition*, p. xxiv.

6. Lyotard, *The Postmodern Condition*, p. 4.

7. Lyotard, *The Postmodern Condition*, p. 15.

8. Lyotard, *The Postmodern Condition*, p. 6.

9. Lyotard, *The Postmodern Condition*, p. 7.

10. Lyotard, *The Postmodern Condition*, p. 51.

11. Lyotard, *The Postmodern Condition*, p. 6. The reader should bear in mind that the concerns over the "piracy" of knowledge were made before the globalization of information on the internet, and the vulnerability of secure databases to computer viruses and hacker-pirates.

12. Lyotard, *The Postmodern Condition*, p. 9.

13. Roland Barthes, "On Reading" in *The Rustle of Language*, trans. Richard Howard (Berkeley: University of California Press, 1984), pp. 36-38.

14. Jürgen Habermas, *The Structural Transformation of the Public Sphere*, pp. 86-88.

15. Jürgen Habermas, *The Structural Transformation of the Public Sphere*, p. 3.

16. Lyotard, *The Postmodern Condition*, p. 6.

17. "Falling through the Net—Defining the Digital Divide." A Report on the Telecommunications and Information Technology Gap in America. National Telecommunications and Information Administration (Washington, DC, July 1999).

18. One exception to this is the work of Theresa Ebert and Mas'ud Zavarzedah. See their op-ed article which appeared in the L.A. Times (March 23rd, 2000).

19. Jean-François Lyotard, *The Postmodern Explained: Correspondence 1982-1985*, trans. Julian Pefanis and Morgan Thomas (Minneapolis: U Minnesota P, 1992), pp. 39-60.

20. Lyotard, *The Postmodern Explained*, p. 40.

21. The second thing I am trying to do in this discussion, consistent with the form of a commentary on Lyotard, is to explain why the Kantian sublime increasingly became the focus of his later work. This, I would argue, is not just some avocation to amuse himself in his retiring years; rather, it concerned the historical conditions of the spirit of philosophy, and a wish to rectify the nature of the "critical" function in knowledge today.

22. David Hume, *Essays: Moral, Political, and Literary* (London: Oxford UP, 1963), p. 278.

23. Hume, *Essays*, p. 280.

24. Hume, *Essays*, p. 279.

25. Hume, *Essays*, p. 280.

26. Emile Benveniste, *The Vocabulary of Indo-European Institutions* (Talahassee: Florida State University Press, 1978), p. 418.
27. Martin Heidegger, *What is Called Thinking?* (New York: Harper & Row, 1978), pp. 156-157.
28. See Clark Kerr, *The Uses of the University, 4e.* (Cambridge: Harvard University Press, 1995).
29. Quoted from Lyotard, *The Postmodern Condition*, p. 32.
30. Jaroslav Pelikan, *The Idea of the University: A Reexamination* (New Haven: Yale University Press, 1992).
31. Quoted from Pelikan, *The Idea of the University*, p. 82.
32. Pelikan, *The Idea of the University*, p. 80.
33. Pelikan, *The Idea of the University*, p. 79.
34. Charles Houston Long, "The University, the Liberal Arts, and the Teaching and Study of Religion" [unpublished paper].
35. Kant, *The Critique of Pure Reason*, p. 203.
36. Wallerstein, Race, Nation, Class, p. 117.
37. Lyotard, *The Differend*, p. 128.
38. Lyotard, *The Postmodern Condition*, p. 47.
39. Lyotard, *The Postmodern Condition*, p. 45.
40. Lyotard, *The Postmodern Condition*, p. 45.
41. Lyotard, *The Postmodern Condition*, p. xxiv.
42. See the following sociological analyses, many of which Lyotard refers to as sources of information: Jürgen Habermas, *Legitimation Crisis*, trans. Thomas McCarthy (Boston: Beacon Press, 1973); and Niklas Luhmann, *Theorie der Gesellschaft oder Sozialtechnologie* (Stuttgart: Suhrkamp, 1971); Talcott Parsons, *Zur Logik der Sozialwissenschaften* (Frankfurt, 1970); Alain Touraine, *The Post-Industrial Society*, trans. Leonard Mayhew (London: Wildwood House, 1974); Daniel Bell, *The Coming of Post-Industrial Society* (New York: Basic Books, 1973).
43. Karl Marx, *The German Ideology*, ed. C. J. Arthur (New York: International Publishers, 1970).
44. Jameson, "Foreword," *The Postmodern Condition*, p. xii.
45. Jameson, "Foreword," *The Postmodern Condition*, pp. xii-xiii.

*Notes to Part III*

1. Lyotard, *The Postmodern Condition*, p. 82.
2. Lyotard, *The Postmodern Condition*, p. 13.
3. Lyotard, *The Postmodern Condition*, pp. 11-12.
4. Lyotard, *The Postmodern Condition*, p. 60.
5. Habermas, *Legitimation Crisis*, p. 141.
6. Habermas, *Legitimation Crisis*, p. 142.
7. Habermas, *Legitimation Crisis*, p. 142.
8. Habermas, *Legitimation Crisis*, p. 143.
9. Jacques Lacan, *Ecrits*, trans. Alan Sheridan (New York: W.W. Norton, 1977), 285.
10. Habermas, *Legitimation Crisis*, p. 142.

11. Habermas, *Legitimation Crisis*, p. 141.
12. Lyotard, *The Differend*, p. 137.
13. Saussure, *The Course in General Linguistics*, trans. Wade Baskin (New York: McGraw-Hill, 1959), p. 71.
14. Saussure, *The Course in General Linguistics*, p. 71.
15. Lyotard, *The Differend*, p. 137.
16. Saussure, *The Course in General Linguistics*, p. 71.
17. Saussure, *The Course in General Linguistics*, p. 74.
18. Saussure, *The Course in General Linguistics*, p. 71.
19. Lyotard, *The Differend*, p. 135.
20. Saussure, *The Course in General Linguistics*, p. 72.
21. Lyotard, *The Differend*, p. 136.
22. Lyotard, *The Differend*, p. 136.
23. Lyotard, *The Differend*, p. 138.
24. Lyotard, *The Postmodern Condition*, "Appendix," pp. 71-84.
25. See Lyotard, *Postmodern Fables*, trans. Georges van den Abbeele (Minneapolis: University of Minnesota Press, 1997).
26. Octavio Paz, *The Children of the Mire* (Cambridge: Harvard University Press, 1991).
27. Michel Foucault, "What is Enlightenment?" *The Foucault Reader*, ed. Paul Rabinow
28. See Gilles Deleuze, *Kant's Critical Philosophy*, "Preface to the English Edition," trans. Hugh Tomlinson (Minneapolis: U of Minnesota Press, 1984), pp. 1-4.
29. Quoted in Derrida, "*Mochlos*, or the Conflict of the Faculties," p. 32.
30. Of course, I realize that this statement would seem to be disproved by the proliferation of critical subjects in the humanities today, and by the visibility of the critical knowledges associated with feminism, race, ethnic or minority issues. I will return to argue below why the critical function of these knowledges do not qualify as "master-narratives," and themselves signal the break-up of an earlier meta-narrative of "the critical." Why? Because they do not address emancipation of a humanity, or the "universal species," but are bound to the emancipation of "particulars." This is why their narrative of emancipation cannot be divorced from the interest that these subjects embody within the political sphere.
31. Lyotard, *The Postmodern Condition*, p. 13.
32. Karl Marx, *Early Writings*, ed. T.B. Bottomore (New York: McGraw-Hill, 1963).
33. Marx, *Early Writings*, p. 12.
34. Jean-Loup Amselle, *Mestizo Logics*, p. 53.
35. Amselle, *Mestizo Logics*, p. 42.
36. Lyotard, *The Postmodern Condition*, p. 14.
37. Lyotard, *The Postmodern Condition*, p. 13.
38. Habermas, *Legitimation Crisis*, p. 143.
39. On this distinction, see Gerard Genette, *Figure,* Volume 1-3, translated by Alan Sheridan; introduction by Marie-Rose Logan (New York : Columbia University Press, 1982).
40. Derrida, *Writing and Difference*, trans. Alan Bass (Chicago: U of Chicago Press, 1978), pp. 278-300.
41. Julia Kristeva, *Revolution of Poetic Language*, trans. Margaret Waller (New York: Columbia University Press, 1984).
42. See Judith Butler, *Bodies That Matter* (New York: Routledge, 1993).
43. See Fredric Jameson, *Postmodernism, or The Cultural Logic of Late-Capitalism* (Durham: Duke University Press, 1991).

44. Jacques Lacan, *Seminar III: The Psychoses*, trans, Russell Grigg (New York: Norton, 1993), p. 258.
45. See Althusser's famous essay, "Ideology and Ideological State Apparatuses," in *Lenin and Philosophy and Other Essays*, trans. Ben Brewster (New York: Monthly Review Press, 1971).
46. I am referring to a passage from Borges that Lacan recounts in his *Seminar XI, The Four Fundamental Concepts of Psychoanalysis*, trans. Alan Sheridan (New York: W.W. Norton, 1977). The passage I am alluding to runs as follows: "When he [Choang-tsu] is a butterfly, the idea does not occur to him to wonder whether, when he is Choang-tsu awake, he is not the butterfly that he is dreaming of being. This is because, when dreaming of being the butterfly, he will no doubt have to bear witness later that he represented himself as a butterfly. But this does not mean that he is captivated by the butterfly — he is a captive butterfly, but captured by nothing, for, in the dream, he is a butterfly for nobody. It is when he is awake that he is Chaong-tsu for others, and is caught in their butterfly net" (76).
47. Lacan, *Seminar XI*, p. 56.
48. For a discussion of the concept of "performativity" in queer theory, see Judith Butler, *Bodies That Matter*, pp. 187-222.
49. Amselle, *Mestizo Logics*, 41. One can see [the] name "queer" as a perfect example of this process, and it was the success of Judith Butler to give "the first name" to the subject of disagreement over gay and lesbian identities.
50. Ernesto Laclau, *Emancipations* (London: Verso Press, 1996), p. 44.
51. Althusser, *For Marx*, 246.
52. Jameson, "Foreword," *The Postmodern Condition*, p. xix.
53. Jameson, "Foreword," *The Postmodern Condition*, p. xix (my emphasis).
54. Lacan, *Seminar XI*, p. 76.
55. Lacan, *Seminar XI*, p. 76.
56. Gilles Deleuze and Claire Parnet, *Dialogues*, trans. Hugh Tomlinson and Barbara Habberjam (New York: Columbia University Press, 1987), p. 144.
57. Wallerstein, *Race, Nation, Class*, p. 118.
58. Thomas Kuhn, *The Structure of Scientific Revolutions* (Chicago: University of Chicago Press, 1996).
59. John Caputo, *The Prayers and Tears of Jacques Derrida: Religion without Religion* (Bloomington: University of Indiana Press, 1997); on "British Radical Orthodoxy," see Phillip Blond (ed.), *Post-Secular Philosophy: Between Philosophy and Theology* (London: Routledge, 1998).
60. Lyotard, *The Postmodern Condition*, p. 66.
61. Thomas L. Friedman, *The Lexus and the Olive Tree* (New York: Anchor Books, 2000), p. 191.
62. Marx, *The Communist Manifesto*, p. 66.
63. For a comparison between the concept of the "bourgeoisie" and its contemporary reality, see especially Wallerstein, "Bourgeois(ie) as Concept and Reality," *Race, Nation, Class*, pp. 135-152.
64. Wallerstein, *Race, Nation, Class*, p. 149.
65. Wallerstein, *Race, Nation, Class*, p. 149.
66. Lyotard, *The Postmodern Condition*, p. 67.
67. Lyotard, *The Postmodern Condition*, p. 36.
68. Jameson, *The Postmodern Condition*, p. xviii.
69. Althusser, For Marx, p. 247.

70. Jameson, *The Postmodern Condition*, p. xix.
71. Jameson, *The Postmodern Condition*, p. xix.
72. Slavoj Žižek, *The Ticklish Subject: The Absent Center of Political Ontology* (London: Verso, 1999), p. 195.
73. Benveniste, *The Vocabulary of Indo-European Institutions*, p. 416.
74. Benveniste, *The Vocabulary of Indo-European Institutions*, p. 389.
75. Benveniste, *The Vocabulary of Indo-European Institutions*, p. 389
76. Benveniste, *The Vocabulary of Indo-European Institutions*, p. 382.
77. Benveniste, *The Vocabulary of Indo-European Institutions*, p. 395.
78. Benveniste, *The Vocabulary of Indo-European Institutions*, p. 396.
79. Benveniste, *The Vocabulary of Indo-European Institutions*, pp. 396-97.
80. Benveniste, *The Vocabulary of Indo-European Institutions*, p. 398.
81. Kant, quoted in Lyotard *The Differend*, p. 121.
82. Benveniste, *The Vocabulary of Indo-European Institutions*, p. 398.
83. On the origin of the stranger and the affiliation with the position of the arbiter-judge, see especially the work of sociologist Georg Simmel, *The Sociology of Georg Simmel*, trans. Kurt Wolff (New York: Free Press, 1950); also my *The Culture of Strangers: On the Marriage of Psychoanalysis and Ethnography in Modern Literature* (forthcoming, Critical Studies in the Humanities, The Davies Group, Publishers).
84. Lyotard, *The Postmodern Condition*, p. 57.

## Notes to Summary and Conclusion

1. A similar strategy of "nomadism" is evident in the critical writings of Deleuze and Guattari as well, although I will reserve a critique of this "strategy" for another occasion.
2. I argue this in my book on "the institution of the stranger," particularly in the context of recent debates concerning over the postcolonial in the field of modern literary criticism. See *The Culture of Strangers: Reflections of Aesthetic Ideology from the Baroque to the Postcolonial*, Critical Studies in the Humanities (Aurora, CO: The Davies Group, Publishers), forthcoming.
3. See Johann Georg Hamann, "Metacritique on the Purism of Reason," in *What is Enlightenment: Eighteenth Century Answers and Twentieth Century Questions*, ed. James Schmidt (Berkeley: University of California Press, 1996), pp. 154-160.
4. Kant, *What is Enlightenment?* p. 63.
5. Kant, *The Conflict of the Faculties*, p. 23 — emphasis in original.
6. See Balibar, "The Nation Form," *Race, Nation, Class*, pp. 86-105.
7. Readings, *The University in Ruins*, p. 191.
8. Readings, *The University in Ruins*, p. 192.
9. Readings, *The University in Ruins*, p. 127.
10. Many of my criticisms of Readings' argument echo those made by Dominique LaCapra in his review article "The University in Ruins?" *Critical Inquiry* (Autumn 1998), pp.32-55. In particular, LaCapra is also suspicious of the lack of class perspective, or perhaps the extremely class-bound nature of some of Readings' arguments for reducing the university to a "language-game" that is perpetuated by a class of petty-bourgeois including the professoriat. He writes: "Indeed one might even suspect in Readings' subject-position (whatever his autobiographical condition might have been) the patrician or quasi-transcendental

perspective of one who is not concerned about social mobility or the way the university may serve it, indeed one who simply takes certain things for granted...." (39).

11. In his book, Readings is actually referring to the impact of various administrative initiatives at Syracuse University, including the promotion of "excellence," the re-definition of the university as a "student-centered research university," and the re-definition of the student as "client" and "customer" under various training programs for faculty and staff. Since Readings departure from Syracuse in the early 1990s, these programs have advanced and have been instituted with a varying degree of success, although not without an equal degree of cynicism on the part of faculty. The term "student-centered research university" has stuck, however, and is often invoked in public brochures and to parents in orientation ceremonies as a quasi-philosophical definition of the idea of Syracuse University. Like Reading's argument concerning the earlier idea of "excellence" — a strategy which was abandoned by Syracuse administrators well before Readings published his book — it is inherently empty of content except in the sense that it appeals to a negative public perception of research universities in order to signal a qualitative difference — i.e., Syracuse is a major research university which still puts the student at the center of the process. Of course, in most if not all matters the priorities of Syracuse University are pretty much identical to many other private research institutions in the country that are dependent on undergraduate tuition revenues, and now to an even greater degree student and parent consumer dollars in any number of local retail venues that Syracuse University owns and especially the income associated with sporting events. But this is not the point. The true effect of the strategy behind the term "student centered research university" is that it was actually promoted in order to stimulate discussion and definition by all the various "university cultures" (see part I[a]), as well as by all the various "publics" of the university (parents, donors, media). As a result of this constant definition or interpretation of what the term actually means by various public constituencies and interior cultures, the term has been provided signification and a quasi-philosophical content even though this content is defined in different and often conflicting ways. For example, recently I was scolded by a student for not being able to meet with him outside of my scheduled office hours, which would be more convenient for his work and class schedule; he said, "but I thought this was a 'student centered research university,' and so what you're telling me is that you refuse to perform your job as your employers have defined it." In addition to this example, I can't count the number of times that I have heard from students that they pay my salary and so I should comply with their demands by virtue of the fact that they are my employer and I am in the position of a service worker. As demonstrated by these two local examples, the function of the term "student-centered research university" is inherently its performativity in changing behaviors and expectations that comprise the current social bond of Syracuse University. Perhaps for this reason it is perhaps a perfect example of a performative mechanism, since the phrase is provided both a theoretical and a practical consistency precisely by the manner in which it is interpreted and applied to concrete relationships by the various subjects to which it is addressed. In the meantime, the real criteria of interest and knowledge that will determine decisions is effectively displaced to "another scene" than the discussion of ideology. In many ways, the manner by which it distorts or consolidates a "false consciousness" concerning the principle of reason that guides the institution's decision-making process fits Marx's classical definition of Ideology.

12. Readings, *The University in Ruins,* p. 178.

13. See Slavoj Žižek, *The Ticklish Subject,* p. 11-22.

14. Jameson's term "the Political Unconscious" has an additional virtue of applying to this situation much in the same way as a dream language. We recall that the dream language is purely idiomatic, a "language game," even though it is constructed according to certain general rules. However, it is the analytical construction of the dream language through the process of secondary elaboration that inserts the idiomatic nature of the dream language into the framework of the Symbolic and thus allows it to speak (*ça parle*) the "reality of the Subject." We might imagine a similar process in decoding and enunciation concerning these new narratives of the "political unconscious," something similar to what I performed in the beginning of this report by reading a fairly innocuous, on first glance, administrative document against the underlying principles it articulated in more classical or philosophical language of the University.

15. On the term *"tautagorical,"* see Lyotard, *Lessons on the Analytic of the Sublime*, trans. Elizabeth Rottenberg (Palo Alto: Stanford University Press, 1991).